# 31 Days Before Your

# Cisco Certified Support Technician (CCST) Networking 100-150 Exam

A Day-By-Day Review Guide for the CCST-Networking Certification Exam

Allan Johnson

**Cisco Press**
Hoboken, NJ

# 31 Days Before Your Cisco Certified Support Technician (CCST) Networking 100-150 Exam

Allan Johnson

Copyright © 2024 Cisco Systems, Inc.

Published by:
Cisco Press

1 2024

Library of Congress Control Number: 2024902156

ISBN-13: 978-0-13-822291-8

ISBN-10: 0-13-822291-6

## Warning and Disclaimer

The opinions expressed in this book belong to the author and are not necessarily those of Cisco Systems, Inc.

## Trademark Acknowledgments

All terms mentioned in this book that are known to be trademarks or service marks have been appropriately capitalized. Cisco Press or Cisco Systems, Inc., cannot attest to the accuracy of this information. Use of a term in this book should not be regarded as affecting the validity of any trademark or service mark.

## Special Sales

For information about buying this title in bulk quantities, or for special sales opportunities (which may include electronic versions; custom cover designs; and content particular to your business, training goals, marketing focus, or branding interests), please contact our corporate sales department at corpsales@pearsoned.com or (800) 382-3419.

For government sales inquiries, please contact governmentsales@pearsoned.com.

For questions about sales outside the U.S., please contact intlcs@pearson.com.

## Feedback Information

At Cisco Press, our goal is to create in-depth technical books of the highest quality and value. Each book is crafted with care and precision, undergoing rigorous development that involves the unique expertise of members from the professional technical community.

Readers' feedback is a natural continuation of this process. If you have any comments regarding how we could improve the quality of this book, or otherwise alter it to better suit your needs, you can contact us through email at feedback@ciscopress.com. Please make sure to include the book title and ISBN in your message.

We greatly appreciate your assistance.

| | |
|---|---|
| GM K12, Early Career and Professional Learning | Soo Kang |
| Alliances Manager, Cisco Press | Caroline Antonio |
| Director, ITP Product Management | Brett Bartow |
| Executive Editor | James Manly |
| Managing Editor | Sandra Schroeder |
| Development Editor | Ellie C. Bru |
| Senior Project Editor | Mandie Frank |
| Copy Editor | Bart Reed |
| Technical Editor | Patrick Gargano |
| Editorial Assistant | Cindy Teeters |
| Designer | Chuti Prasertsith |
| Composition | CodeMantra |
| Indexer | Ken Johnson |
| Proofreader | Jennifer Hinchliffe |

# About the Author

**Allan Johnson** entered the academic world in 1999 after 10 years as a business owner/operator to dedicate his efforts to his passion for teaching. He holds both an MBA and an MEd in training and development. He taught CCNA courses at the high school level for seven years and has taught both CCNA and CCNP courses at Del Mar College in Corpus Christi, Texas. In 2003, Allan began to commit much of his time and energy to the CCNA Instructional Support Team, providing services to Networking Academy instructors worldwide and creating training materials. He now splits his time between working as a curriculum lead for Cisco Networking Academy and as an account lead for Unicon (unicon.net) supporting Cisco's educational efforts.

# About the Technical Reviewer

**Patrick Gargano** is a lead content advocate and instructor on the Technical Education team within Learning & Certifications at Cisco. Before joining Cisco in 2021, he worked as a Cisco Networking Academy instructor and instructor-trainer since 2000, and as a Certified Cisco Systems Instructor (CCSI) since 2005 for Fast Lane UK, Skyline ATS, and NterOne teaching CCNA and CCNP courses. Recently, he was responsible for developing Cisco's official ENARSI, ENSDWI, ENCC, SDWFND, and SDWSCS course content. He has published four Cisco Press books, and he holds CCNA, CyberOps Associate, and CCNP Enterprise certifications. He also holds BEd and BA degrees from the University of Ottawa and has a Master of Professional Studies (MPS) degree in computer networking from Fort Hays State University. He is a regular speaker at Cisco Live, presenting on topics related to SD-WAN and network troubleshooting. He lives in Quebec, Canada with his wife and son.

# Dedications

For my wife, Becky. Thank you for all your support during this crazy whirlwind of a year. You are the stabilizing force that keeps me grounded.

# Acknowledgments

As a technical author, I rely heavily on my technical editor; Patrick Gargano had my back for this work. Thankfully, when James Manly contacted him, he was willing and able to do the arduous review work necessary to make sure that you get a book that is both technically accurate and unambiguous.

Russ White's *Cisco Certified Support Technician CCST Networking 100-150 Official Cert Guide, First Edition* was one of my main sources. Russ is well known in the computer networking community where he is a highly respected expert. I recommend subscribing to the podcast *Hedge*, where Russ is a co-host.

The Cisco Network Academy authors for the online curriculum take the reader deeper, past the CCST Networking exam topics, with the ultimate goal of preparing the student not only for CCST Networking certification, but for more advanced college-level technology courses and degrees as well. Thank you especially to Rick Graziani, Bob Vachon, John Pickard, Dave Holzinger, Martin Benson, Suk-Yi Pennock, Allan Reid, Anna Bolen and the rest of the ACE team. Their excellent treatment of the material is reflected throughout this book.

James Manly, executive editor, effectively juggles multiple projects simultaneously, steering each from beginning to end. Thank you, James, for shepherding this project for me.

Thank you to the professional and thorough review of this work by development editor Ellie Bru, project editor Mandie Frank, and copy editor Bart Reed. Their combined efforts ensure that what I authored is ready for publication.

And to the rest of the Pearson family who contributes in countless ways to bring a book to the reader, thank you for all your hard work.

# Contents at a Glance

# Reader Services

**Register your copy** at www.ciscopress.com/title/9780138222918 for convenient access to downloads, updates, and corrections as they become available. To start the registration process, go to www.ciscopress.com/register and log in or create an account.* Enter the product ISBN 9780138222918 and click Submit. When the process is complete, you will find any available bonus content under Registered Products.

*Be sure to check the box that you would like to hear from us to receive exclusive discounts on future editions of this product.

# Contents

# Icons Used in This Book

 Access Point

 Switch

 Router

 Printer

 Clock

 Server

WWW Server

 ASA 5500

Phone

 Laptop

 File Server

Cisco Nexus 1000

Cloud

Firewall

Terminal

# Command Syntax Conventions

The conventions used to present command syntax in this book are the same conventions used in the IOS Command Reference. The Command Reference describes these conventions as follows:

- **Boldface** indicates commands and keywords that are entered literally as shown. In actual configuration examples and output (not general command syntax), boldface indicates commands that are manually input by the user (such as a **show** command).

- *Italic* indicates arguments for which you supply actual values.

- Vertical bars (|) separate alternative, mutually exclusive elements.

- Square brackets ([ ]) indicate an optional element.

- Braces ({ }) indicate a required choice.

- Braces within brackets ([{ }]) indicate a required choice within an optional element.

# Introduction

If you're reading this introduction, you've probably already spent a considerable amount of time and energy pursuing your CCST Networking certification. Regardless of how you got to this point in your travels through your studies, *31 Days Before Your Cisco Certified Support Technician (CCST) Networking 100-150 Exam* most likely represents the last leg of your journey on your way to the destination: to become a Cisco Certified Support Technician in Networking. However, if you are like me, you might be reading this book at the *beginning* of your studies. If so, this book provides an excellent overview of the material you must now spend a great deal of time studying and practicing. But I must warn you: unless you are extremely well-versed in networking technologies and have considerable experience supporting networks, this book will *not* serve you well as the sole resource for your exam preparations. Therefore, let me spend some time discussing my recommendations for study resources.

# Study Resources

Cisco Press and Pearson IT Certification offer an abundance of networking-related books to serve as your primary source for learning how to install, configure, operate, and troubleshoot small to medium-size routed and switched networks.

## Safari Books Online

All the resources I reference in the book are available with a subscription to Safari Books Online (https://www.safaribooksonline.com). If you don't have an account, you can try it free for ten days.

## Primary Resources

First on the list must be Russ White's *Cisco Certified Support Technician CCST Networking 100-150 Official Cert Guide 1st Edition* (ISBN: 9780138213428). If you do not buy any other books, buy this one. Russ's method of teaching, combined with his technical expertise and down-to-earth style, is unsurpassed in our industry. As you read through his book, you sense that he is sitting right there next to you walking you through the material. With your purchase, you get access to practice exams and study materials and other online resources that are worth the price of the book. There is no better resource on the market for a CCST Networking candidate.

If you are a Cisco Networking Academy student, you are blessed with access to the online version of the Networking Essentials version 3 curriculum and the wildly popular Packet Tracer network simulator. However, this content is also available for free to anyone who signs up at https://skills-forall.com. After registering and logging in, look for the Network Technician Career Path (https://skillsforall.com/career-path/network-technician). Here, you can gain access to the following four mini-courses that add up to 70 hours of training:

- Networking Basics

- Networking Devices and Initial Configuration

- Network Addressing and Basic Troubleshooting

- Network Support and Security

You can also buy *Networking Essentials Companion Guide v3: Cisco Certified Support Technician (CCST) Networking 100-150, Second Edition* (ISBN: 978-0-13-832133-8), which maps to both the Networking Essentials version 3 instructor-led online course and the four self-enroll mini-courses. You might also consider purchasing *Networking Essentials Lab Manual v3: Cisco Certified Support Technician (CCST) Networking 100-150, 2nd Edition* (ISBN: 9780138293727). You can find these books at http://www.ciscopress.com by clicking the Cisco Networking Academy link.

## The Cisco Learning Network

Finally, if you have not done so already, you should register with The Cisco Learning Network at https://learningnetwork.cisco.com. Sponsored by Cisco, The Cisco Learning Network is a free social learning network where IT professionals can engage in the common pursuit of enhancing and advancing their IT careers. Here, you can find many resources to help you prepare for your CCST Networking exam, in addition to a community of like-minded people ready to answer your questions, help you with your struggles, and share in your triumphs.

So which resources should you buy? The answer to that question depends largely on how deep your pockets are or how much you like books. If you're like me, you must have it all! I admit it; my bookcase is a testament to my Cisco "geekness." Whatever you choose, you will be in good hands. Any or all of these resources will serve you well.

# Goals and Methods

The main goal of this book is to provide you with a clear and succinct review of the CCST Networking objectives. Each day, we will review an exam topic, starting with the first one and proceeding through the list objectives until they are all covered. Each day is structured using the following format:

- A title for the day that concisely states the overall topic

- A list of one or more CCST Networking 100-150 exam topics to be reviewed

- A "Key Topics" section to introduce the review material and quickly orient you to the day's focus

- An extensive review section consisting of short paragraphs, lists, tables, examples, and graphics

- A "Study Resources" section to give you a quick reference for locating more in-depth treatment of the day's topics

The book counts down starting with Day 31 and continues through exam day to provide post-test information. Inside this book is also a calendar and checklist that you can tear out and use during your exam preparation.

Use the calendar to enter each actual date beside the countdown day and the exact day, time, and location of your CCST Networking exam. The calendar provides a visual for the time you can dedicate to each exam topic.

The checklist highlights important tasks and deadlines leading up to your exam. Use it to help you map out your studies.

# Who Should Read This Book?

The audience for this book is anyone finishing preparation for taking the CCST Networking 100-150 exam. A secondary audience is anyone needing a refresher review of CCST Networking exam topics, possibly as a review before attempting to sit for another certification for which the CCST Networking exam topics provide a foundation.

# Getting to Know the CCST Networking 100-150 Exam

Cisco announced the current CCST Networking 100-150 exam in January 2023. This certification is aimed at entry-level network technicians, networking students, and interns. It tests foundational knowledge and skills in network operation, including the understanding of devices, media, and protocols vital for network communication. This certification serves as an entry point into the Cisco certification program, with CCNA being the next level. The exam is targeted toward secondary and post-secondary students, as well as entry-level IT and Networking professionals. To qualify, candidates should have a minimum of 150 hours of instruction and hands-on experience, and successful candidates will be recognized as qualified entry-level network technicians and customer support technicians.

To earn your certification, you must pass a 50-minute exam composed of 35 to 50 questions. Certiport has an exam tutorial here:

https://certiport.pearsonvue.com/Educator-resources/Exam-details/Exam-tutorials/Cisco_Tutorial.pdf

If that link doesn't work, be sure to register at https://www.certiport.com and then look for the exam tutorials link. One of the nice features of the CCST Networking exam is that you can move forward and back through test items, changing your answers if desired, before the exam ends or you select **Finish**.

## What Topics Are Covered on the CCST Networking Exam

The six domains of the CCST Networking 100-150 exam are as follows:

- 1.0 Standards and Concepts

- 2.0 Addressing and Subnet Formats

- 3.0 Endpoints and Media Types

- 4.0 Infrastructure

- 5.0 Diagnosing Problems

- 6.0 Security

Although Cisco outlines general exam topics, not all topics might appear on the CCST Networking exam; likewise, topics that are not specifically listed might appear on the exam. The exam topics that Cisco provides and this book covers are a general framework for exam preparation. Be sure to check Cisco's website for the latest exam topics.

## Purchase an Exam Voucher and Schedule Your Exam

If you are starting *31 Days Before Your Cisco Certified Support Technician (CCST) Networking 100-150 Exam* today, register with Certiport (https://www.certiport.com) and purchase your exam voucher right now. Next, use Certiport's locator to find a testing center (https://www.certiport.com/locator). Many testing centers provide remote testing in your chosen space. In my testing experience, there is no better motivator than a scheduled test date staring me in the face. I'm willing to bet the same holds true for you. So, if you're ready, gather the following information and register right now!

- Legal name
- Social Security or passport number
- Company name
- Valid email address
- Method of payment

You can schedule your exam at any time. I recommend that you schedule it for 31 days from now. The process and available test times vary based on the local testing center you choose.

Remember, there is no better motivation for study than an actual test date. *Sign up today.*

# Credits

Figures 2.3–2.6, 2.8–2.19: Linksys Holdings

Figures 5.4, 7.1, 7.2, 16.1–16.5: Microsoft Corporation

Figure 7.3: PuTTY

Figures 9.1- 9.3: Wireshark Foundation

Figure 14.5a: Wavebreakmedia/Shutterstock

Figure 14.5b: WhiteYura/Shutterstock

Figure 16.6: The Linux Foundation

Figures 16.7, 16.8, 16.10: Apple Inc

Figures 16.9, 16.11: Google LLC

Figure 19.1a: Galushko Sergey/Shutterstock

Figure 19.1b: ZayacSK/Shutterstock

Figure 19.1c: Ra3rn/Shutterstock

Figure 19.4b: Monte_a/Shutterstock

Figure 19.4c: Nattapan72/Shutterstock

Figure 19.4d: Darkroom Graphic/Shutterstock

Figure 19.5a: Peter Kotoff/Shutterstock

Figure 19.5b: Rogerutting/123RF

Figure 19.6a: Shaffandi/123RF

Figure 19.6b: Shahril KHMD/Shutterstock

Figure 19.10: Datskevich Aleh/Shutterstock

Figure 19.11: tom_tom_13/Shutterstock

Figure 19.12: Artush/123RF

Figure 19.13: Horvathta/Shutterstock

Figure 19.15: Suyanawut/123RF

Figures 19.14, 19.16, 19.17: Andrey Renteev/Shutterstock

Figures 28.5, 28.6: Ookla, LLC

# Networking Models

## CCST Networking Exam Topic

- 1.1. Identify the fundamental building blocks of networks.
  - *TCP/IP model, OSI model, frames and packets, addressing*

## Key Topics

Both the Open Systems Interconnection (OSI) and Transmission Control Protocol/Internet Protocol (TCP/IP) networking models are important conceptual frameworks for understanding networks. Today we review the layers and functions of each model.

## The OSI and TCP/IP Models

To understand how communication occurs across the network, you can use layered models as a framework for representing and explaining networking concepts and technologies. Layered models, such as the TCP/IP and OSI models, support interoperability between competing vendor product lines.

The OSI model principally serves as a tool for explaining networking concepts and troubleshooting. However, the protocols of the TCP/IP suite are the rules by which networks now operate. Because both models are important, you should be well versed in each model's layers and know how the models map to each other. Figure 31-1 summarizes the two models.

Using two models can be confusing; however, these simple guidelines might help:

- When discussing layers of a model, we are usually referring to the OSI model.
- When discussing protocols, we are usually referring to the TCP/IP model.

The next sections quickly review the OSI layers and the TCP/IP protocols.

**Figure 31-1   OSI and TCP/IP Models**

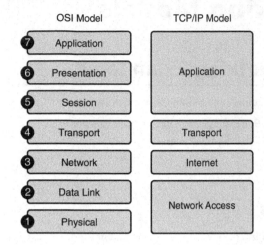

## OSI Layers

Table 31-1 summarizes the layers of the OSI model and provides a brief functional description.

**Table 31-1   OSI Model Layers and Functions**

| Layer | Functional Description |
|---|---|
| Application (7) | Refers to interfaces between network and application software and selects the application service. |
| Presentation (6) | Defines the format and organization of data. Includes encryption. |
| Session (5) | Establishes and maintains end-to-end bidirectional flows between endpoints. Includes managing transaction flows. Coordinates application interaction. |
| Transport (4) | Provides end-to-end data integrity and quality of service (QoS), including connection establishment and termination, flow control, error recovery, and segmentation of large data blocks into smaller parts for transmission. |
| Network (3) | Refers to logical addressing, routing, and path determination. Routes data between hosts. |
| Data link (2) | Formats data into frames appropriate for transmission onto some physical medium. Defines rules for when the medium can be used. Defines the means by which to recognize transmission errors. Transfers data across a single physical link. |
| Physical (1) | Defines the electrical, optical, cabling, connectors, and procedural details required for transmitting bits, represented as some form of energy passing over a physical medium. |

As networking theory evolved, the OSI model was adapted by generalizing some layers and minimizing others:

- Application and presentation layers are usually a single protocol rather than two separate ones.

- Session and transport layers are often combined into one protocol rather than two.

- QoS is often provided through the network layer rather than the transport layer.

- The data link and physical layers are conceptually combined but often involve two distinct protocols or functions.

The following mnemonic phrase, in which the first letter represents the layer (A stands for Application), can help in memorizing the name and order of the layers from top to bottom:

All People Seem To Need Data Processing

## TCP/IP Layers and Protocols

The TCP/IP model defines four categories of functions that must occur for communications to succeed. Most protocol models describe a vendor-specific protocol stack. However, because the TCP/IP model is an open standard, one company does not control the definition of the model.

Table 31-2 summarizes the TCP/IP layers, their functions, and the most common protocols.

**Table 31-2  TCP/IP Layer Functions**

| TCP/IP Layer | Function | Example Protocols |
| --- | --- | --- |
| Application | Represents data to the user and controls dialog | DNS, Telnet, SMTP, POP3, IMAP, DHCP, HTTP, FTP, SNMP |
| Transport | Supports communication between diverse devices across diverse networks | TCP, UDP, QUIC |
| Internet | Determines the best path through the network | IP, ARP, ICMP |
| Network access | Controls the hardware devices and media that make up the network | Ethernet, Wireless |

In the coming days, we review these protocols in more detail. For now, a brief description of the main TCP/IP protocols follows:

- **Domain Name System (DNS)**: Provides the IP address of a website or domain name so that a host can connect to it

- **Telnet**: Enables administrators to log in to a host from a remote location

- **Simple Mail Transfer Protocol (SMTP), Post Office Protocol (POP3), and Internet Message Access Protocol (IMAP)**: Facilitates sending email messages between clients and servers

- **Dynamic Host Configuration Protocol (DHCP)**: Assigns IP addressing to requesting clients

- **Hypertext Transfer Protocol (HTTP)**: Transfers information between web clients and web servers

- **File Transfer Protocol (FTP)**: Facilitates the download and upload of files between an FTP client and FTP server

- **Simple Network Management Protocol (SNMP)**: Enables network management systems to monitor devices attached to the network

- **Transmission Control Protocol (TCP)**: Supports virtual connections between hosts on the network to provide reliable delivery of data

- **User Datagram Protocol (UDP)**: Supports faster, unreliable delivery of lightweight or time-sensitive data

- **Quick UDP Internet Connections (QUIC)**: Encapsulated in a UDP packet but provides the same flow control mechanisms as TCP

- **Internet Protocol (IP)**: Provides a unique global address to computers for communicating over the network

- **Address Resolution Protocol (ARP)**: Finds a host's hardware address when only the IP address is known

- **Internet Control Message Protocol (ICMP)**: Sends error and control messages, including reachability to another host and availability of services

- **Ethernet**: Serves as the most popular LAN standard for framing and preparing data for transmission onto the media

- **Wireless**: Includes both IEEE 802.11 standards for wireless local area networks (WLANs) and cellular access options

# Study Resources

For today's exam topics, refer to the following resources for more study:

| Resource | Module or Chapter |
| --- | --- |
| SFA Self Enroll: Networking Basics | 5 |
| SFA Instructor Led: Networking Essentials | 5 |
| CCST Networking 100–150 Official Cert Guide | 6 |

**NOTE**   SFA: https://skillsforall.com/

# TCP/IP Layer Functions

## CCST Networking 100-150 Exam Topic

- 1.1. Identify the fundamental building blocks of networks.
  - *TCP/IP model, OSI model, frames and packets, addressing*

## Key Topics

Today we spend some time on the layers of the TCP/IP model, reviewing how each layer operates. We pay particular attention to the transport layer and its three protocols: Transmission Control Protocol (TCP), User Datagram Protocol (UDP), and Quick UDP Internet Connections (QUIC).

## The TCP/IP Application Layer

The application layer of the TCP/IP model provides an interface between software such as a web browser and the network itself. The process of requesting and receiving a web page works like this:

1. An HTTP request is sent, including an instruction to "get" a file (which is often a website's home page).

2. An HTTP response is sent from the web server with a code in the header, usually either 200 (request succeeded and information is returned in response) or 404 (page not found).

The HTTP request and the HTTP response are encapsulated in headers. The content of the headers allows the application layers on each end device to communicate. Regardless of the application layer protocol (HTTP, FTP, DNS, and so on), all use the same general process for communicating between application layers on the end devices.

## The TCP/IP Transport Layer

The transport layer, through TCP, provides a mechanism to guarantee delivery of data across the network. TCP supports error recovery to the application layer through the use of basic acknowledgment logic. Adding to the process for requesting a web page, TCP operation works like this:

1. The web client sends an HTTP request for a specific web server down to the transport layer.

2. TCP encapsulates the HTTP request with a TCP header and includes the destination port number for HTTP.

**3.** Lower layers process and send the request to the web server.

**4.** The web server receives HTTP requests and sends a TCP acknowledgment back to the requesting web client.

**5.** The web server sends the HTTP response down to the transport layer.

**6.** TCP encapsulates the HTTP data with a TCP header.

**7.** Lower layers process and send the response to the requesting web client.

**8.** The requesting web client sends an acknowledgment back to the web server.

If data is lost at any point during this process, TCP must recover the data. HTTP at the application layer does not get involved in error recovery.

In addition to TCP, the transport layer provides UDP, a connectionless, unreliable protocol for sending data that does not require or need error recovery. Table 30-1 lists the main features that the transport protocols support. Both TCP and UDP support the first function; only TCP supports the rest.

**Table 30-1   TCP/IP Transport Layer Features**

| Function | Description |
| --- | --- |
| Multiplexing using ports | Function that enables receiving hosts to choose the correct application for which the data is destined, based on the destination port number. |
| Error recovery (reliability) | Process of numbering and acknowledging data with Sequence and Acknowledgment header fields. |
| Flow control using windowing | Process that uses a sliding window size that the two end devices dynamically agree upon at various points during the virtual connection. The window size, represented in bytes, is the maximum amount of data the source will send before receiving an acknowledgment from the destination. |
| Connection establishment and termination | Process used to initialize port numbers and Sequence and Acknowledgment fields. |
| Ordered data transfer and data segmentation | A continuous stream of bytes from an upper-layer process that is "segmented" for transmission and delivered to upper-layer processes at the receiving device, with the bytes in the same order. |

# The TCP/IP Internet Layer

The Internet layer of the TCP/IP model and its Internet Protocol (IP) define addresses so that each host computer can have a different IP address. In addition, the Internet layer defines the process of routing so that routers can determine the best path to send packets to the destination. Continuing with the web page example, IP addresses the data as it passes from the transport layer to the Internet layer:

**1.** The web client sends an HTTP request.

**2.** TCP encapsulates the HTTP request.

3. IP encapsulates the transport segment into a packet, adding source and destination addresses.

4. Lower layers process and send the request to the web server.

5. The web server receives HTTP requests and sends a TCP acknowledgment back to the requesting web client.

6. The web server sends the HTTP response down to the transport layer.

7. TCP encapsulates the HTTP data.

8. IP encapsulates the transport segment into a packet, adding source and destination addresses.

9. Lower layers process and send the response to the requesting web client.

10. The requesting web client sends an acknowledgment back to the web server.

The operation of IP includes not only addressing but also the process of routing the data from source to destination. IP is further discussed and reviewed in the upcoming days.

# The TCP/IP Network Access Layer

IP depends on the network access layer to deliver IP packets across a physical network. Therefore, the network access layer defines the protocols and hardware required to deliver data across some physical network by specifying exactly how to physically connect a networked device to the physical media over which data can be transmitted.

The network access layer includes many protocols to deal with the different types of media that data can cross on its way from source device to destination device. For example, data might need to travel first on an Ethernet link and then cross a Point-to-Point Protocol (PPP) link, then a Frame Relay link, then a Multiprotocol Label Switching (MPLS) link, and then finally an Ethernet link to reach the destination. At each transition from one media type to another, the network access layer provides the protocols, cabling standards, headers, and trailers to send data across the physical network.

Many times, a local link address is needed to transfer data from one hop to the next. For example, in an Ethernet LAN, Media Access Control (MAC) addresses are used between the sending device and its local gateway router. At the gateway router (depending on the needs of the outbound interface), the Ethernet header might be replaced with an MPLS label. The label serves the same purpose as MAC addresses in Ethernet: to get the data across the link from one hop to the next so that the data can continue its journey to the destination. Some protocols, such as PPP, do not need a link address because only one other device on the link can receive the data.

With the network access layer, we can now finalize our web page example. The following greatly simplifies and summarizes the process of requesting and sending a web page:

1. The web client sends an HTTP request.

2. TCP encapsulates the HTTP request.

3. IP encapsulates the transport segment into a packet, adding source and destination addresses.

4. The network access layer encapsulates the packet in a frame, addressing it for the local link.

5. The network access layer sends the frame as bits on the media.

6. Intermediary devices process the bits at the network access and Internet layers and then forward the data toward the destination.

7. The web server receives the bits on the physical interface and sends them up through the network access and Internet layers.

8. The web server sends a TCP acknowledgment back to the requesting web client.

9. The web server sends the HTTP response down to the transport layer.

10. TCP encapsulates the HTTP data.

11. IP encapsulates the transport segment into a packet, adding source and destination addresses.

12. The network access layer encapsulates the packet in a frame, addressing it for the local link.

13. The network access layer sends the frame as bits on the media.

14. Lower layers process and send the response to the requesting web client.

15. The response travels back to the source over multiple data links.

16. The requesting web client receives the response on the physical interface and sends the data up through the network access and Internet layers.

17. The requesting web client sends a TCP acknowledgment back to the web server.

18. The web page is displayed in the requesting device's browser.

# Study Resources

For today's exam topics, refer to the following resources for more study:

| Resource | Module or Chapter |
| --- | --- |
| SFA Self Enroll: Networking Basics | 5 |
| SFA Instructor Led: Networking Essentials | 5 |
| CCST Networking 100–150 Official Cert Guide | 6 |

**NOTE**   SFA: https://skillsforall.com/

# Data Encapsulation

## CCST Networking 100-150 Exam Topic

- 1.1. Identify the fundamental building blocks of networks.

  - *TCP/IP model, OSI model, frames and packets, addressing*

## Key Topics

Today's review focuses on how data is encapsulated into packets and frames. This concept is important for understanding normal traffic flow as well as traffic that is encapsulated in a tunnel.

## Data Encapsulation Summary

As application data is passed down the protocol stack on its way to be transmitted across the network media, various protocols add information to it at each level. This is commonly known as the *encapsulation process*.

The data structure at any given layer is called a *protocol data unit (PDU)*. Table 29-1 lists the PDUs at each layer of the OSI model.

**Table 29-1   PDUs at Each Layer of the TCP/IP Model**

| TCP/IP Layer | PDU |
|---|---|
| Application | Data |
| Transport | Segment |
| Internet | Packet |
| Network accesss | Frame |
| | Bits |

Each layer of the TCP/IP model adds its own header information. As the data travels down through the layers, it is encapsulated with a new header. At the network access layer, a trailer is also added. This encapsulation process is described in five steps:

**Step 1.**   Create and encapsulate the application data with any required application layer headers. For example, the HTTP OK message can be returned in an HTTP header, followed by part of the contents of a web page.

**Step 2.**   Encapsulate the data supplied by the application layer inside a transport layer header. For end-user applications, a TCP or UDP header is typically used.

**Step 3.**   Encapsulate the data supplied by the transport layer inside an Internet layer (IP) header. IP is the only addressing protocol available in the TCP/IP network model at the Internet layer.

**Step 4.**   Encapsulate the data supplied by the Internet layer inside a network access layer header and trailer. This is the only layer that uses both a header and a trailer.

**Step 5.**   Transmit the bits. The physical layer encodes a signal onto the medium to transmit the frame.

The numbers in Figure 29-1 correspond to the five steps in the list, graphically showing the same encapsulation process.

**Figure 29-1   Five Steps of Data Encapsulation**

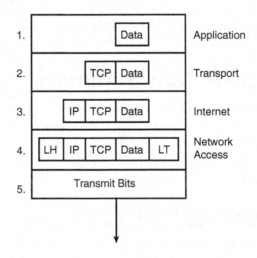

NOTE   The letters *LH* and *LT* stand for link header and link trailer, respectively, and refer to the data link layer header and trailer.

# Encapsulating in Tunnels

The process of encapsulating data in each PDU effectively hides the previous layer's data from the current layer. For example, the frame at the network access layer cannot "see" the IP addressing in the upper layer packet.

This hiding of data is called tunnelling when we use the word *tunnel* to refer to any packet that is encapsulated into another packet before being sent across the network. The original packet can be encrypted so that the data is hidden as the packet crosses the public Internet. To accomplish this tunnelling, two devices near the edge of the Internet are configured to create a virtual private network (VPN). The devices agree on a suite of protocols, typically IPsec, for encrypting the original packet. They then add some VPN header information and encapsulate the packet into a new IP packet with a new header.

Figure 29-2 shows a site-to-site VPN created between a branch office router and a Cisco firewall.

**Figure 29-2    VPN Tunnel Example**

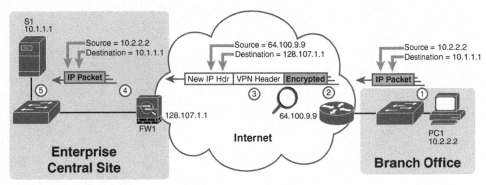

The figure shows the following steps, which explain the overall flow:

**Step 1.**    Host PC1 (10.2.2.2) on the right sends a packet to the web server (10.1.1.1), just as it would without a VPN.

**Step 2.**    The branch office router encrypts the packet, adds some VPN headers, adds another IP header (with public IP addresses), and forwards the packet.

**Step 3.**    An attacker on the Internet copies the packet (called a man-in-the-middle attack). However, the attacker cannot change the packet without being noticed and cannot read the contents of the original packet.

**Step 4.**    The Enterprise Central Site firewall (FW1) receives the packet, confirms the authenticity of the sender, confirms that the packet has not been changed, and then decrypts the original packet.

**Step 5.**    Server S1 receives the unencrypted packet.

# Study Resources

For today's exam topics, refer to the following resources for more study:

| Resource | Module or Chapter |
| --- | --- |
| SFA Self Enroll: Networking Devices and Initial Configuration | 5 |
| SFA Instructor Led: Networking Essentials | 22 |
| CCST Networking 100–150 Official Cert Guide | 1 |

**NOTE**    SFA: https://skillsforall.com/

# Measuring Network Performance

## CCST Networking 100-150 Exam Topic

- 1.2. Differentiate between bandwidth and throughput.
  - *Latency, delay, speed test vs. iPerf*

## Key Topics

Today's review focuses on the different measurements for network performance, the sources of delay, testing network performance online, and testing network performance using the Windows iPerf tool.

## Bandwidth, Throughput, and Goodput

There are three basic measurements for network performance: bandwidth, throughput, and goodput.

### Bandwidth

Bandwidth is determined by the medium's physical properties and is measured in bits per second. For example, 10GBASE-T Ethernet has a maximum capacity of 10Gbps (gigabits per second). The available bandwidth of a connection is how Internet service providers (ISPs) advertise and charge for their services.

### Throughput

Throughput is the actual rate of data transfer across the network and will be less than the bandwidth. This is because there is overhead on the link, such as routing protocols, Layer 2 minimum frame sizes (Ethernet), network congestion, and more.

Another important reason that throughput is less than bandwidth is because network engineers want to ensure the link has enough capacity to adjust to new demand bursts. For example, in Figure 28-1, Application 4 might not be able to start if the other three applications are consuming closer to 100% of the link's capacity. For this reason, it is common for network designers to consider a link at 80% bandwidth utilization as full utilization.

**Figure 28-1   Providing Enough Bandwidth for Another Application to Start**

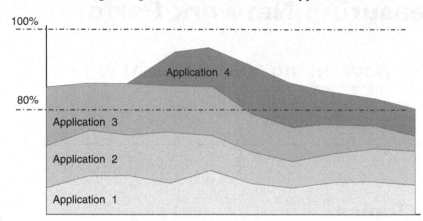

## Goodput

Although less commonly mentioned, goodput is the measure of the actual payload of data that is transmitted across the network. Goodput will always be less than throughput because every data packet contains fields of overhead. For example, Ethernet has a 20-byte header and IPv6 has a 40-byte header. In addition, there will always be a small number of errors in data transmission where packets must be recent.

## End-to-End Bandwidth

The bandwidth of an end-to-end path is limited by the lowest bandwidth link along the path. For example, a 1Gbps local link does not guarantee 1Gbps to all destinations. In Figure 28-2, Host A will have an end-to-end bandwidth of 1Gbps to Server E. However, Host A will be limited to 100Mbps to Server G and 10Mbps to Server H.

**Figure 28-2   Lowest Bandwidth Link Determines End-to-End Bandwidth**

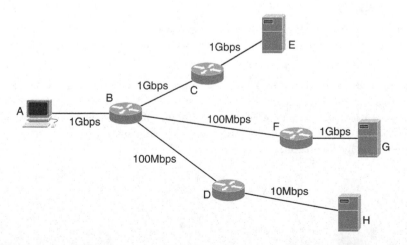

# Sources of Delay

Delay is the time it takes for a packet to travel from source to destination. Sources of delay include the following:

- The physical path length

- The time it takes to transmit data onto the wire (serialization delay)

- Queueing when there is congestion between the source and destination

- Jitter, which is the measure of difference in delay between packets

## Physical Path Length

Physical path length is the actual distance that packets need to travel from the source to the destination. The physical path length is a fundamental factor in determining delay, as it contributes to the overall time it takes for a signal to traverse the distance. In general, longer physical paths result in higher delays.

## Serialization Delay

Serialization delay refers to the time it takes to convert digital data into a stream of bits and transmit it onto the network. This process involves encoding the data and sending it out as a series of bits, as shown for the 8 bits in Figure 28-3.

**Figure 28-3   Converting Digital Bits to the Physical Medium**

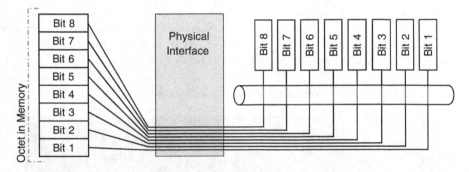

## Queueing Delay

Queueing delay occurs when there is congestion or contention for resources within the network. When multiple packets are trying to traverse the same network link simultaneously, they may have to wait in a queue before they can be transmitted. This queueing delay is directly related to network traffic and the network's capacity. Higher levels of congestion lead to longer queueing delays.

## Jitter

Jitter is the measure of variation in delay between packets. In an ideal network, packets would all arrive at the destination with consistent and predictable delays, as shown for the top row of packets in Figure 28-4. However, in real-world networks, factors such as varying traffic loads, different routing paths, and queueing delays can introduce variation in the arrival times of packets, as shown in the bottom row of packets in Figure 28-4.

**Figure 28-4   An Example of Equally Spaced and Jittered Packets**

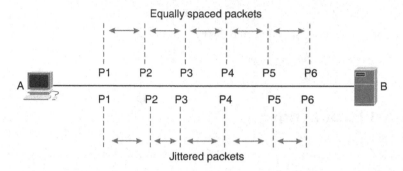

Jitter can be a significant issue in real-time applications like Voice over Internet Protocol (VoIP) or video streaming applications, where consistent timing is essential. To mitigate jitter, network engineers often use techniques like quality of service (QoS) to prioritize certain types of traffic and reduce variability in delay.

# Speed Tests

It's relatively easy for you to test the speed of your personal Internet connections. A quick Internet search will reveal several ad-supported sites that provide this service for free. Speed tests measure the throughput of your link. Specifically, they measure the throughput between you and the destination server that the speed test chooses for your test. Some speed tests, such as the one provided by Ookla, allow you to change the destination server, as shown in Figure 28-5.

**Figure 28-5   Example of a Web-Based Speed Test by Ookla**

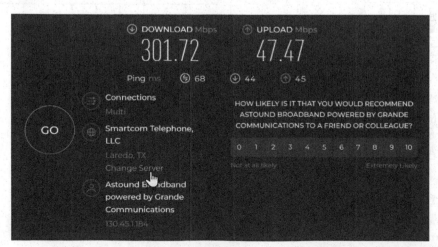

Ookla also has an app you can use to test the throughput of your cellular bandwidth, as shown in Figure 28-6.

**Figure 28-6    Ookla's Mobile App Speedtest**

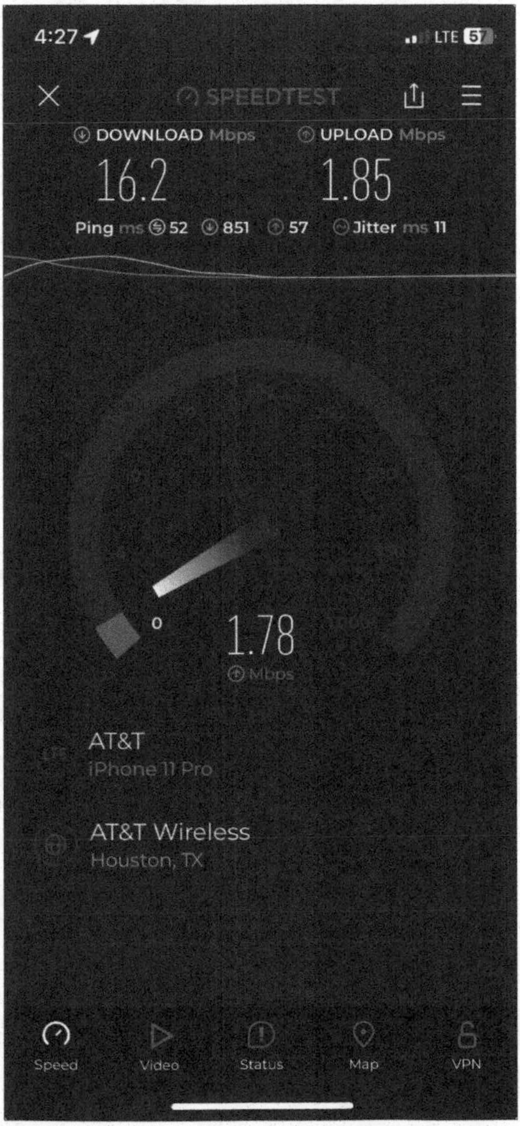

## The iPerf Tool

Although there are a variety of other tools you could download for measuring your network's performance, the CCST-Networking exam specifically calls out the iPerf tool. As of this writing, iPerf is in version 3 and can be downloaded for all the major operating systems at https://iperf.fr.

Example 28-1 shows the iPerf tool running on a Windows machine, testing the connection to a public iPerf server in Dallas.

**Example 28-1  Output from the iPerf Windows Tool**

```
C:\tools\iperf-3.1.3-win32> iperf3 -c dal.speedtest.clouvider.net
Connecting to host dal.speedtest.clouvider.net, port 5200
[  4] local 192.168.68.106 port 61680 connected to 2.56.188.136 port 5200
[ ID] Interval           Transfer      Bandwidth
[  4]   0.00-1.00   sec   441 KBytes   3.60 Mbits/sec
[  4]   1.00-2.00   sec   756 KBytes   6.19 Mbits/sec
[  4]   2.00-3.01   sec   756 KBytes   6.18 Mbits/sec
[  4]   3.01-4.00   sec   693 KBytes   5.68 Mbits/sec
[  4]   4.00-5.00   sec   756 KBytes   6.20 Mbits/sec
[  4]   5.00-6.00   sec   756 KBytes   6.19 Mbits/sec
[  4]   6.00-7.00   sec   756 KBytes   6.21 Mbits/sec
[  4]   7.00-8.00   sec   756 KBytes   6.20 Mbits/sec
[  4]   8.00-9.01   sec   819 KBytes   6.62 Mbits/sec
[  4]   9.01-10.01  sec   819 KBytes   6.71 Mbits/sec
- - - - - - - - - - - - - - - - - - - - - - - - -
[ ID] Interval           Transfer      Bandwidth
[  4]   0.00-10.01  sec  7.14 MBytes   5.98 Mbits/sec                sender
[  4]   0.00-10.01  sec  7.14 MBytes   5.98 Mbits/sec                receiver

iperf Done.

C:\tools\iperf-3.1.3-win32>
```

**NOTE**  You can easily find available iPerf public servers by doing an Internet search. The server chosen for Example 28-1 was found at https://github.com/R0GGER/public-iperf3-servers.

In Example 28-1, the number of kilobytes of data being transferred is measured every second. This value is then converted into the number of bits per second. After 10 seconds, we can see that the average throughput is 5.98Mbps for both the sender and the receiver.

Be sure you review the documentation for iPerf at https://iperf.fr/iperf-doc.php and practice different command-line options, including the following:

- **-s** sets the device to run in server mode.

- **-t** changes the amount of time in seconds to something other than the default 10 seconds.

- **-w** can be used to set the TCP window size.

- **-4** or **-6** indicate to only use IPv4 or IPv6, respectively.

Example 28-2 shows all the available options for iPerf on Windows.

**Example 28-2    Windows iPerf Options**

```
C:\tools\iperf-3.1.3-win32> iperf3 -h
Usage: iperf [-s|-c host] [options]
       iperf [-h|--help] [-v|--version]

Server or Client:
  -p, --port      #         server port to listen on/connect to
  -f, --format    [kmgKMG]  format to report: Kbits, Mbits, KBytes, MBytes
  -i, --interval  #         seconds between periodic bandwidth reports
  -F, --file name           xmit/recv the specified file
  -B, --bind      <host>    bind to a specific interface
  -V, --verbose             more detailed output
  -J, --json                output in JSON format
  --logfile f               send output to a log file
  -d, --debug               emit debugging output
  -v, --version             show version information and quit
  -h, --help                show this message and quit
Server specific:
  -s, --server              run in server mode
  -D, --daemon              run the server as a daemon
  -I, --pidfile file        write PID file
  -1, --one-off             handle one client connection then exit
Client specific:
  -c, --client    <host>    run in client mode, connecting to <host>
  -u, --udp                 use UDP rather than TCP
  -b, --bandwidth #[KMG][/#] target bandwidth in bits/sec (0 for unlimited)
                            (default 1 Mbit/sec for UDP, unlimited for TCP)
                            (optional slash and packet count for burst mode)
  -t, --time      #         time in seconds to transmit for (default 10 secs)
  -n, --bytes     #[KMG]    number of bytes to transmit (instead of -t)
  -k, --blockcount #[KMG]   number of blocks (packets) to transmit
(instead of -t or -n)
  -l, --len       #[KMG]    length of buffer to read or write
                            (default 128 KB for TCP, 8 KB for UDP)
  --cport         <port>    bind to a specific client port (TCP and UDP,
default: ephemeral port)
  -P, --parallel  #         number of parallel client streams to run
  -R, --reverse             run in reverse mode (server sends, client receives)
  -w, --window    #[KMG]    set window size / socket buffer size
  -M, --set-mss   #         set TCP/SCTP maximum segment size (MTU - 40 bytes)
  -N, --no-delay            set TCP/SCTP no delay, disabling Nagle's Algorithm
  -4, --version4            only use IPv4
  -6, --version6            only use IPv6
```

```
-S, --tos N              set the IP 'type of service'
-Z, --zerocopy           use a 'zero copy' method of sending data
-O, --omit N             omit the first n seconds
-T, --title str          prefix every output line with this string
--get-server-output      get results from server
--udp-counters-64bit     use 64-bit counters in UDP test packets


[KMG] indicates options that support a K/M/G suffix for kilo-, mega-, or giga-


iperf3 homepage at: http://software.es.net/iperf/
Report bugs to:     https://github.com/esnet/iperf


C:\tools\iperf-3.1.3-win32>
```

If you want to test the performance in your own network, download iPerf on the computer that will receive the iPerf packets. Use the **-s** option to start an iPerf server, as shown in Example 28-3.

**Example 28-3   iPerf Running in Server Mode**

```
C:\tools\iperf-3.1.3-win32> iperf3 -s
------------------------------------------------------------
Server listening on 5201
------------------------------------------------------------
```

**NOTE**   You will most likely need to configure a rule on your local firewalls to allow iPerf traffic.

# Study Resources

For today's exam topics, refer to the following resources for more study:

| Resource | Module or Chapter |
| --- | --- |
| SFA Self Enroll: Networking Basics | 1 |
| SFA Self Enroll: Network Support and Security | 1 |
| SFA Instructor Led: Networking Essentials | 1, 37 |
| CCST Networking 100–150 Official Cert Guide | 9 |

**NOTE**   SFA: https://skillsforall.com/

# Network Topologies

## CCST Networking 100-150 Exam Topic

- 1.3. Differentiate between LAN, WAN, MAN, CAN, PAN, and WLAN.
  - *Identify and illustrate common physical and logical network topologies*

## Key Topics

A network topology is typically a conceptual framework that defines the structure and connections within a network. These topologies can be very generic or they can be quite detailed, showing the precise architecture of the network. These detailed topologies or network diagrams are blueprints that help engineers visualize, build, and manage their network effectively. Today we will review the basic types of topologies.

## LANs and WANs

Local area networks (LANs) and wide area networks (WANs) are the two major classifications of network topologies.

### LANs

A LAN is a network of computers and other components located relatively close together in a limited area. LANs can vary widely in size—from one computer connected to a router in a home office, to hundreds of computers in a corporate office. However, in general, a LAN spans a limited geographical area. The fundamental components of a LAN include the following:

- Computers
- Interconnections (NICs and the media)
- Networking devices (access points, switches, and routers)
- Protocols (Ethernet, IP, ARP, DHCP, DNS, and so on)

### LAN Topologies

In multiaccess LANs, end devices are interconnected using star or extended star topologies, as shown in Figure 27-1. In this type of topology, end devices are connected to a central intermediary device, such as an Ethernet switch (not shown in Figure 27-1). An extended star extends this topology by interconnecting multiple Ethernet switches. The star and extended topologies are easy to install, very scalable, and easy to troubleshoot.

**Figure 27-1   LAN Topologies**

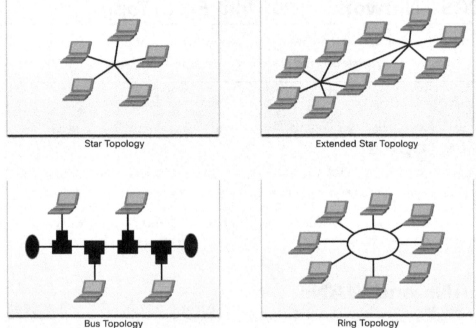

Star Topology          Extended Star Topology

Bus Topology          Ring Topology

---

**NOTE**   Also shown in Figure 27-1 are two legacy LAN topologies. Early Ethernet used a bus topology in which all end systems were chained to each other and terminated in some form on each end. Legacy Token Ring and legacy Fiber Distributed Data Interface (FDDI) used a ring topology in which end systems were connected to their respective neighbor, forming a ring. The ring does not need to be terminated, unlike in the bus topology.

---

# WANs

A WAN generally connects LANs that are geographically separated. A collection of LANs connected by one or more WANs is called an *internetwork*—thus, we have the Internet. The term *intranet* is often used to refer to a privately owned connection of LANs and WANs.

Depending on the type of service, connecting to the WAN normally works in one of six ways:

- 60-pin serial connection to a CSU/DSU (legacy)

- RJ-45 T1 controller connection to a CSU/DSU (legacy)

- RJ-11 connection to a dialup or DSL modem

- Cable coaxial connection to a cable modem

- Fiber Ethernet connection to a service provider's switch

## WAN Topologies

The three most common topologies used to interconnect WANs are point-to-point, hub-and-spoke, and mesh.

In Figure 27-2, the simplest and most common WAN topology is shown. It consists of a permanent link between two endpoints.

**Figure 27-2    Point-to-Point Topology**

In Figure 27-3, the WAN version of the star topology is shown. Here, a central site interconnects branch sites through the use of point-to-point links. Branch sites cannot exchange data with other branch sites without going through the central site.

**Figure 27-3    Hub-and-Spoke Topology**

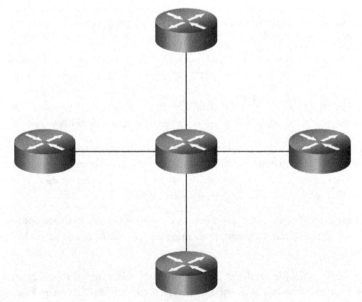

In Figure 27-4, the full mesh topology provides high availability but requires that every end system is interconnected to every other system. Therefore, the administrative and physical costs can be significant. Each link is essentially a point-to-point link to the other node.

**Figure 27-4  Full Mesh Topology**

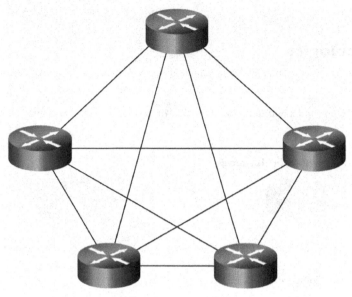

---

**NOTE**  A variation of any of these three topologies is called a hybrid topology. For example, a partial mesh topology is a hybrid in which one or more of the full mesh links are not present.

---

## Physical and Logical Topologies

Two types of network diagrams are used when describing LAN and WAN networks:

- **Physical topology**: Identifies the physical connections and how end devices and intermediary devices (that is, routers, switches, and wireless access points) are interconnected. The topology may also include specific device locations such as room number and location on the equipment rack. Physical topologies are usually point-to-point or star.

- **Logical topology**: Refers to the way a network transfers frames from one node to the next. This topology identifies virtual connections using device interfaces and Layer 3 IP addressing schemes.

Figures 27-5 and 27-6 display examples of physical topology and a logical topology for a small network. Notice that the LAN topology type is extended star and the WAN topology type (the connection to the Internet) is point-to-point.

**Figure 27-5   Physical Topology**

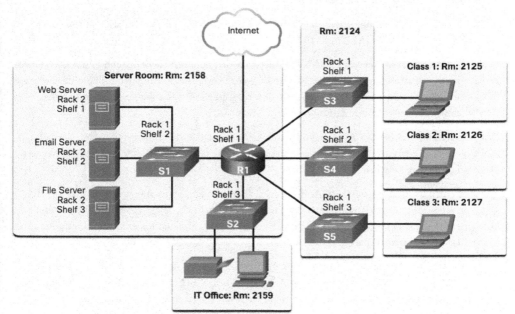

**Figure 27-6   Logical Topology**

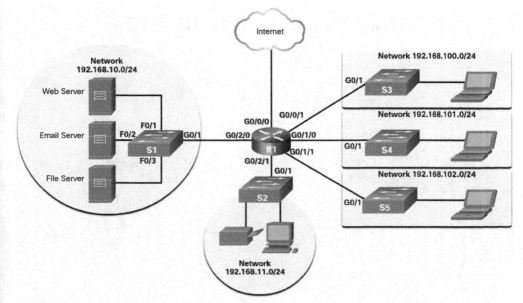

# Topology Variations

The CCST-Networking objectives call out some specific topology types we have yet to review, including PAN, WLAN, CAN, and MAN:

- A **personal area network (PAN)** is a network that connects devices, such as mice, keyboards, printers, smartphones, and tablets, within the range of an individual person. These devices are most often connected with Bluetooth technology. Bluetooth is a wireless technology that enables devices to communicate over short distances.

- A **wireless LAN (WLAN)** is similar to a LAN but wirelessly connects users and devices in a small geographical area instead of using a wired connection. A WLAN uses radio waves to transmit data between wireless devices.

- A **campus area network (CAN)** covers a slightly larger geographic area than a LAN, such as a university campus, corporate campus, or an industrial complex. CANs are used to connect multiple buildings within the defined campus area, allowing for efficient communication between different departments or units.

- A **metropolitan area network (MAN)** covers a larger geographical area than a CAN but is smaller than a WAN. It typically spans a city or a very large campus. MANs are designed to connect multiple LANs within a metropolitan area to provide high-speed connectivity. They are commonly used by businesses, educational institutions, and government organizations to interconnect their local networks.

# Small Office/Home Office (SOHO)

With the growing number of remote workers, enterprises have an increasing need for secure, reliable, and cost-effective ways to connect people working in small offices or home offices (SOHO) or other remote locations to resources on corporate sites. For SOHO workers, this is typically done through a cable or DSL connection, as shown in Figure 27-7.

**Figure 27-7   SOHO Connections to the Internet**

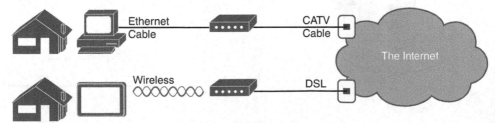

Remote connection technologies to support teleworkers include the following:

- Traditional private WAN technologies, including Frame Relay, ATM, and leased lines, although these technologies are now considered legacy

- Remote secure virtual private network (VPN) access through a broadband connection over the public Internet

Components needed for teleworker connectivity include the following:

- **Home office components**: Computer, broadband access (cable or DSL), and a VPN router or VPN client software installed on the computer

- **Corporate components**: VPN-capable routers, VPN concentrators, multifunction security appliances, authentication, and central management devices for resilient aggregation and termination of the VPN connections

## SOHO Routers

The gateway to the Internet for a SOHO is typically an integrated, multifunction router. SOHO routers have the following features:

- They use the Internet and virtual private network (VPN) technology for their WAN connections to send data back and forth to the rest of the enterprise.

- They use a multifunction device that offers routing, LAN switching, VPN, wireless, and other features, as shown in Figure 27-8.

In reality, the access point and switch are integrated into the router.

**Figure 27-8    Internal Functions of a SOHO Router**

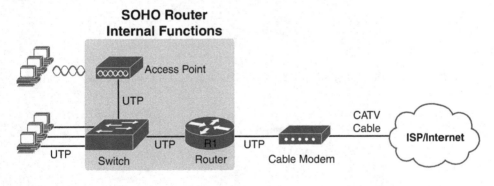

NOTE    UTP in Figure 27-8 stands for *unshielded twisted pair*.

# Hierarchical Campus Design

Hierarchical campus design involves dividing the network into discrete layers. Each layer provides specific functions that define its role within the overall network. When the various functions that exist on a network are separated, the network design becomes modular, which facilitates scalability and performance. The hierarchical design model is divided into three layers:

- **Access layer**: Provides local and remote user access

- **Distribution layer**: Controls the flow of data between the access and core layers

- **Core layer**: Acts as the high-speed redundant backbone

Figure 27-9 shows an example of the three-tiered hierarchical campus network design.

**Figure 27-9   Three-Tiered Campus Design**

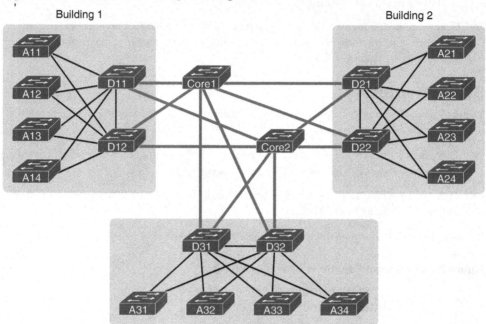

For smaller networks, the core is often collapsed into the distribution layer for a two-tiered design, as in Figure 27-10.

**Figure 27-10   Two-Tiered Campus Design**

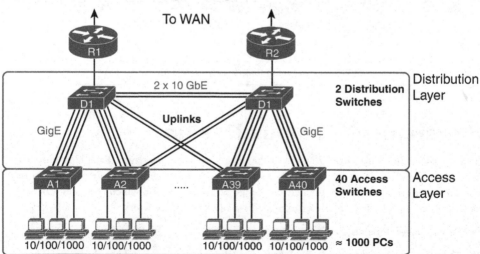

A two-tier design solves two major design needs:

- It provides a place to connect end-user devices (the access layer, with access switches).

- It connects the switches with a reasonable number of cables and switch ports by connecting all 40 access switches to two distribution switches.

For very small networks and home networks, all three tiers can be seen in one device, such as the Cisco Meraki wireless router shown in Figure 27-11.

**Figure 27-11    Cisco Meraki MX68 Wireless VPN Router**

# Study Resources

For today's exam topics, refer to the following resources for more study:

| Resource | Module or Chapter |
|---|---|
| SFA Self Enroll: Networking Devices and Initial Configuration | 18 |
| SFA Self Enroll: Network Addressing and Basic Troubleshooting | 2 |
| SFA Instructor Led: Networking Essentials | 18, 31 |
| CCST Networking 100-150 Official Cert Guide | 12, 13 |

**NOTE**    SFA: https://skillsforall.com/

# Cloud Computing

## CCST Networking 100-150 Exam Topic

- 1.4. Compare and contrast cloud and on-premises applications and services.

  - *Public, private, hybrid, SaaS, PaaS, IaaS, remote work/hybrid work*

## Key Topics

Just about everything you do online today involves the cloud in some way or another. When you use email services like Gmail, your emails are stored on and accessed from the cloud. Dropbox and Google Drive store your files on cloud servers. Netflix delivers content from the cloud. Microsoft 365 is delivered as a service over the cloud. Instagram and TikTok store and process data in the cloud. Xbox Game Pass has a cloud feature for game streaming. Today we review how different cloud configurations enable a variety of network configurations and enable remote and hybrid work.

## On-Premises Computing

On-premises is a type of computing infrastructure that is located physically within an organization's properties. The infrastructure is maintained, operated, and controlled by IT staff employed by the organization. This type of computing has the following advantages and disadvantages:

**On-Premises Advantages**

- **Control:** The organization has complete control of its data, applications, and server infrastructure.

- **Performance**: On-premises hardware can provide more predictable performance, as you're not competing with other businesses for resources or dependent on Internet connections.

- **Security:** The organization has full control over security measures.

**On-Premises Disadvantages**

- **High upfront costs:** The organization is responsible for purchasing and installing the necessary hardware and software.

- **Maintenance and updates**: The organization is responsible for maintaining the hardware, updating software, and applying patches, which can be time-consuming and require dedicated IT staff.

- **Limited scalability**: Scaling up requires purchasing, installing, and configuring new hardware, which can be slow and expensive.

# Cloud Computing

*Cloud* refers to the delivery of computing services, including servers, storage, databases, networking, software, analytics, and intelligence, over the Internet to offer faster innovation, flexible resources, and economies of scale.

Cloud computing involves large numbers of computers connected through a network that can be physically located anywhere. Cloud computing provides the following benefits:

- Enables access to organizational data anywhere and at any time

- Streamlines IT operations by subscribing only to needed services

- Eliminates or reduces the need for onsite IT equipment, maintenance, and management

- Reduces cost for equipment, energy, physical plant requirements, and personnel training needs

- Enables rapid responses to increasing data volume requirements

Cloud computing has the following advantages and disadvantages:

**Cloud Computing Advantages**

- **Scalability**: The organization can scale its purchase of cloud services very quickly to meet demand.

- **Cost-effectiveness**: The organization is not responsible for large capital expenditures for hardware and ensuing maintenance.

- **Accessibility**: The organization does not need to manage multiple incoming remote worker VPN connections because cloud services can be accessed from anywhere with an Internet connection.

- **Automatic updates**: The organization benefits from software that is updated by the service provider, instead of the organization's IT staff, to the most current version.

**Cloud Computing Disadvantages**

- **Internet connection**: The organization must depend on its Internet connections to be able to access applications and data.

- **Long-term cost**: The organization's cost might be more in the long term if recurring costs exceed purchasing and maintaining on-premises hardware.

- **Data security and privacy**: While most cloud providers offer robust security measures, storing sensitive data in the cloud can still be a concern for some businesses due to potential data breaches or privacy issues.

# Cloud Computing Services

To understand the value of cloud computing, consider the effort it takes to manage virtual machines (VMs) in a traditional data center. The workflow follows:

1. A customer requests a VM or a new set of VMs.

2. The data center engineer configures virtualization software.

3. Virtualization software creates VMs.

Although this process works, it does not have the characteristics of a cloud computing service as defined by the U.S. National Institute of Standards and Technology (NIST):

- **On-demand self-service**: The user can order, modify, and end service without human interaction.

- **Broad network access**: The service can be accessed from a variety of devices across any network.

- **Resource pooling**: The provider has a pool of resources that can be dynamically allocated to users. The user typically requires no awareness of the physical location of the resources.

- **Rapid elasticity**: To the user, the resource pool appears to be unlimited; it can expand and contract as needed.

- **Measured service**: The provider can measure the usage and then report that usage to the consumer, for both transparency and billing.

Cloud providers can offer a variety of services to meet the needs of their customers, including these:

- **Software as a Service (SaaS)**: The cloud provider is responsible for access to services that are delivered over the Internet, such as email, communication, and Microsoft 365. Users only need to provide their data.

- **Platform as a Service (PaaS)**: The cloud provider is responsible for access to the development tools and services used to deliver the applications. Customers can customize the virtualized hardware.

- **Infrastructure as a Service (IaaS)**: The cloud provider is responsible for access to the network equipment, virtualized network services, and network infrastructure support.

Four primary cloud models exist:

- **Public clouds**: Cloud-based applications and services offered in a public cloud are made available to the general population. The public cloud uses the Internet to provide services.

- **Private clouds**: Cloud-based applications and services offered in a private cloud are intended for a specific organization or entity, such as the government. A private cloud uses the organization's private network.

- **Hybrid clouds**: A hybrid cloud is made up of two or more clouds (for example, part private/ part public). Each part remains a distinct object, but both are connected using a single architecture.

- **Community clouds**: A community cloud is created for exclusive use by a specific community. The differences between public clouds and community clouds are the functional needs that have been customized for the community.

# Server Virtualization

Although not specifically called out in the CCST-Networking objectives, cloud providers rely heavily on virtualization to enable the solutions they offer to clients. Let's spend some time reviewing some fundamental aspects of virtualization.

Historically, organizations bought multiple hardware servers, and the server administrator installed one or more network applications on the server, such as an email server or file server (see Figure 26-1).

**Figure 26-1  Dedicated Server with One OS**

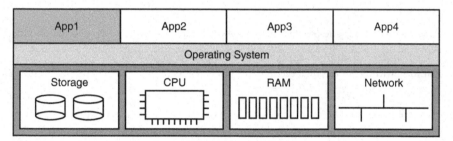

Each of these servers had its own CPU, memory, network interface card (NIC), and disk space. However, this model faces several challenges:

- If a component fails, the service is unavailable until the component is repaired or replaced.
- Servers sometimes sit idle for long periods of time waiting for clients to use them.
- Servers take up space and waste energy.

Server virtualization takes advantage of idle resources and consolidates the number of required servers. Virtualization separates the operating system (OS) from the hardware. This also makes it possible for multiple OSs to exist on a single hardware platform. Each instance of an OS is called a virtual machine (VM).

A server with multiple VMs uses a hypervisor to manage access to the server's physical resources. The hypervisor sits between the VMs and the hardware, as shown in Figure 26-2.

Another method for managing a set of VMs on a server, especially in a data center environment, is to use a virtual switch that connects the VMs to physical NICs, as shown in Figure 26-3. Instead of a hypervisor, an external controller (not shown) manages the server hardware.

**Figure 26-2  Hypervisor Managing Four VMs**

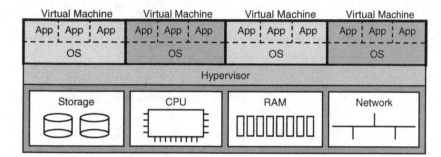

**Figure 26-3  Virtual Switch and VMs**

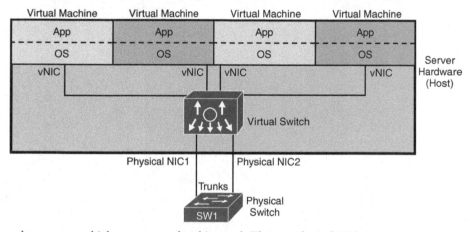

In a data center, multiple servers are placed in a rack. The two physical NICs in Figure 26-3 are attached to two redundant top-of-rack (ToR) switches. Racks are lined up in rows and managed by two redundant end-of-row (EoR) switches. Figure 26-4 shows this physical layout of a traditional data center.

**Figure 26-4  Traditional Data Center Physical Topology**

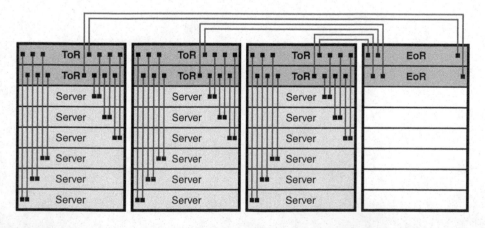

# Study Resources

For today's exam topics, refer to the following resources for more study:

| Resource | Module or Chapter |
|---|---|
| SFA Self Enroll: Networking Devices and Initial Configuration | 2 |
| SFA Instructor Led: Networking Essentials | 19 |
| CCST Networking 100-150 Official Cert Guide | 17 |

**NOTE**   SFA: https://skillsforall.com/

# Transport Protocols

## CCST Networking 100-150 Exam Topic

- 1.5. Describe common network applications and protocols.

    - *TCP vs. UDP (connection-oriented vs. connectionless), FTP, SFTP, TFTP, HTTP, HTTPS, DHCP, DNS, ICMP, NTP*

## Key Topics

We will spend the next three days reviewing this exam topic. Today, we will focus on the two main transport layer protocols, Transport Control Protocol (TCP) and User Datagram Protocol (UDP).

## TCP and UDP

TCP and UDP are the two primary protocols that operate at the transport layer. TCP is connection-oriented, which means it establishes a connection before transmitting data, and ensures that all data packets arrive at the destination in the correct order. It's like a phone call where you dial a number, wait for the call to be answered, and then start a conversation, asking the other person to repeat themselves if you did not understand them.

UDP, on the other hand, is connectionless. It sends data without setting up a connection, which can result in faster transmission but with the risk of packets being lost or arriving out of order. It's like sending a postcard, where you write the address and send it without knowing whether or not it will reach the destination. You might send a postcard every day, but there is no guarantee that the addressee will receive the postcards in the same order.

Table 25-1 reviews the differences between connection-oriented and connectionless protocols.

**Table 25-1  Connectionless versus Connection-Oriented Protocols**

| Characteristic | Connection-Oriented | Connectionless |
|---|---|---|
| Basic description | Looks like a circuit, or a direct connection between two devices. | Simple "send-and-forget" protocol. |
| Connection process | Uses some form of handshake to verify devices on either end of the circuit can communicate. | None; source just sends packets to the destination. |

| Characteristic | Connection-Oriented | Connectionless |
|---|---|---|
| Reaction to dropped packets, segments, or data | Tracks transmitted data and requests retransmission if anything is missing. | None. |
| Reaction to transmission errors | Requests retransmission if detected. | If errors are detected, data is dropped. |
| Flow control | Transmitter and receiver communicate to ensure data is being transmitted at a rate both can support. | None; transmitter sends at its own pace. |
| Data reordering | Reorders data correctly if detected. | Not detected. |

## TCP Header

TCP provides error recovery, but to do so, it consumes more bandwidth and uses more processing cycles than UDP. TCP and UDP rely on IP for end-to-end delivery. TCP is concerned with providing services to the applications of the sending and receiving computers. To provide all these services, TCP uses a variety of fields in its header (see Figure 25-1).

**Figure 25-1  TCP Header**

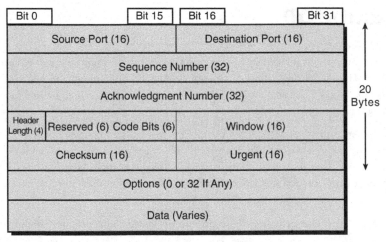

## Port Numbers

The first two fields of the TCP header—the source and destination ports—are also part of the UDP header that appears later in Figure 25-6. Port numbers provide TCP (and UDP) with a way to multiplex multiple applications on the same computer. Web browsers now support multiple tabs or pages. Each time you open a new tab and request another web page, TCP assigns a different source port number and sometimes multiple port numbers. For example, you might have five web pages open. TCP almost always assigns destination port 80 for all five sessions. However, the source port for each is different. This is how TCP (and UDP) multiplexes the conversation so that the web browser knows in which tab to display the data.

TCP and UDP usually dynamically assign the source ports, starting with 1024 and going up to a maximum of 65535. Port numbers below 1024 are reserved for well-known applications. Table 25-2 lists several popular applications and their well-known port numbers.

**Table 25-2    Popular Applications and Their Well-Known Port Numbers**

| Port Number | Protocol | Application |
| --- | --- | --- |
| 20 | TCP | FTP data |
| 21 | TCP | FTP control |
| 22 | TCP | SSH |
| 23 | TCP | Telnet |
| 25 | TCP | SMTP |
| 53 | UDP, TCP | DNS |
| 67, 68 | UDP | DHCP |
| 69 | UDP | TFTP |
| 80 | TCP | HTTP (WWW) |
| 110 | TCP | POP3 |
| 161 | UDP | SNMP |
| 443 | TCP | HTTPS (SSL) |
| 16384–32767 | UDP | RTP-based voice (VoIP) and video |

# Error Recovery

Also known as *reliability*, TCP provides error recovery during data transfer sessions between two end devices that have established a connection. The Sequence and Acknowledgment fields in the TCP header track every byte of data transfer and ensure that missing bytes are retransmitted.

In Figure 25-2, the Acknowledgment field sent by the web client (4000) implies the next byte to be received; this is called *positive acknowledgment*.

**Figure 25-2    TCP Acknowledgment Without Errors**

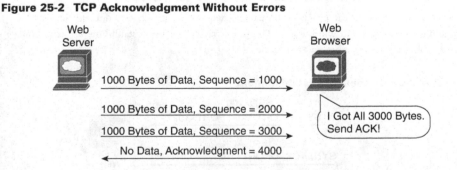

Figure 25-3 depicts the same scenario, except now with some errors. The second TCP segment was lost in transmission. Therefore, the web client replies with an ACK field set to 2000. This is called a positive acknowledgment with retransmission (PAR) because the web client is requesting that some of the data be retransmitted. The web server will now resend data starting at segment 2000. In this way, lost data is recovered.

**Figure 25-3  TCP Acknowledgment with Errors**

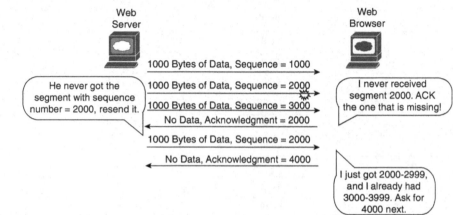

Although not shown, the web server also sets a retransmission timer and awaits acknowledgment, just in case the acknowledgment is lost or all transmitted segments are lost. If that timer expires, the web server sends all segments again.

## Flow Control

TCP handles flow control through a process called *windowing*. The two end devices negotiate the window size when initially establishing the connection; then they dynamically renegotiate window size during the life of the connection, increasing its size until it reaches the maximum window size of 65,535 bytes or until errors occur. Window size is specified in the Window field of the TCP header. After sending the amount of data specified in the window size, the source must receive an acknowledgment before sending the next window size of data.

## Connection Establishment and Termination

Connection establishment is the process of initializing sequence and acknowledgment fields and agreeing on port numbers and window size. The three-way connection establishment phase shown in Figure 25-4 must occur before data transfer can proceed.

**Figure 25-4  TCP Connection Establishment**

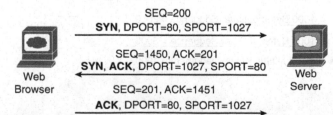

In the figure, DPORT and SPORT are the destination port and the source port, respectively. SEQ is the sequence number. In bold are SYN and ACK, with each representing a 1-bit flag in the TCP header used to signal connection establishment. TCP initializes the Sequence Number and Acknowledgment Number fields to any number that fits into the 4-byte fields. The initial Sequence Number is a random 32-bit number generated with each new transmission. The Acknowledgment Number is received back and increments the sender's sequence number by 1.

When data transfer is complete, a four-way termination sequence occurs that uses an additional flag, called the FIN bit (see Figure 25-5).

**Figure 25-5  TCP Connection Termination**

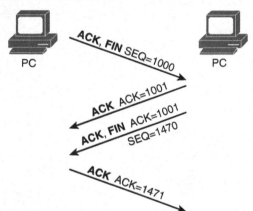

# UDP

TCP establishes and terminates connections between endpoints, whereas UDP does not. Therefore, UDP is called a *connectionless protocol*. It provides no reliability, no windowing, and no reordering of the data. However, UDP does provide data transfer and multiplexing using port numbers, and it does so with fewer bytes of overhead and less processing than TCP. Applications that use UDP, such as VoIP, can trade the possibility of some data loss for less delay. Figure 25-6 compares the two headers.

**Figure 25-6  TCP and UDP Headers**

| 2 | 2 | 4 | 4 | 4 bits | 6 bits | 6 bits | 2 | 2 | 2 | 3 | 1 |
|---|---|---|---|--------|--------|--------|---|---|---|---|---|
| Source Port | Dest. Port | Sequence Number | Ack. Number | Offset | Reserved | Flags | Window Size | Checksum | Urgent | Options | PAD |

TCP Header

| 2 | 2 | 2 | 2 |
|---|---|---|---|
| Source Port | Dest. Port | Length | Checksum |

UDP Header

* Unless Specified, Lengths Shown
  Are the Numbers of Bytes

# Study Resources

For today's exam topics, refer to the following resources for more study:

| Resource | Module or Chapter |
| --- | --- |
| SFA Self-Enroll: Networking Basics | 15 |
| SFA Instructor Led: Networking Essentials | 15 |
| CCST Networking 100-150 Official Cert Guide | 14 |

**NOTE**   SFA: https://skillsforall.com/

# FTP, NTP, and ICMP

## CCST Networking 100-150 Exam Topic

- 1.5. Describe common network applications and protocols.

  - *TCP vs. UDP (connection-oriented vs. connectionless), FTP, SFTP, TFTP, HTTP, HTTPS, DHCP, DNS, ICMP, NTP*

## Key Topics

Security is a real concern when you are using a file transfer application. Rarely do you want to send unencrypted files over a network. Network Time Protocol (NTP) is essential for maintaining accurate and synchronized time across all devices on a network, which is fundamental for data consistency, accurate logging, and authentication. The Internet Control Message Protocol (ICMP) allows network devices to exchange error messages and operational information, indicating the success or failure of data transmission. This helps in diagnosing network-related issues, maintaining network health, and improving performance. Today, we review file transfer protocols, NTP, and ICMP.

## File Transfer Protocols

Common file transfer protocols include the following:

- **File Transfer Protocol (FTP)** is used to transfer files in plaintext between a client and a server over a network.

- **Secure File Transfer Protocol (SFTP)** is an extension of Secure Shell (SSH) that provides file transfer capabilities. SFTP adds encryption to enhance security.

- **Trivial File Transfer Protocol (TFTP)** is a simplified version of FTP that allows files to be transferred but lacks security or file management features. It's mainly used in scenarios where security isn't a concern, like updating the configuration or firmware on a network device.

### FTP

FTP uses a separate control connection and data connection. The control connection is used to send control information (commands and responses) while the data connection is used to send the actual files. FTP can be used with a command-line interface (CLI) such as the Windows command prompt or the Linux terminal window. However, it can also be used in a web-based interface or standalone program with a graphical user interface (GUI) such as FileZilla or Cyberduck.

Table 24-1 lists some of the more common FTP commands.

**Table 24-1 FTP Commands**

| Command | Description |
|---|---|
| ftp *user@servername*<br><br>or<br><br>ftp *user:pass@servername* | This command is used to connect to the FTP server with *user* at *servername*. The *servername* can be an IP address or a fully qualified domain name (FQDN). The FTP server will prompt you for a password (*pass*) if you do not include it in the command. |
| Pwd | Displays the current directory on the FTP server. |
| cd *directory-path* | Changes the current directory to another directory on the FTP server. |
| Ls | Lists the files and directories in the current directory on the FTP server. |
| Binary | This command is used to set the mode of file transfer to binary, which is suitable for non-text files, such as images and executable files. |
| Ascii | This command is used to set the mode of file transfer to ASCII, which is suitable for text files. |
| get *filename* | Downloads *filename* from the current directory on the FTP server. |
| put *filename* | Uploads a file to the current directory on the FTP server. |
| Quit | Closes the FTP connection. |

Example 24-1 shows how you might use these commands on a Linux FTP client to connect to an FTP server and manage files.

**Example 24-1 Using FTP Commands on a Linux or Mac Client**

```
$ ftp admin@ftp.example.com
Password: letmein
ftp> pwd
257 "/home/admin" is your current location
ftp> cd files
250 Directory successfully changed.
ftp> ls
200 PORT command successful. Consider using PASV.
150 Here comes the directory listing.
-rw-r--r--    1 1000     1000         4096 Oct 20 13:58 myfile1.jpg
-rw-r--r--    1 1000     1000         2048 Oct 20 13:59 myfile2.txt
226 Directory send OK.
ftp> binary
200 Switching to Binary mode.
ftp> get myfile1.jpg
200 PORT command successful.
150 Opening BINARY mode data connection for myfile1.jpg (4096 bytes).
226 Transfer complete.
```

```
4096 bytes received in 0.01 secs (409.6 kB/s)
ftp> ascii
200 Switching to ASCII mode.
ftp> put myfile3.txt
200 PORT command successful.
150 Opening ASCII mode data connection for myfile3.txt.
226 Transfer complete.
ftp> quit
221 Goodbye.
```

FTP doesn't encrypt its data, meaning that information such as usernames, passwords, and files can be intercepted easily. Because of this, it's recommended to use FTPS (FTP over SSL) or SFTP (SSH File Transfer Protocol) when security is a concern.

# SFTP

SFTP is a protocol that provides file transfer and manipulation capabilities. Unlike FTPS, it does not utilize the File Transfer Protocol. It is built as an extension of SSH, which was designed as secure replacement for Telnet. SFTP encrypts both the data being transferred and the commands being sent, preventing passwords and sensitive information from being transmitted in the plaintext over the network. It only needs a single port to establish a server connection, as opposed to FTP and FTPS, which both require a data port and a command port. This single-port feature makes it easier to configure access rules in firewalls. Example 24-2 demonstrates a simple SFTP session.

**Example 24-2   Using SFTP Commands on a Linux or Mac Client**

```
$ sftp admin@ftp.example.com
admin@ftp.example.com's password: letmein
sftp> pwd
Remote working directory: /home/admin
sftp> ls
myfile1.jpg    myfile2.txt
sftp> cd files
sftp> get myfile2.txt
Fetching /home/admin/files/myfile2.txt to myfile2.txt
myfile2.txt                          100%   180     0.2KB/s    00:00
sftp> put myfile3.txt
Uploading myfile3.txt to /home/admin/files/myfile3.txt
myfile3.txt                          100%   180     0.2KB/s    00:00
sftp> exit
```

Another benefit to using SFTP is access to familiar Linux file and directory commands, such as the ones shown in Table 24-2.

**Table 24-2  SFTP Supports Linux File and Directory Commands**

| Command | Description |
|---|---|
| `mkdir` | Create a new directory. |
| `rmdir` | Remove an empty directory. |
| `rename` `old_filename` `new_filename` | Rename a file or directory. |
| `rm` filename | Remove a file. |
| `chmod` `permissions` `filename` | Change the permissions for *filename*. The *permissions* are specified as a three-digit number. For example, for *filename*, the three digits 755 would permit read-write-execute for the owner (7) and read-execute for the group (5) and others (5). |

## TFTP

The first *T* in TFTP stands for "Trivial" because it is a very simplistic protocol with very limited features. It was designed for simplicity and ease of implementation, rather than security or functionality.

You typically see TFTP in controlled environments where there is no connection to the Internet or other networks. TFTP is commonly used to configure a network device or upgrade it with new firmware.

# NTP

NTP is the standard protocol for synchronizing network devices and hosts within a few milliseconds of one another across a global network. NTP has a hierarchy of stratums, shown in Figure 24-1, that devices use to determine which NTP source is the most trusted.

**Figure 24-1  NTP Stratums**

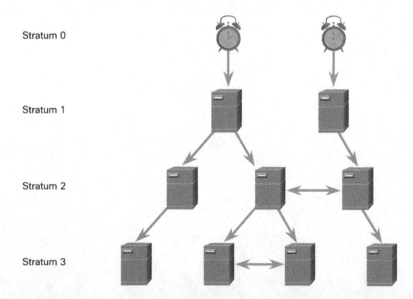

Stratum 0

Stratum 1

Stratum 2

Stratum 3

**Stratum 0** devices are high-precision timekeeping devices such as atomic clocks, Global Positioning System (GPS) radio clocks, or devices using Precision Time Protocol (PTP) to obtain sub-microsecond time from another stratum 0 device. They are used by Stratum 1 servers to determine the precise time. Stratum 0 devices are technically not part of the NTP network, but they are connected to Stratum 1 servers and are used to set their time.

**Stratum 1** are the servers directly connected to Stratum 0 devices. They query Stratum 0 devices for the time and then distribute the time from these reference clocks to other, lower-stratum servers on the network. Stratum 1 servers may be connected to several stratum 0 devices and may also query other stratum 1 servers.

Stratum 2 servers are connected to one or more Stratum 1 servers, and Stratum 2 servers are connected to one or more Stratum 3 servers. Not shown in Figure 24-1 are Stratum 16 devices, which are devices that are unsynchronized with any time source.

# NTP Configuration and Verification

Network devices issue log messages in response to different events. For example, when an interface fails, the device creates log messages. With default settings, Cisco IOS sends these messages to the console port. But Cisco IOS can be configured to also send messages to a syslog server, where they can be stored for administration review and troubleshooting. Figure 24-2 shows a topology with a syslog server.

**Figure 24-2  Sample Network with a Syslog Server**

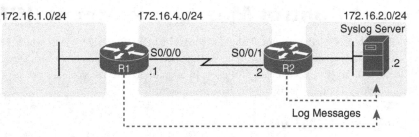

Most log messages list the date and time as part of the message so that when a network engineer looks back at the message, they know exactly when that message occurred.

The Network Time Protocol (NTP) provides a way to synchronize the time-of-day clock so that timestamps are consistent across devices, making troubleshooting easier.

To configure a router or switch to synchronize its time with an existing NTP server, use the **ntp server** command, as in Example 24-3.

**Example 24-3  Configuration and Verification of an NTP Client**

```
R1(config)# ntp server 172.16.2.2
R1(config)# end
%SYS-5-CONFIG_I: Configured from console by console
R1#
```

```
R1# show ntp status
Clock is synchronized, stratum 8, reference is 172.16.2.2
nominal freq is 250.0000 Hz, actual freq is 250.0000 Hz, precision is 2**21
ntp uptime is 4700 (1/100 of seconds), resolution is 4000
reference time is D42BD899.5FFCE014 (13:48:09.374 UTC Fri Oct 19 2023)
clock offset is -0.0033 msec, root delay is 1.28 msec
root dispersion is 3938.51 msec, peer dispersion is 187.59 msec
loopfilter state is 'CTRL' (Normal Controlled Loop), drift is 0.000000000 s/s
system poll interval is 64, last update was 42 sec ago.
R1# show ntp associations
address ref clock st when poll reach delay offset disp
*172.16.2.2 127.127.1.1 7 36 64 1 1.261 -0.001 7937.5
 * sys.peer, # selected, + candidate, - outlyer, x falseticker, configured
```

The output of the **show ntp status** command gives the NTP status in the very first line—R1 is synchronized with the NTP server at 172.16.2.2. The **show ntp associations** command lists a single line of output for every other NTP device with which the router has associated.

Routers and switches can actually be the NTP server with just one command (**ntp master**) as well. In addition, NTP can use authentication so that a router or switch does not get fooled into changing its timestamp.

# Internet Control Message Protocol (ICMP)

Because IP is only a best-effort protocol, the developers of TCP/IP created ICMP, which provides feedback about issues related to the processing of IP packets under certain conditions. However, ICMP does not make IP reliable. That's TCP's job. In addition, ICMP messages are not required and are often not allowed within a network for security reasons.

## ICMPv4 and ICMPv6

ICMP is available for both IPv4 and IPv6. ICMPv4 is the messaging protocol for IPv4. ICMPv6 provides these same services for IPv6 but includes additional functionality. The types of ICMP messages, and the reasons why they are sent, are extensive. The following are the ICMP messages common to both ICMPv4 and ICMPv6 and most pertinent for our review:

- **Host reachability**: ICMP Echo messages are used to test the reachability of a host on an IP network. If the host is available, the destination host responds with an Echo Reply. This use of the ICMP Echo messages is the basis of the **ping** utility.

- **Destination or Service Unreachable**: When a host or gateway receives a packet that it cannot deliver, it can use an ICMP Destination Unreachable message to notify the source that the destination or service is unreachable. The message will include a code that indicates why the packet could not be delivered.

- **Time Exceeded:** An ICMPv4 Time Exceeded message is used by a router to indicate that a packet cannot be forwarded because the Time to Live (TTL) field of the packet was decremented to 0. If this happens, the router discards the packet and sends a Time Exceeded message to the source. ICMPv6 also sends a Time Exceeded message if the router cannot forward an IPv6 packet because the packet has expired. Instead of the IPv4 TTL field, ICMPv6 uses the IPv6 Hop Limit field to determine if the packet has expired.

# Ping and Traceroute

ICMP includes the **ping** and **traceroute** (**tracert** on Windows) commands. The **ping** command is used to test connectivity. Type of connectivity tests include the following:

- Pinging the local loopback
- Pinging the default gateway
- Pinging the remote host

Example 24-4 shows **ping** output from my computer to a remote host, www.cisco.com.

### Example 24-4   Using `ping` on a Windows PC

```
C:\Windows\System32> ping www.cisco.com

Pinging e2867.dsca.akamaiedge.net [23.59.109.220] with 32 bytes of data:
Reply from 23.59.109.220: bytes=32 time=18ms TTL=55
Reply from 23.59.109.220: bytes=32 time=21ms TTL=55
Reply from 23.59.109.220: bytes=32 time=20ms TTL=55
Reply from 23.59.109.220: bytes=32 time=19ms TTL=55

Ping statistics for 23.59.109.220:
    Packets: Sent = 4, Received = 4, Lost = 0 (0% loss),
Approximate round trip times in milli-seconds:
    Minimum = 18ms, Maximum = 21ms, Average = 19ms

C:\Windows\System32>
```

However, **ping** does not provide information about the details of devices between the hosts; **traceroute** generates a list of hops that were successfully reached along the path. This list can provide important verification and troubleshooting information.

**traceroute** provides round-trip time (RTT) for each hop along the path and indicates if a hop fails to respond. The round-trip time is the time a packet takes to reach the remote host and for the response from the host to return. An asterisk (*) is used to indicate a lost or missing packet that received no reply, as shown in Example 24-5.

**Example 24-5   Using** `tracert` **on a Windows PC**

```
C:\Windows\System32> tracert www.cisco.com


Tracing route to e2867.dsca.akamaiedge.net [23.59.109.220]
over a maximum of 30 hops:


  1     3 ms      <1 ms     <1 ms   192.168.68.1
  2       *          *         *     Request timed out.
  3    10 ms       7 ms      11 ms   24-155-250-86.dyn.grandenetworks.net
     [24.155.250.86]
  4    12 ms      25 ms      10 ms   ae0.0.aggr01.crchtx.grandecom.net
     [24.155.121.166]
  5    23 ms      18 ms      24 ms   24-155-121-16.static.grandenetworks.net
     [24.155.121.16]
  6    21 ms      21 ms      19 ms   24-155-121-238.static.grandenetworks.net
     [24.155.121.238]
  7    19 ms      29 ms      45 ms   66-90-138-97.static.grandenetworks.net
     [66.90.138.97]
  8    21 ms      20 ms      19 ms   192.168.224.49
  9    20 ms      20 ms      21 ms   192.168.237.149
 10    19 ms      24 ms      20 ms   192.168.247.159
 11    19 ms      22 ms      18 ms   a23-59-109-220.deploy.static.akamaitechnologies.
     com [23.59.109.220]


Trace complete.


C:\Windows\System32>
```

This information can be used to locate a problematic router in the path or may indicate that the router is configured not to reply. If the display shows high response times or data losses from a particular hop, this is an indication that the resources of the router or its connections may be stressed.

Traceroute makes use of a function of the TTL field in IPv4 and the Hop Limit field in IPv6 in the Layer 3 headers, along with the ICMP Time Exceeded message.

The first sequence of messages sent from **traceroute** will have a TTL field value of 1. This causes the TTL to time out the IPv4 packet at the first router. This router then responds with an ICMPv4 Time Exceeded message. **traceroute** now has the address of the first hop and the RTT.

**traceroute** then progressively increments the TTL field (2, 3, 4 …) for each sequence of messages. This provides the trace with the address of each hop as the packets time out further down the path. The TTL field continues to be increased until the destination is reached, or it is incremented to a predefined maximum.

After the final destination is reached, the host responds with either an ICMP Port Unreachable message or an ICMP Echo Reply message instead of the ICMP Time Exceeded message.

# ICMPv6 Messages

ICMPv6 includes four new protocols as part of the Neighbor Discovery Protocol (ND or NDP). Messaging types between an IPv6 router and an IPv6 device, including dynamic address allocation, are as follows:

- Router Solicitation (RS) message

- Router Advertisement (RA) message

Messaging types between IPv6 devices, including duplicate address detection and address resolution, are as follows:

- Neighbor Solicitation (NS) message

- Neighbor Advertisement (NA) message

## RA Message

RA messages are sent by IPv6-enabled routers every 200 seconds, as shown in Figure 24-3, to provide addressing information to IPv6-enabled hosts. A host using Stateless Address Autoconfiguration (SLAAC) will set its default gateway to the link-local address of the router that sent the RA. More on SLAAC tomorrow on Day 23 when we review DHCPv6.

**Figure 24-3   R1 Sends an RA Message Every 200 Seconds**

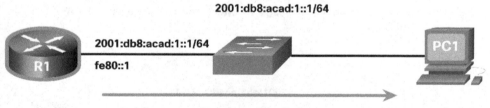

In Figure 24-3, the RA message sent by R1 is saying, "Hi all IPv6-enabled devices. I'm R1, and you can use SLAAC to create an IPv6 global unicast address. The prefix is 2001:db8:acad:1::/64. By the way, use my link-local address fe80::1 as your default gateway."

## RS Message

An IPv6-enabled router will also send out an RA message in response to an RS message. In Figure 24-4, PC1 just booted and has not yet received any RA messages. It sends an RS message to determine how to receive its IPv6 address information dynamically.

Figure 24-4 shows the following exchanges between R1 and PC1:

1. PC1 sends an RS message: "Hi, I just booted up. Is there an IPv6 router on the network? I need to know how to get my IPv6 address information dynamically."

2. R1 replies with an RA message: "Hi all IPv6-enabled devices. I'm R1, and you can use SLAAC to create an IPv6 global unicast address. The prefix is 2001:db8:acad:1::/64. By the way, use my link-local address fe80::1 as your default gateway."

**Figure 24-4   PC1 Sends an RS and R1 Replies with an RA**

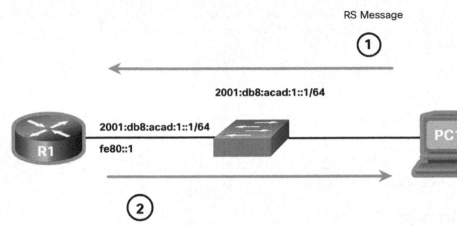

## NS Message

To check the uniqueness of an address, a device will send an NS message with its own IPv6 address as the targeted IPv6 address. In Figure 24-5, PC1 sends an NS message to check the uniqueness of its address: "Will whoever has the IPv6 address 2001:db8:acad:1::10 send me your MAC address?"

**Figure 24-5   PC1 Sends an NS Message to Check the Uniqueness of Its IPv6 Address**

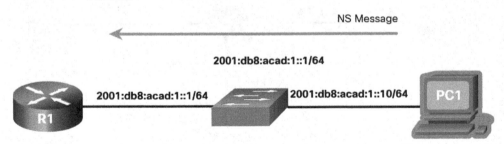

If another device on the network has this address, it will respond with an NA message. This NA message will notify the sending device that the address is in use. If a corresponding NA message is not returned within a certain amount of time, the unicast address is unique and acceptable for use.

## NA Message

NA messages are also used for address resolution to discover the MAC address of a destination on the local network. In Figure 24-6, R1 sends an NS message to 2001:db8:acad:1::10 asking for its MAC address.

**Figure 24-6   R1 Sends an NS Message to Discover the MAC Address of a Destination**

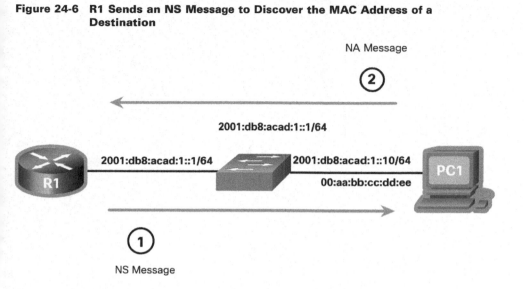

The following explains the exchanges in Figure 24-6:

1. R1 sends an address resolution NS message: "Will whoever has the IPv6 address 2001:db8:acad:1::10 send me your MAC address?"

2. PC1 replies with an NA message: "I'm 2001:db8:acad:1::10 and my MAC address is 00:aa:bb:cc:dd:ee."

# Study Resources

For today's exam topics, refer to the following resources for more study:

| Resource | Module or Chapter |
|---|---|
| SFA Self Enroll: Networking Basics | 16, 17 |
| SFA Self Enroll: Networking Devices and Initial Configuration | 12 |
| SFA Instructor Led: Networking Essentials | 16, 17, 29 |
| CCST Networking 100-150 Official Cert Guide | 15, 16 |

**NOTE**   SFA: https://skillsforall.com/

# HTTP, DHCP, and DNS

## CCST Networking 100-150 Exam Topic

- 1.5. Describe common network applications and protocols.

  - *TCP vs. UDP (connection-oriented vs. connectionless), FTP, SFTP, TFTP, HTTP, HTTPS, DHCP, DNS, ICMP, NTP*

## Key Topics

Today we review three important protocols. Hypertext Transfer Protocol (HTTP) is the most common method of data exchange on the Internet. HTTP functions as a request-response protocol. Dynamic Host Configuration Protocol (DHCP) is used to automatically assign an IP address and other network configuration parameters to each device on the network. It allows computers and other devices to join a network without requiring manual configuration. Domain Name System (DNS) is a hierarchical and decentralized system used on the Internet to translate human-friendly domain names, like www.cisco.com, into the numerical IP addresses needed for locating and identifying computer services and devices.

## HTTP

HTTP carries all the different kinds of information needed to build a web page, including the following:

- The Hypertext Markup Language (HTML) and Cascading Style Sheets (CSS), which describe the content and styling of a web page

- Images, videos, and other files

- Apps written in JavaScript and other languages that run within the web browser

---

**NOTE** This book uses HTTP and HTTPs interchangeably. You should make sure you are not navigating to unsecure websites. You do this by ensuring the protocol in the address bar starts with **https://**, which means that your HTTP session is encrypted.

---

HTTP is a client/server protocol. The web browser acts as a client, requesting from or posting to a web server. Important HTTP messages include the following:

- **GET**: Requests a specific resource from the server

- **POST**: Sends data to the server to create/update a resource

- **PUT**: Updates an existing resource with new data

- **DELETE**: Deletes a specific resource

- **HEAD**: Similar to GET but used to retrieve the headers only, not the body of the resource

## HTTP Operation

When a web address or Uniform Resource Locator (URL) is typed into a web browser, the web browser establishes a connection to the web server. To better understand how the web browser and web server interact, examine how a web page is opened in a browser. For the example shown in Figures 23-1 through 23-4, we are using the URL http://www.cisco.com/index.html.

In Figure 23-1, the browser running on the client interprets the three parts of the URL:

- http (the protocol or scheme)

- www.cisco.com (the server name)

- index.html (the specific filename requested)

**Figure 23-1   HTTP Operation: Step 1**

In Figure 23-2, the browser then checks with a name server to convert www.cisco.com into a numeric IP address, which it uses to connect to the server. The client initiates an HTTP GET request to the IP address of the www.cisco.com server asking for the index.html file.

**Figure 23-2   HTTP Operation: Step 2**

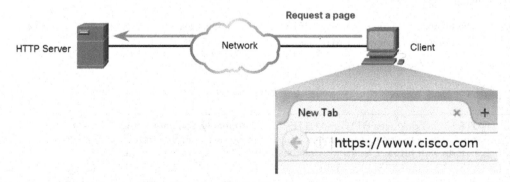

In response to the request, the server sends the HTML code for this web page to the browser, as shown in Figure 23-3.

**Figure 23-3   HTTP Operation: Step 3**

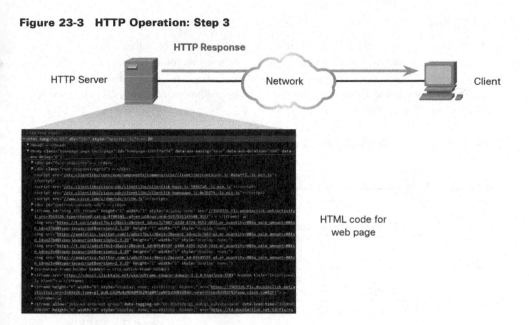

HTTP code for
web page

In Figure 23-4, the browser deciphers the HTML code and formats the page for the browser window.

**Figure 23-4   HTTP Operation: Step 4**

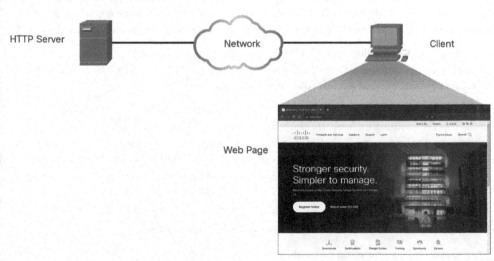

# DHCP

DHCP dynamically assigns IP addressing information to clients that request the service. DHCPv4 supports IPv4 addressing and DHCPv6 supports IPv6 addressing.

# DHCPv4

DHCPv4 allows a host to obtain an IP address dynamically when it connects to the network. The DHCPv4 client contacts the DHCPv4 server by sending a request for an IP address. The DHCPv4 server chooses an address from a configured range of addresses called a pool and assigns it to the host client for a set period. Figure 23-5 graphically shows the process for how a DHCPv4 server fulfills a request from a DHCPv4 client.

**Figure 23-5   Allocating IP Addressing Information Using DHCPv4**

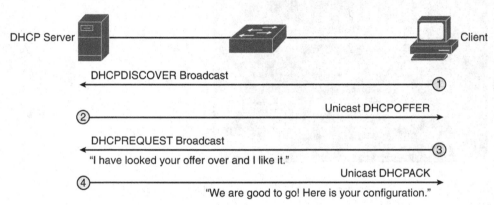

When a DHCPv4-configured device boots up or connects to the network, the client broadcasts a DHCPDISCOVER packet to identify any available DHCPv4 servers on the network. A DHCPv4 server replies with a DHCPOFFER, which is a lease offer message with an assigned IP address, subnet mask, DNS server, and default gateway information, as well as the duration of the lease.

The client can receive multiple DHCPOFFER packets if the local network has more than one DHCPv4 server. The client chooses the first offer and broadcasts a DHCPREQUEST packet that identifies the explicit server and lease offer that it is accepting.

Assuming that the IP address is still valid, the chosen server returns a DHCPACK (acknowledgment) message finalizing the lease. If the offer is no longer valid for some reason, the chosen server responds to the client with a DHCPNAK (negative acknowledgment) message. After it is leased, the client renews before the lease expiration through another DHCPREQUEST. If the client is powered down or taken off the network, the address is returned to the pool for reuse.

# DHCPv6

IPv6 has two methods for automatically obtaining a global unicast address:

- Stateless address autoconfiguration (SLAAC)
- Stateful DHCPv6 (Dynamic Host Configuration Protocol for IPv6)

# SLAAC

SLAAC uses ICMPv6 Router Solicitation (RS) and Router Advertisement (RA) messages to provide addressing and other configuration information. A client then uses the RA information to build an IPv6 address and verify it with a special type of Neighbor Solicitation (NS) known as

Duplicate Address Detection (DAD). These three message types—RA, RS, and NS—belong to the Neighbor Discovery Protocol:

- **Router Solicitation (RS) message:** When a client is configured to obtain its addressing information automatically using SLAAC, the client sends an RS message to the router. The RS message is sent to the IPv6 all-routers multicast address, FF02::2.

- **Router Advertisement (RA) message:** A client uses this information to create its own IPv6 global unicast address. A router sends an RA message periodically or in response to an RS message. The RA message includes the prefix and prefix length of the local segment. By default, Cisco routers send RA messages every 200 seconds. RA messages are sent to the IPv6 all-nodes multicast address, FF02::1.

- **Neighbor Solicitation (NS) message:** An NS message is normally used to learn the data-link layer address of a neighbor on the same network. In the SLAAC process, a host uses DAD by inserting its own IPv6 address as the destination address in an NS. The NS is sent out on the network to verify that a newly minted IPv6 address is unique. If a Neighbor Advertisement is received, the host knows that the IPv6 address is not unique.

Figure 23-6 shows the SLAAC process using three messages of the Neighbor Discovery Protocol (NDP).

**Figure 23-6   Neighbor Discovery and the SLAAC Process**

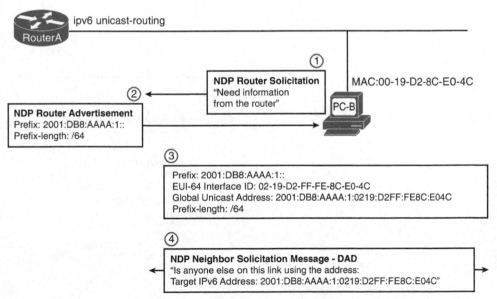

Let's briefly review the steps in Figure 23-6:

**Step 1.**    PC-B sends an RS message to the all-routers multicast address, FF02::2, to inform the local IPv6 router that it needs an RA.

**Step 2.**    RouterA receives the RS message and responds with an RA message. Included in the RA message are the prefix and prefix length of the network. The RA message is sent to the IPv6 all-nodes multicast address, FF02::1, with the link-local address of the router as the IPv6 source address.

**Step 3.**   PC-B uses this information to create its own IPv6 global unicast address. It appends the 64-bit prefix address to its own locally generated 64-bit interface ID, which it creates using either the EUI (Extended Unique Identifier) process or a random number generator. It uses RouterA's link-local address as the default gateway.

**Step 4.**   Before PC-B can use this newly created IPv6 address, it uses the DAD process, sending out an NS to verify that the address is unique.

## Stateless and Stateful DHCPv6 Operation

Figure 23-7 shows the full operation of DHCPv6, regardless of the method used: SLAAC, stateless DHCPv6, or stateful DHCPv6.

**Figure 23-7   DHCPv6 Operations**

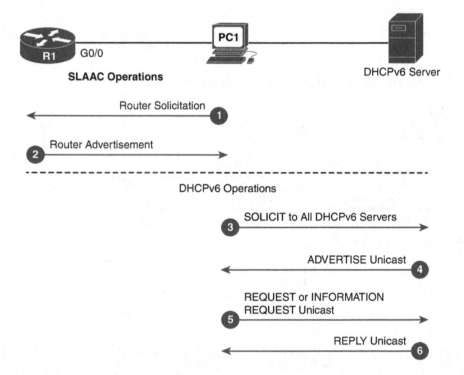

The following steps summarize Figure 23-7:

**Step 1.**   PC1 sends an RS on bootup to begin the process of obtaining IPv6 addressing.

**Step 2.**   R1 replies with an RA. Assuming R1 does not specify to use SLAAC, PC1 begins the DHCPv6 process.

**Step 3.**   PC1 sends a DHCPv6 SOLICIT message to the all-DHCPv6-servers address, FF02::1:2—a link-local multicast address that will not be forwarded by routers.

**Step 4.** A DHCPv6 server responds with a DHCPv6 ADVERTISE unicast message informing the client of its presence.

**Step 5.** The client then sends either a unicast DHCPv6 REQUEST for stateful DHCPv6 or a unicast DHCPv6 INFORMATION-REQUEST for stateless DHCPv6.

**Step 6.** The server replies with the information requested.

# DNS Operation

DNS is a distributed system of servers that resolve domain names to IP addresses. The domain name is part of the Uniform Resource Identifier (URI), as Figure 23-8 shows.

**Figure 23-8   URI Structure**

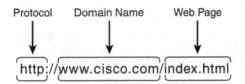

> **NOTE**  Many people use the terms *web address* and *Universal Resource Locator (URL)*. However, *Uniform Resource Identifier (URI)* is the correct formal term.

When you type a new URI in your browser, your computer uses DNS to send out a request to resolve the URI into an IP address. Figure 23-9 summarizes the DNS process.

The DNS server stores different types of resource records used to resolve names. These records contain the name, address, and type of record. Some of these record types follow:

- **A**: An end-device IPv4 address
- **NS**: An authoritative name server
- **AAAA**: An end-device IPv6 address (pronounced "quad-A")
- **MX**: A mail exchange record

When a client makes a query, the server's DNS process first looks at its own records to resolve the name. If it cannot resolve the name using its stored records, it contacts other servers to resolve the name.

DNS root servers manage the top-domain suffixes, such as these:

- **.com**: Commercial businesses
- **.edu**: Educational organizations
- **.gov**: Government organizations
- **.mil**: Military organizations

- **.net**: Networking organizations, such as ISPs

- **.org**: Noncommercial organizations

Top-level DNS servers also exist for each country code, such as .ca (Canada), .de (Germany), .ru (Russia), and .cn (China).

**Figure 23-9   DNS Process**

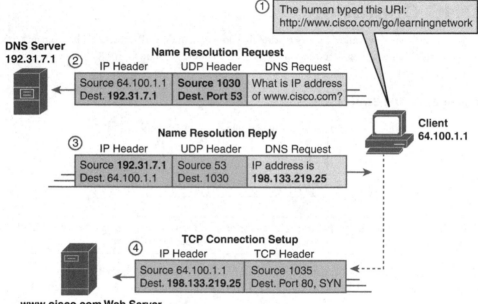

## Study Resources

For today's exam topics, refer to the following resources for more study:

| Resource | Module or Chapter |
|---|---|
| SFA Self Enroll: Networking Basics | 11, 16 |
| SFA Instructor Led: Networking Essentials | 11, 16 |
| CCST Networking 100-150 Official Cert Guide | 15, 16 |

**NOTE**   SFA: https://skillsforall.com/

# Private Addressing and NAT

## CCST Networking 100-150 Exam Topic

- 2.1. Compare and contrast private addresses and public addresses.
  - *Each IP address must be unique on the network*

# Key Topics

To cope with the depletion of IPv4 addresses, several short-term solutions were developed. One short-term solution is to use private addresses and network address translation (NAT). Although not explicitly called out in the exam objectives, NAT is why networks can use a private IP addressing scheme and still be able to communicate with other networks, some of which might be using the exact same addressing. Today we review private addressing and NAT.

# Private Addressing

RFC 1918, "Address Allocation for Private Internets," eased the demand for IP addresses by reserving the following addresses for use in private internetworks:

- **Class A**: 10.0.0.0/8 (10.0.0.0–10.255.255.255)
- **Class B**: 172.16.0.0/12 (172.16.0.0–172.31.255.255)
- **Class C**: 192.168.0.0/16 (192.168.0.0–192.168.255.255)

If you are addressing a nonpublic intranet, these private addresses are normally used instead of globally unique public addresses. This provides flexibility in your addressing design. Any organization can take full advantage of an entire Class A address (10.0.0.0/8). Forwarding traffic to the public Internet requires translation to a public address using network address translation (NAT). However, by overloading an Internet-routable address with many private addresses, a company needs only a handful of public addresses.

## Reserved Addresses

Some addresses should never be used either for private networks or for connecting to the global Internet. These are called reserved addresses, and they are considered unroutable by service providers. Table 22-1 lists some of these addresses and their usage.

**Table 22-1    Reserved IP Addresses**

| Address Space | Usage |
| --- | --- |
| 100.64.0.0/10 | Assigned by service providers using Carrier Grade Network Address Translation (CGNAT). |
| 127.0.0.0/8 ::1/128 | Loopback; most host network software implementations will send any packets sent to an address in this address range back to the host itself. |
| 169.254.0.0/16 | Link local addresses; not widely used. |
| 172.16.0.0/12 | Private networks. |
| 192.0.2.0/24 | Documentation. |
| 192.88.99.0/24 | No longer used, but still reserved. |
| 198.18.0.0/15 | Benchmarking. |
| 198.51.100.0/24 | Documentation. |
| 203.0.113.0/24 | Documentation. |
| 224.0.0.0/4 | Multicast distribution. |
| 233.252.0.0/24 | Documentation. |
| 240.0.0.0/4 | Reserved. |
| ::ffff:0:0/96 ::ffff:0:0:0/96 64:ff9b::/96 64:ff9b:1::/48 2002::/16 | IPv4 to IPv6 translation services; not widely used and/or deprecated. |
| 100::/64 | Discard prefix; any packets sent to this address will be discarded. |
| 2001:0000::/32 2001:20::/28 | Special applications like Teredo. |
| 2001:db8::/32 | Documentation. |
| fe80::/64 | Link local addresses. |
| ff00::/8 | Multicast. |

# NAT Concepts

NAT, defined in RFC 3022, has many uses. Its key use is to conserve IPv4 addresses by allowing networks to use private IPv4 addresses. NAT translates unroutable, private, internal addresses into routable, public addresses. NAT also has the benefit of hiding internal IPv4 addresses from outside networks.

A NAT-enabled device typically operates at the border of a stub network. Figure 22-1 shows the master topology used during today's review. R2 is the border router and is the device used for today's example configurations.

**Figure 22-1   NAT Topology**

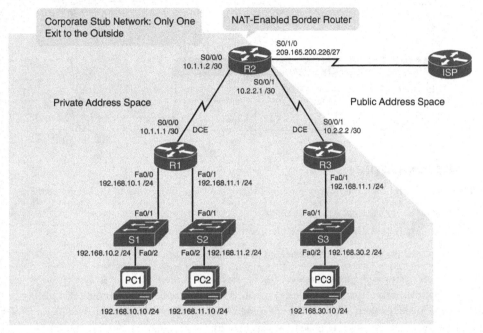

In NAT terminology, the inside network is the set of networks that are subject to translation (every network in the shaded region in Figure 22-1). The outside network refers to all other addresses. Figure 22-2 and the following list explain how to refer to the addresses when you're configuring NAT:

- **Inside local address**: Most likely a private address. In the figure, the IPv4 address 192.168.10.10 assigned to PC1 is an inside local address.

- **Inside global address**: A valid public address that the inside host is given when it exits the NAT router. When traffic from PC1 is destined for the web server at 209.165.201.1, R2 must translate the inside local address to an inside global address, which is 209.165.200.226, in this case.

- **Outside global address**: A reachable IPv4 address assigned to a host on the Internet. For example, the web server can be reached at IPv4 address 209.165.201.1.

- **Outside local address**: The local IPv4 address assigned to a host on the outside network. In most situations, this address is identical to the outside global address of that outside device. (Outside local addresses are beyond the scope of the CCNA.)

**Figure 22-2   NAT Terminology**

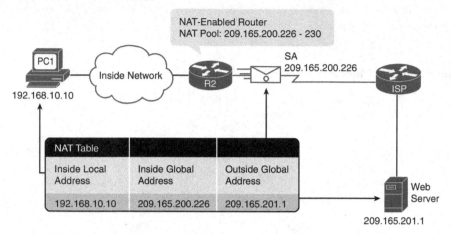

## A NAT Example

Referring to Figure 22-1, the following steps illustrate the NAT process when PC1 sends traffic to the Internet:

1. PC1 sends a packet destined for the Internet to R1, the default gateway.

2. R1 forwards the packet to R2, as directed by its routing table.

3. R2 refers to its routing table and identifies the next hop as the ISP router. It then checks to see whether the packet matches the criteria specified for translation. R2 has an ACL that identifies the inside network as a valid host for translation. Therefore, it translates an inside local IPv4 address to an inside global IPv4 address, which, in this case, is 209.165.200.226. It stores this mapping of the local address to global address in the NAT table.

4. R2 modifies the packet with the new source IPv4 address (the inside global address) and sends it to the ISP router.

5. The packet eventually reaches its destination, which then sends its reply to the inside global address 209.165.200.226.

6. When replies from the destination arrive back at R2, it consults the NAT table to match the inside global address to the correct inside local address. R2 then modifies the packet, inserting the inside local address (192.168.10.10) as the destination address and sending it to R1.

7. R1 receives the packet and forwards it to PC1.

## Dynamic and Static NAT

The two types of NAT translation are as follows:

- **Dynamic NAT**: Uses a pool of public addresses and assigns them on a first-come, first-served basis, or reuses an existing public address configured on an interface. When a host with a private IPv4 address requests access to the Internet, dynamic NAT chooses an IPv4 address from the pool that another host is not already using. Instead of using a pool, dynamic NAT can be configured to overload an existing public address configured on an interface.

- **Static NAT**: Uses a one-to-one mapping of local and global addresses. These mappings remain constant. Static NAT is particularly useful for web servers or hosts that must have a consistent address that is accessible from the Internet.

# NAT Overload

NAT overloading, also called port address translation (PAT), maps multiple private IPv4 addresses to a single public IPv4 address or a few addresses. To do this, a port number also tracks each private address. When a response comes back from the outside, source port numbers determine the correct client for the NAT router to translate the packets.

Figure 22-3 and the following steps illustrate the NAT overload process.

**Figure 22-3  NAT Overload Example**

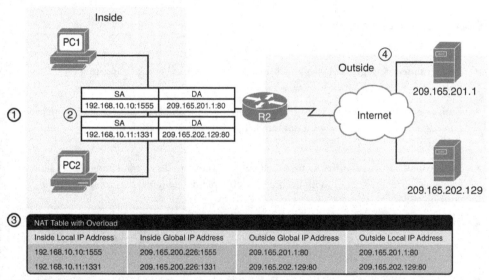

1. PC1 and PC2 send packets destined for the Internet.

2. When the packets arrive at R2, NAT overload changes the source address to the inside global IPv4 address and keeps a record of the assigned source port numbers (1555 and 1331, in this example) to identify the client from which the packets originated.

3. R2 updates its NAT table. Notice the assigned ports. R2 then routes the packets to the Internet.

4. When the web server replies, R2 uses the destination source port to translate the packet to the correct client.

NAT overload attempts to preserve the original source port. However, if this source port is already used, NAT overload assigns the first available port number, starting from the beginning of the appropriate port group 0–511, 512–1023, or 1024–65535.

## NAT Benefits

Using NAT offers the following benefits:

- NAT conserves registered IPv4 address space because, with NAT overload, internal hosts can share a single public IPv4 address for all external communications.

- NAT increases the flexibility of connections to the public network. Multiple pools, backup pools, and load-balancing pools can be implemented to ensure reliable public network connections.

- NAT allows the existing scheme to remain while supporting a new public addressing scheme. This means that an organization can change ISPs and not need to change any of its inside clients.

- NAT provides a layer of network security because private networks do not advertise their inside local addresses outside the organization. However, the phrase *NAT firewall* is misleading; NAT does not replace firewalls.

## NAT Limitations

The limitations of using NAT include the following:

- **Performance is degraded**: NAT increases switching delays because translating each IPv4 address within the packet headers takes time.

- **End-to-end functionality is degraded**: Many Internet protocols and applications depend on end-to-end functionality, with unmodified packets forwarded from the source to the destination.

- **End-to-end IP traceability is lost**: Tracing packets that undergo numerous packet address changes over multiple NAT hops becomes much more difficult, making troubleshooting challenging.

- **Tunneling is more complicated**: Using NAT also complicates tunneling protocols, such as IPsec, because NAT modifies values in the headers that interfere with the integrity checks that IPsec and other tunneling protocols do.

- **Services can be disrupted**: Services that require the initiation of TCP connections from the outside network, or stateless protocols such as those using UDP, can be disrupted.

# Study Resources

For today's exam topics, refer to the following resources for more study:

| Resource | Module or Chapter |
|---|---|
| SFA Self Enroll: Networking Basics | 9, 12 |
| SFA Instructor Led: Networking Essentials | 9, 12 |
| CCST Networking 100-150 Official Cert Guide | 2 |

**NOTE**   SFA: https://skillsforall.com/

# IPv4 Addressing

## CCST Networking 100-150 Exam Topic

- 2.2. Identify IPv4 addresses and subnet formats.

  - *Subnet concepts, subnet calculator, slash notation, and subnet mask; broadcasts do not go outside the subnet*

# Key Topics

Today we focus on reviewing the structure of an IPv4 address, the classes, and IPv4 subnetting. The exam topic for today only calls out "subnet concepts" and "subnet calculator." However, we will review the steps to subnet a basic network address so that you are more than ready for any potential questions on subnetting. But also know that there are plenty of subnet calculators available online. You only need to search for them. Network administrators rarely subnet by hand but instead rely on a subnetting tool—possibly one that is built into the network management software they use to configure and monitor their network.

# IPv4 Addressing

Although IPv6 is rapidly permeating the networks of the world, most networks still have a large IPv4 implementation. Especially on private networks, migration away from IPv4 will take years to complete. Clearly, IPv4 and your skill in its use are still in demand.

## Header Format

Figure 21-1 shows the layout of the IPv4 header.

Note that each IP packet carries this header, which includes a source IP address and destination IP address.

An IP address consists of two parts:

- The high-order (leftmost) bits specify the network address component (network ID) of the address.

- The low-order (rightmost) bits specify the host address component (host ID) of the address.

**Figure 21-1   IPv4 Header Format**

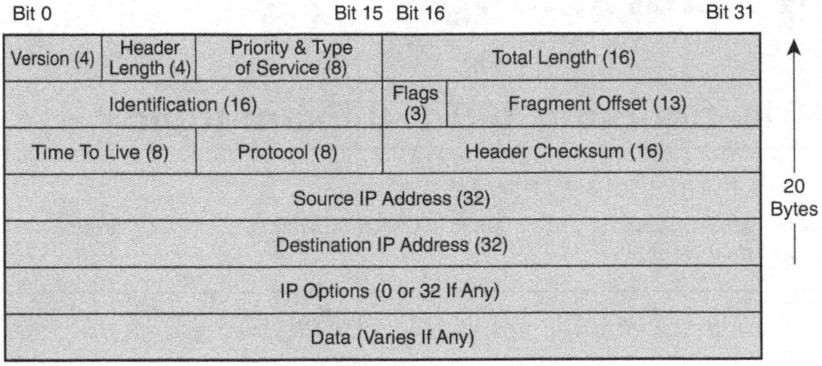

**Classes of Addresses**

From the beginning, IPv4 was designed with a class structure: Classes A, B, C, D, and E. Class D is used for multicasting addresses, and Class E is reserved for experimentation. Classes A, B, and C are assigned to network hosts. To provide a hierarchical structure, these classes are divided into network and host portions, as Figure 21-2 shows. The high-order bits specify the network ID, and the low-order bits specify the host ID.

**Figure 21-2   Network/Host Boundary for Each Class of IPv4 Address**

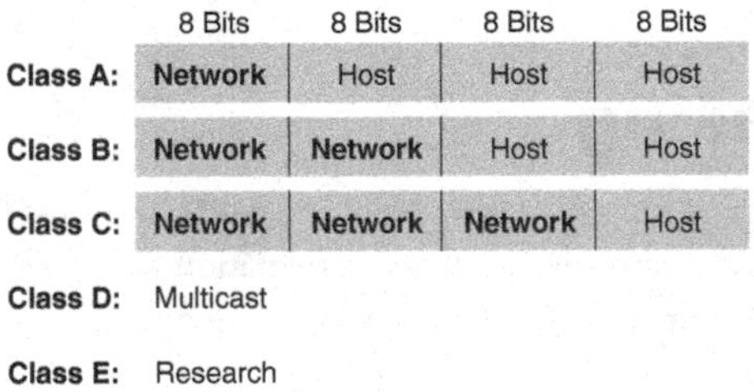

In a classful addressing scheme, devices that operate at Layer 3 can determine the address class of an IP address from the format of the first few bits in the first octet. Initially, this was important so that a networking device could apply the default subnet mask for the address and determine the host address. Table 21-1 summarizes how addresses are divided into classes, the default subnet mask, the number of networks per class, and the number of hosts per classful network address.

**Table 21-1   IPv4 Address Classes**

| Address Class | First Octet Range (Decimal) | First Octet Bits (Highlighted Bits Do Not Change) | Network (N) and Host (H) Portions of Addresses | Default Subnet Mask (Decimal and Binary) | Number of Possible Networks and Hosts per Network |
|---|---|---|---|---|---|
| A | 1–127 | 00000000–01111111 | N.H.H.H | 255.0.0.0 | $2^7$ or 128 networks |
|  |  |  |  | 11111111.00000000. 00000000.00000000 | $2^{24} - 2$ or 16,777,214 hosts per network |

| Address Class | First Octet Range (Decimal) | First Octet Bits (Highlighted Bits Do Not Change) | Network (N) and Host (H) Portions of Addresses | Default Subnet Mask (Decimal and Binary) | Number of Possible Networks and Hosts per Network |
|---|---|---|---|---|---|
| B | 128–191 | 10000000–10111111 | N.N.H.H | 255.255.0.0 | $2^{14}$ or 16,384 networks |
| | | | | 11111111.11111111. 00000000.00000000 | $2^{16} - 2$ or 65,534 hosts per network |
| C | 192–223 | 11000000–11011111 | N.N.N.H | 255.255.255.0 | $2^{21}$ or 2,097,152 networks |
| | | | | 11111111.11111111. 11111111.00000000 | $2^{8} - 2$ or 254 hosts per network |
| D | 224–239 | 11100000–11101111 | Not used for host addressing | | |
| E | 240–255 | 11110000–11111111 | Not used for host addressing | | |

In the last column, the −2 for hosts per network is to account for the reserved network and broadcast addresses for each network. These two addresses cannot be assigned to hosts.

**NOTE** We do not review the process of converting between binary and decimal. At this point in your studies, you should be comfortable moving between the two numbering systems. If not, take some time to practice this necessary skill. You can search the Internet for binary conversion tricks, tips, and games to help you practice.

## Purpose of the Subnet Mask

Subnet masks are always a series of 1 bits followed by a series of 0 bits. The boundary where the series changes from 1s to 0s is the boundary between the network and the host. This is how a device that operates at Layer 3 determines the network address for a packet, by finding the bit boundary where the series of 1 bits ends and the series of 0 bits begins. The bit boundary for default subnet masks breaks on the octet boundary. Determining the network address for an IP address that uses a default mask is easy.

For example, a router receives a packet destined for 192.168.1.51. By ANDing the IP address and the subnet mask, the router determines the network address for the packet. Per the ANDing rules, a 1 AND a 1 equals 1. All other possibilities equal 0. Table 21-2 shows the results of the ANDing operation. Notice that the host bits in the last octet are ignored.

**Table 21-2   ANDing an IP Address and Subnet Mask to Find the Network Address**

| Destination Address | 192.168.1.51 | 11000000.10101000.00000001.00110011 |
|---|---|---|
| Subnet Mask | 255.255.255.0 | 11111111.11111111.11111111.00000000 |
| Network Address | 192.168.1.0 | 11000000.10101000.00000001.00000000 |

The bit boundary can now occur in just about any place in the 32 bits. Table 21-3 summarizes the values for the last nonzero octet in a subnet mask.

**Table 21-3   Subnet Mask Binary Values**

| Mask (Decimal) | Mask (Binary) | Network Bits | Host Bits |
| --- | --- | --- | --- |
| 0 | 00000000 | 0 | 8 |
| 128 | 10000000 | 1 | 7 |
| 192 | 11000000 | 2 | 6 |
| 224 | 11100000 | 3 | 5 |
| 240 | 11110000 | 4 | 4 |
| 248 | 11111000 | 5 | 3 |
| 252 | 11111100 | 6 | 2 |
| 254 | 11111110 | 7 | 1 |
| 255 | 11111111 | 8 | 0 |

# Subnetting in Four Steps

Everyone has a preferred method of subnetting. Each teacher uses a slightly different strategy to help students master this crucial skill, and each of the suggested study resources has a slightly different way of approaching this subject.

The method I prefer consists of four steps:

**Step 1.**   Determine how many bits to borrow, based on the host requirements.

**Step 2.**   Determine the new subnet mask.

**Step 3.**   Determine the subnet multiplier.

**Step 4.**   List the subnets, including subnetwork address, host range, and broadcast address.

The best way to demonstrate this method is to use an example. Assume that you are given the network address 192.168.1.0 with the default subnet mask 255.255.255.0. The network address and subnet mask can be written as 192.168.1.0/24. The /24 represents the subnet mask in a shorter notation and means that the first 24 bits are network bits.

Now further assume that you need 30 hosts per network and want to create as many subnets for the given address space as possible. With these network requirements, you can now subnet the address space.

## Determine How Many Bits to Borrow

To determine the number of bits you can borrow, you first must know how many host bits you have to start with. Because the first 24 bits are network bits in this example, the remaining 8 bits are host bits.

Because our requirement specifies 30 host addresses per subnet, we need to first determine the minimum number of host bits to leave. The remaining bits can be borrowed:

Host Bits = Bits Borrowed + Bits Left

To provide enough address space for 30 hosts, we need to leave 5 bits. Use the following formula:

$2^{BL} - 2$ = number of host addresses

The exponent BL is bits left in the host portion.

Remember, the $-2$ is to account for the network and broadcast addresses that cannot be assigned to hosts.

In this example, leaving 5 bits in the host portion provides the right number of host addresses:

$2^5 - 2 = 30$

Because we have 3 bits remaining in the original host portion, we borrow all these bits to satisfy the requirement to "create as many subnets as possible." To determine how many subnets we can create, use the following formula:

$2^{BB}$ = number of subnets

The exponent BB is bits borrowed from the host portion.

In this example, borrowing 3 bits from the host portion creates eight subnets: $2^3 = 8$.

As Table 21-4 shows, the 3 bits are borrowed from the leftmost bits in the host portion. The highlighted bits in the table show all possible combinations of manipulating the 8 bits borrowed to create the subnets.

**Table 21-4    Binary and Decimal Value of the Subnetted Octet**

| Subnet Number | Last Octet Binary Value | Last Octet Decimal Value |
|---|---|---|
| 0 | 00000000 | .0 |
| 1 | 00100000 | .32 |
| 2 | 01000000 | .64 |
| 3 | 01100000 | .96 |
| 4 | 10000000 | .128 |
| 5 | 10100000 | .160 |
| 6 | 11000000 | .192 |
| 7 | 11100000 | .224 |

# Determine the New Subnet Mask

Notice in Table 21-4 that the network bits now include the 3 borrowed host bits in the last octet. Add these 3 bits to the 24 bits in the original subnet mask, and you have a new subnet mask, /27.

In decimal format, you turn on the 128, 64, and 32 bits in the last octet, for a value of 224. The new subnet mask is thus 255.255.255.224.

## Determine the Subnet Multiplier

Notice in Table 21-4 that the last octet decimal value increments by 32 with each subnet number. The number 32 is the subnet multiplier. You can quickly find the subnet multiplier using one of two methods:

- **Method 1**: Subtract the last nonzero octet of the subnet mask from 256. In this example, the last nonzero octet is 224. The subnet multiplier is therefore 256 − 224 = 32.

- **Method 2**: The decimal value of the last bit borrowed is the subnet multiplier. In this example, we borrowed the 128 bit, the 64 bit, and the 32 bit. The 32 bit is the last bit we borrowed and is, therefore, the subnet multiplier.

By using the subnet multiplier, you no longer have to convert binary subnet bits to decimal.

## List the Subnets, Host Ranges, and Broadcast Addresses

Listing the subnets, host ranges, and broadcast addresses helps you see the flow of addresses within one address space. Table 21-5 documents our subnet addressing scheme for the 192.168.1.0/24 address space.

**Table 21-5   Subnet Addressing Scheme for 192.168.1.0/24: 30 Hosts Per Subnet**

| Subnet Number | Subnet Address | Host Range | Broadcast Address |
|---|---|---|---|
| 0 | 192.168.1.0 | 192.168.1.1–192.168.1.30 | 192.168.1.31 |
| 1 | 192.168.1.32 | 192.168.1.33–192.168.1.62 | 192.168.1.63 |
| 2 | 192.168.1.64 | 192.168.1.65–192.168.1.94 | 192.168.1.95 |
| 3 | 192.168.1.96 | 192.168.1.97–192.168.1.126 | 192.168.1.127 |
| 4 | 192.168.1.128 | 192.168.1.129–192.168.1.158 | 192.168.1.159 |
| 5 | 192.168.1.160 | 192.168.1.161–192.168.1.190 | 192.168.1.191 |
| 6 | 192.168.1.192 | 192.168.1.193–192.168.1.222 | 192.168.1.223 |
| 7 | 192.168.1.224 | 192.168.1.225–192.168.1.254 | 192.168.1.255 |

Following are three examples using the four subnetting steps. For brevity, Step 4 lists only the first three subnets.

## Subnetting Example 1

Subnet the address space 172.16.0.0/16 to provide at least 80 host addresses per subnet while creating as many subnets as possible.

   1. There are 16 host bits. Leave 7 bits for host addresses ($2^7 − 2 = 126$ host addresses per subnet). Borrow the first 9 host bits to create as many subnets as possible ($2^9 = 512$ subnets).

**2.** The original subnet mask is /16, or 255.255.0.0. Turn on the next 9 bits, starting in the second octet, for a new subnet mask of /25, or 255.255.255.128.

**3.** The subnet multiplier is 128, which can be found as $256 - 128 = 128$, or because the 128 bit is the last bit borrowed.

**4.** Table 21-6 lists the first three subnets, host ranges, and broadcast addresses.

**Table 21-6    Subnet Addressing Scheme for Example 1**

| Subnet Number | Subnet Address | Host Range | Broadcast Address |
|---|---|---|---|
| 0 | 172.16.0.0 | 172.16.0.1–172.16.0.126 | 172.16.0.127 |
| 1 | 172.16.0.128 | 172.16.0.129–172.16.0.254 | 172.16.0.255 |
| 2 | 172.16.1.0 | 172.16.1.1–172.16.1.126 | 172.16.1.127 |

## Subnetting Example 2

Subnet the address space 172.16.0.0/16 to provide at least 80 subnet addresses.

**1.** There are 16 host bits. Borrow the first 7 host bits to create at least 80 subnets ($2^7 = 128$ subnets). That leaves 9 bits for host addresses, or $2^9 - 2 = 510$ host addresses per subnet.

**2.** The original subnet mask is /16, or 255.255.0.0. Turn on the next 7 bits, starting in the second octet, for a new subnet mask of /23, or 255.255.254.0.

**3.** The subnet multiplier is 2, which can be found as $256 - 254 = 2$, or because the 2 bit is the last bit borrowed.

**4.** Table 21-7 lists the first three subnets, host ranges, and broadcast addresses.

**Table 21-7    Subnet Addressing Scheme for Example 2**

| Subnet Number | Subnet Address | Host Range | Broadcast Address |
|---|---|---|---|
| 0 | 172.16.0.0 | 172.16.0.1–172.16.1.254 | 172.16.1.255 |
| 1 | 172.16.2.0 | 172.16.2.1–172.16.3.254 | 172.16.3.255 |
| 2 | 172.16.4.0 | 172.16.4.1–172.16.5.254 | 172.16.5.255 |

## Subnetting Example 3

Subnet the address space 172.16.10.0/23 to provide at least 60 host addresses per subnet while creating as many subnets as possible.

**1.** There are 9 host bits. Leave 6 bits for host addresses ($2^6 - 2 = 62$ host addresses per subnet). Borrow the first 3 host bits to create as many subnets as possible ($2^3 = 8$ subnets).

**2.** The original subnet mask is /23, or 255.255.254.0. Turn on the next 3 bits, starting with the last bit in the second octet, for a new subnet mask of /26, or 255.255.255.192.

3. The subnet multiplier is 64, which can be found as 256 − 192 = 64, or because the 64 bit is the last bit borrowed.

4. Table 21-8 lists the first three subnets, host ranges, and broadcast addresses.

**Table 21-8   Subnet Addressing Scheme for Example 3**

| Subnet Number | Subnet Address | Host Range | Broadcast Address |
|---|---|---|---|
| 0 | 172.16.10.0 | 172.16.10.1–172.16.10.62 | 172.16.10.63 |
| 1 | 172.16.10.64 | 172.16.10.65–172.16.10.126 | 172.16.10.127 |
| 2 | 172.16.10.128 | 172.16.10.129–172.16.10.190 | 172.16.10.191 |

# Study Resources

For today's exam topics, refer to the following resources for more study:

| Resource | Module or Chapter |
|---|---|
| SFA Self Enroll: Networking Basics | 8, 9 |
| SFA Self Enroll: Networking Devices and Initial Configuration | 3, 5, 6 |
| SFA Instructor Led: Networking Essentials | 8, 9, 20, 22, 23 |
| CCST Networking 100-150 Official Cert Guide | 2, 14 |

**NOTE**   SFA: https://skillsforall.com/

# IPv6 Addressing

## CCST Networking 100-150 Exam Topic

- 2.3. Identify IPv6 addresses and prefix formats.

  - *Types of addresses, prefix concepts*

## Key Topics

In the early 1990s, the Internet Engineering Task Force (IETF) grew concerned about the exhaustion of the IPv4 network addresses and began to look for a replacement for this protocol. This activity led to the development of what is now known as IPv6. Today's review focuses on the IPv6 protocol and IPv6 address types.

## Overview and Benefits of IPv6

Scaling networks today requires a limitless supply of IP addresses and improved mobility that private addressing and network address translation (NAT) alone cannot meet. IPv6 satisfies the increasingly complex requirements of hierarchical addressing that IPv4 does not provide. The main benefits and features of IPv6 include the following:

- **Extended address space**: A 128-bit address space represents about 340 trillion trillion trillion addresses.

- **Stateless address autoconfiguration**: IPv6 provides host devices with a method for generating their own routable IPv6 addresses. IPv6 also supports stateful configuration using DHCPv6.

- **No need for NAT/PAT**: NAT/PAT was conceived as part of the solution to IPv4 address depletion. With IPv6, address depletion is no longer an issue. NAT64, however, does play an important role in providing backward compatibility with IPv4.

- **Simpler header**: A simpler header offers several advantages over IPv4:

  - Better routing efficiency for performance and forwarding-rate scalability

  - No broadcasts and, thus, no potential threat of broadcast storms

- No requirement for processing checksums

- Simpler and more efficient extension header mechanisms

- **Mobility and security**: Mobility and security help ensure compliance with mobile IP and IPsec standards:

    - IPv4 does not automatically enable mobile devices to move without breaks in established network connections.

    - In IPv6, mobility is built in, which means that any IPv6 node can use mobility when necessary.

    - IPsec is enabled on every IPv6 node and is available for use, making the IPv6 Internet more secure.

- **Transition strategies**: You can incorporate existing IPv4 capabilities with the added features of IPv6 in a couple of ways:

    - You can implement a dual-stack method, with both IPv4 and IPv6 configured on the interface of a network device.

    - You can use tunneling, which will become more prominent as the adoption of IPv6 grows.

# The IPv6 Protocol

Table 20-1 compares the binary and alphanumeric representations of IPv4 and IPv6 addresses.

**Table 20-1  IPv4 and IPv6 Address Comparison**

| | IPv4 (4 Octets) | IPv6 (8 Hextets) |
|---|---|---|
| **Binary Representation** | 11000000.101010 00.00001010. 01100101 | 1010010100100100:0111001011010011:00101100 10000000:1101110100000010:0000000000101001 :1110110001111010:0000000000101011:1110101 001110011 |
| **Alphanumeric Representation** | 192.168.10.101 | A524:72D3:2C80:DD02:0029:EC7A:002B:EA73 |
| **Total IP Addresses** | 4,294,967,296, or $2^{32}$ | $3.4 \times 10^{38}$, or $2^{128}$ |

Figure 20-1 compares the IPv4 header with the main IPv6 header. Notice that the IPv6 header is represented in 64-bit words instead of the 32-bit words used by IPv4.

**Figure 20-1    IPv6 Header Format**

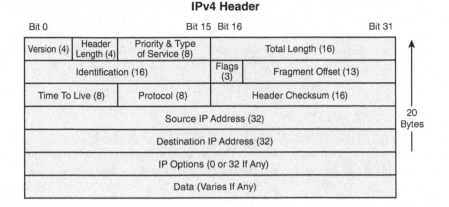

## IPv4 Header

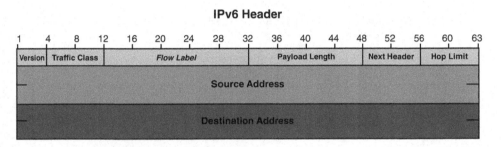

## IPv6 Header

# IPv6 Address Types

IPv4 has three address types: unicast, multicast, and broadcast. IPv6 does not use broadcasts. Instead, IPv6 uses unicast, multicast, and anycast. Figure 20-2 illustrates these three types of IPv6 addresses.

**Figure 20-2    IPv6 Address Types**

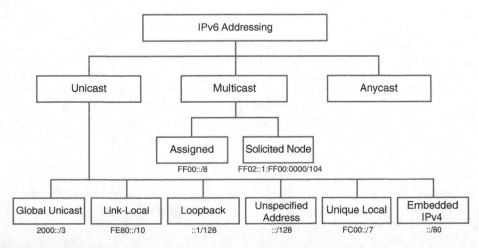

# Unicast

The first classification of IPv6 address types shown in Figure 20-2 is the unicast address. A unicast address uniquely identifies an interface on an IPv6 device. A packet sent to a unicast address is received by the interface that is assigned to that address. Similar to IPv4, source IPv6 addresses must be a unicast address. Because unicast addressing—as opposed to multicast and anycast addressing—is the major focus for a CCNA candidate, we spend some time reviewing the unicast branch in Figure 20-2.

## Global Unicast Address

IPv6 has an address format that enables aggregation upward, eventually to the Internet service provider (ISP). An IPv6 global unicast address is globally unique. Similar to a public IPv4 address, it can be routed in the Internet without modification. An IPv6 global unicast address consists of a 48-bit global routing prefix, a 16-bit subnet ID, and a 64-bit interface ID. Use Rick Graziani's method of breaking down the IPv6 address with the 3-1-4 Rule (also known as the *pi rule* for 3.14), shown in Figure 20-3.

**Figure 20-3   Graziani's 3-1-4 Rule for Remembering the Global Unicast Address Structure**

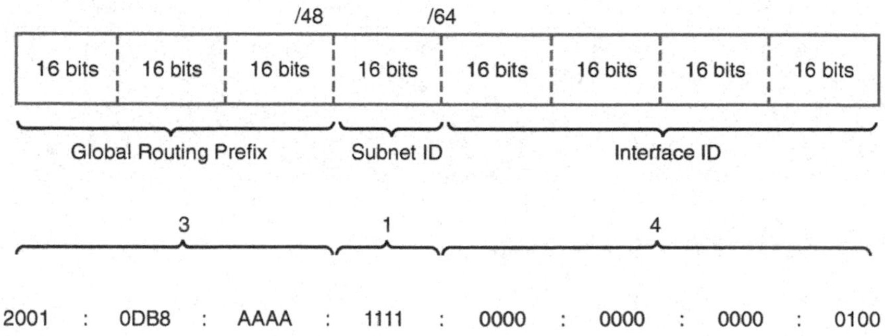

Each number refers to the number of hextets, or 16-bit segments, of that portion of the address:

- **3**: Three hextets for the global routing prefix
- **1**: One hextet for the subnet ID
- **4**: Four hextets for the interface ID

Global unicast addresses that are currently assigned by the Internet Assigned Numbers Authority (IANA) use the range of addresses that start with binary value 001 (2000::/3). This range represents one-eighth of the total IPv6 address space and is the largest block of assigned addresses. Figure 20-4 shows how the IPv6 address space is divided into an eight-piece pie based on the value of the first 3 bits.

Using the 2000::/3 pie piece, the IANA assigns /23 or shorter address blocks to the five Regional Internet Registries (RIR). From there, ISPs are assigned /32 or shorter address blocks. ISPs then assign sites—their customers—a /48 or shorter address block. Figure 20-5 shows the breakdown of global routing prefixes.

**Figure 20-4    Allocation of IPv6 Address Space**

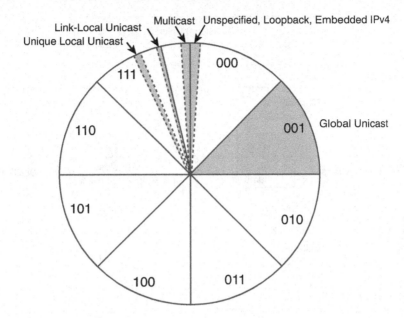

**Figure 20-5    Classification of Global Routing Prefix Sizes**

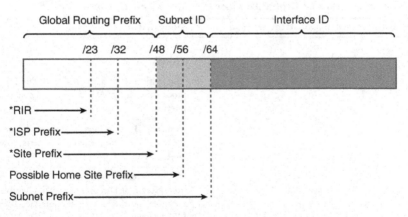

*This is a minimum allocation. The prefix length may be less if it can be
justified.

In IPv6, an interface can be configured with multiple global unicast addresses, which can be on the same or different subnets. In addition, an interface does not have to be configured with a global unicast address, but it must at least have a link-local address.

A global unicast address can be further classified into the various configuration options available, as Figure 20-6 shows.

**Figure 20-6    Global Unicast Address Configuration Options**

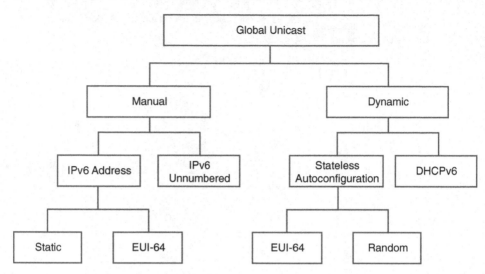

We review EUI-64 and stateless address autoconfiguration in more detail later in this day. We review the rest of the configuration options in Figure 20-6 in more detail in the upcoming days. For now, Table 20-2 summarizes them as follows.

**Table 20-2    Summary of Global Unicast Configuration Options**

| Global Unicast Configuration Option | | Description |
|---|---|---|
| Manual | Static | Similar to IPv4, the IPv6 address and prefix are statically configured on the interface. |
| | EUI-64 | The prefix is configured manually. The EUI-64 process uses the MAC address to generate the 64-bit interface ID. |
| | IPv6 unnumbered | Similar to IPv4, an interface can be configured to use the IPv6 address of another interface on the same device. |
| Dynamic | Stateless address autoconfiguration | SLAAC determines the prefix and prefix length from Neighbor Discovery Router advertisement messages and then creates the interface ID using the EUI-64 method. |
| | DHCPv6 | Similar to IPv4, a device can receive some or all of its addressing from a DHCPv6 server. |

## Link-Local Address

As Figure 20-2 shows, link-local addresses are a type of unicast address. Link-local addresses are confined to a single link. They need to be unique only to that link because packets with a link-local source or destination address are not routable off the link.

Link-local addresses are configured in one of three ways:

- Dynamically, using EUI-64

- Randomly generated interface ID

- Statically, entering the link-local address manually

Link-local addresses provide a unique benefit in IPv6. A device can create its link-local address completely on its own. Link-local unicast addresses are in the range of FE80::/10 to FEBF::/10, as Table 20-3 shows.

**Table 20-3    Range of Link-Local Unicast Addresses**

| Link-Local Unicast Address | Range of First Hextet | Range of First Hextet in Binary |
|---|---|---|
| FE80::/10 | FE80 | 1111 1110 10 00 0000 |
| | FEBF | 1111 1110 10 11 1111 |

Figure 20-7 shows the format of a link-local unicast address.

**Figure 20-7    Link-Local Unicast Address**

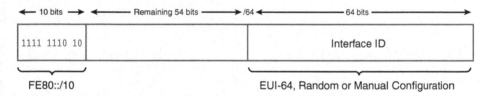

## Loopback Address

The loopback address for IPv6 is an all-0s address except for the last bit, which is set to a 1. As in IPv4, an end device uses the IPv6 loopback address to send an IPv6 packet to itself to test the TCP/IP stack. The loopback address cannot be assigned to an interface and is not routable outside the device.

## Unspecified Address

The unspecified unicast address is the all-0s address, represented as ::. It cannot be assigned to an interface but is reserved for communications when the sending device does not have a valid IPv6 address yet. For example, a device uses :: as the source address when using the duplicate address detection (DAD) process. The DAD process ensures a unique link-local address. Before a device can begin using its newly created link-local address, it sends out an all-nodes multicast to all devices on the link with its new address as the destination. If the device receives a response, it knows that link-local address is in use and, therefore, needs to create another link-local address.

## Unique Local Address

Unique local addresses (ULAs) are defined by RFC 4193, "Unique Local IPv6 Unicast Addresses." Figure 20-8 shows the format for ULAs.

**Figure 20-8   Unique Local Address**

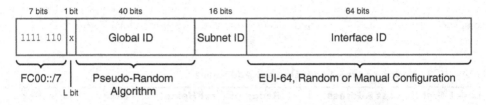

These are private addresses. However, unlike in IPv4, IPv6 ULAs are globally unique. This is possible because of the relatively large amount of address space in the Global ID portion shown in Figure 20-8: 40 bits, or more than 1 trillion unique global IDs. As long as a site uses the Pseudo-Random Global ID Algorithm, it will have a very high probability of generating a unique global ID.

Unique local addresses have the following characteristics:

- Possess a globally unique prefix or at least have a very high probability of being unique.

- Allow sites to be combined or privately interconnected without address conflicts or addressing renumbering.

- Remain independent of any Internet service provider and can be used within a site without having Internet connectivity.

- If accidentally leaked outside a site by either routing or the Domain Name System (DNS), don't cause a conflict with any other addresses.

- Can be used just like a global unicast address.

## IPv4 Embedded Address

IPv4 and IPv6 packets are not compatible. Features such as NAT-PT (now deprecated) and NAT64 are required to translate between the two address families. IPv4-mapped IPv6 addresses are used by transition mechanisms on hosts and routers to create IPv4 tunnels that deliver IPv6 packets over IPv4 networks.

---

**NOTE**   NAT64 is beyond the scope of the CCST Networking exam topics.

---

To create an IPv4-mapped IPv6 address, the IPv4 address is embedded within the low-order 32 bits of IPv6. Basically, IPv6 just puts an IPv4 address at the end, adds 16 all-1 bits, and pads the rest of the address. The address does not have to be globally unique. Figure 20-9 illustrates this IPv4-mapped IPv6 address structure.

**Figure 20-9    Pv4-Mapped IPv6 Address**

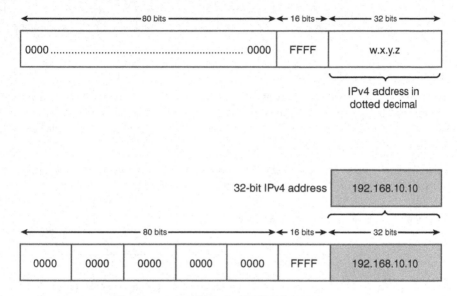

IPv6 compressed format ::FFFF.192.168.10.10

# Multicast

The second major classification of IPv6 address types in Figure 20-2 is multicast. Multicast is a technique used for a device to send a single packet to multiple destinations simultaneously. An IPv6 multicast address defines a group of devices known as a multicast group and is equivalent to IPv4 224.0.0.0/4. IPv6 multicast addresses have the prefix FF00::/8.

Two types of IPv6 multicast addresses are used:

- Assigned multicast
- Solicited-node multicast

## Assigned Multicast

Assigned multicast addresses are used in context with specific protocols.

The following are two common IPv6 assigned multicast groups:

- **FF02::1 All-nodes multicast group**: This is a multicast group that all IPv6-enabled devices join. Similar to a broadcast in IPv4, all IPv6 interfaces on the link process packets sent to this address. For example, a router sending an ICMPv6 Router Advertisement (RA) uses the all-nodes FF02::1 address. IPv6-enabled devices can then use the RA information to learn the link's address information such as prefix, prefix length, and the default gateway.

- **FF02::2 All-routers multicast group**: This is a multicast group that all IPv6 routers join. A router becomes a member of this group when it is enabled as an IPv6 router with the **ipv6**

**unicast-routing** global configuration command. A packet sent to this group is received and processed by all IPv6 routers on the link or network. For example, IPv6-enabled devices send ICMPv6 Router Solicitation (RS) messages to the all-routers multicast address requesting an RA message.

## Solicited-Node Multicast

In addition to every unicast address assigned to an interface, a device has a special multicast address known as a solicited-node multicast address (see Figure 20-2). These multicast addresses are automatically created using a special mapping of the device's unicast address with the solicited-node multicast prefix FF02:0:0:0:0:1:FF00::/104.

As Figure 20-10 shows, solicited-node multicast addresses are used for two essential IPv6 mechanisms, both part of the Neighbor Discovery Protocol (NDP):

**Figure 20-10   Uses of Solicited-Node Multicasts**

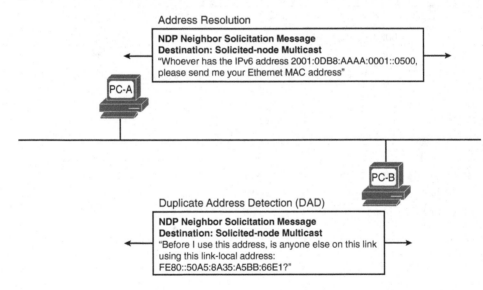

- **Address resolution**: In this mechanism, which is equivalent to ARP in IPv4, an IPv6 device sends an NS message to a solicited-node multicast address to learn the link-layer address of a device on the same link. The device recognizes the IPv6 address of the destination on that link but needs to know its data-link address.

- **Duplicate address detection (DAD)**: As reviewed earlier, DAD allows a device to verify that its unicast address is unique on the link. An NS message is sent to the device's own solicited-node multicast address to determine whether anyone else has this same address.

As Figure 20-11 shows, the solicited-node multicast address consists of two parts:

**Figure 20-11   Solicited-Node Multicast Address Structure**

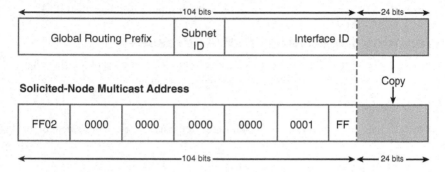

**Unicast/Anycast Address**

| Global Routing Prefix | Subnet ID | Interface ID | |
|---|---|---|---|

104 bits | 24 bits

**Solicited-Node Multicast Address**

| FF02 | 0000 | 0000 | 0000 | 0000 | 0001 | FF | |
|---|---|---|---|---|---|---|---|

104 bits | 24 bits

Copy

FF02:0:0:0:0:1:FF00::/104

- **FF02:0:0:0:0:FF00::/104 multicast prefix:** This is the first 104 bits of the all solicited-node multicast address.

- **Least significant 24 bits:** These bits are copied from the far-right 24 bits of the global unicast or link-local unicast address of the device.

# Anycast

The last major classification of IPv6 address types in Figure 20-2 is the anycast address. It is an address that can be assigned to more than one device or interface. A packet sent to an anycast address is routed to the "nearest" device that is configured with the anycast address, as Figure 20-12 shows.

**Figure 20-12   Example of Anycast Addressing**

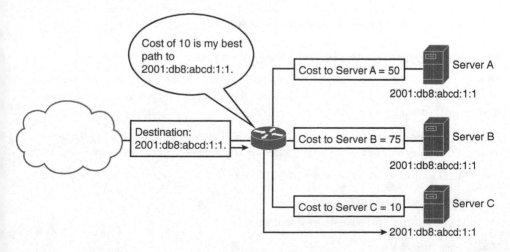

# Representing the IPv6 Address

The IPv6 address can look rather intimidating to someone who is used to IPv4 addressing. However, the IPv6 address can be easier to read and is much simpler to subnet than IPv4.

## Conventions for Writing IPv6 Addresses

IPv6 conventions use 32 hexadecimal numbers, organized into eight hextets of four hex digits separated by a colon, to represent a 128-bit IPv6 address. For example:

2340:1111:AAAA:0001:1234:5678:9ABC

To make things a little easier, two rules allow you to shorten what must be configured for an IPv6 address:

- **Rule 1**: Omit the leading 0s in any given hextet.

- **Rule 2**: Omit the all-0s hextets. Represent one or more consecutive hextets of all hex 0s with a double colon (::), but only for one such occurrence in a given address.

For example, consider the following address. The highlighted hex digits represent the portion of the address that can be abbreviated.

FE00:0000:0000:0001:0000:0000:0000:0056

This address has two locations in which one or more hextets have four hex 0s, so two main options work for abbreviating this address, using the :: abbreviation in one of the locations. The following two options show the two briefest valid abbreviations:

- FE00::1:0:0:0:56

- FE00:0:0:1::56

In the first example, the second and third hextets preceding 0001 were replaced with ::. In the second example, the fifth, sixth, and seventh hextets were replaced with ::. In particular, note that the :: abbreviation, meaning "one or more hextets of all 0s," cannot be used twice because that would be ambiguous. Therefore, the abbreviation FE00::1::56 would not be valid.

## Conventions for Writing IPv6 Prefixes

IPv6 prefixes represent a range or block of consecutive IPv6 addresses. The number that represents the range of addresses, called a *prefix*, is usually seen in IP routing tables, just as you see IP subnet numbers in IPv4 routing tables.

As with IPv4, when you're writing or typing a prefix in IPv6, the bits past the end of the prefix length are all binary 0s. The following IPv6 address is an example of an address assigned to a host:

2000:1234:5678:9ABC:1234:5678:9ABC:1111/64

The prefix in which this address resides is as follows:

2000:1234:5678:9ABC:**0000:0000:0000:0000**/64

When abbreviated, this is

2000:1234:5678:9ABC::/64

If the prefix length does not fall on a hextet boundary (is not a multiple of 16), the prefix value should list all the values in the last hextet. For example, assume that the prefix length in the previous example is /56. By convention, the rest of the fourth hextet is written, after being set to binary 0s, as follows:

2000:1234:5678:9A00::/56

The following list summarizes some key points about how to write IPv6 prefixes:

- The prefix has the same value as the IP addresses in the group for the first number of bits, as defined by the prefix length.

- Any bits after the prefix length number of bits are binary 0s.

- The prefix can be abbreviated with the same rules as IPv6 addresses.

- If the prefix length is not on a hextet boundary, write down the value for the entire hextet.

Table 20-4 shows several sample prefixes, their formats, and a brief explanation.

**Table 20-4    Example IPv6 Prefixes and Their Meanings**

| Prefix | Explanation | Incorrect Alternative |
|---|---|---|
| 2000::/3 | All addresses whose first 3 bits are equal to the first 3 bits of hex number 2000 (bits are 001) | 2000/3 (omits ::) or 2::/3 (omits the rest of the first hextet) |
| 2340:1140::/26 | All addresses whose first 26 bits match the listed hex number | 2340:114::/26 (omits the last digit in the second hextet) |
| 2340:1111::/32 | All addresses whose first 32 bits match the listed hex number | 2340:1111/32 (omits ::) |

# Migration to IPv6

Two major transition strategies are currently used to migrate to IPv6:

- **Dual-stacking**: In this integration method, a node has implementation and connectivity to both an IPv4 and IPv6 network. This is the recommended option and involves running IPv4 and IPv6 at the same time.

- **Tunneling**: Tunneling is a method for transporting IPv6 packets over IPv4-only networks by encapsulating the IPv6 packet inside IPv4. Several tunneling techniques are available.

Because of the simplicity of running dual-stack, it will most likely be the preferred strategy as IPv4-only networks begin to disappear. However, it will probably still be decades before we see enterprise networks running exclusively IPv6. Figure 20-13 illustrates one way Wendell Odom thinks about the transition to IPv6: "But who knows how long it will take?"

**NOTE** Wendell Odom is a Cisco Certified Internet Expert (CCIE No. 1624) and the author of the widely popular *CCNA 200-301 Official Cert Guide Library* (ISBN 978-1587147142).

Remember this advice: "Dual-stack where you can; tunnel where you must." These two methods are the most common techniques to transition from IPv4 to IPv6. Dual-stacking is easy enough. Just configure all your devices to use both IPv4 and IPv6 addressing. Tunneling, however, is more complex and beyond the scope of the CCST Networking exam topics.

**Figure 20-13  Transition to IPv6 Using Dual-Stack**

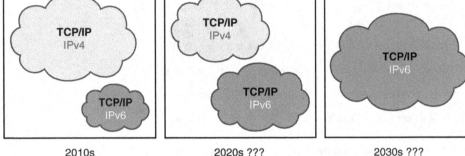

| 2010s | 2020s ??? | 2030s ??? |

# Study Resources

For today's exam topics, refer to the following resources for more study:

| Resource | Module or Chapter |
| --- | --- |
| SFA Self Enroll: Networking Basics | 10 |
| SFA Self Enroll: Network Addressing and Basic Troubleshooting | 5 |
| SFA Instructor Led: Networking Essentials | 10, 33 |
| CCST Networking 100-150 Official Cert Guide | 2, 14 |

**NOTE**  SFA: https://skillsforall.com/

# Cables and Connectors

## CCST Networking 100-150 Exam Topic

- 3.1. Identify cables and connectors commonly used in local area networks.

  - *Cable types: fiber, copper, twisted pair; Connector types: coax, RJ-45, RJ-11, fiber connector types*

- 3.2. Differentiate between Wi-Fi, cellular, and wired network technologies.

  - *Copper, including sources of interference; fiber; wireless, including 802.11 (unlicensed, 2.4 GHz, 5 GHz, 6 GHz), cellular (licensed), sources of interference*

## Key Topics

For the next two days, we review the media that devices use to physically connect to the network. Today, we focus on cabling and connectors. Tomorrow, we will turn our attention to wireless connections.

## Network Media Forms and Standards

Three basic forms of network media exist:

- **Copper cable:** The signals are patterns of electrical pulses.

- **Fiber-optic cable:** The signals are patterns of light.

- **Wireless:** The signals are patterns of microwave transmissions.

Messages are encoded and then placed onto the media. Encoding is the process of converting data into patterns of electrical, light, or electromagnetic energy so that it can be carried on the media.

Table 19-1 summarizes the three most common types of networking media in use today.

**Table 19-1   Networking Media**

| Media | Physical Components | Frame Encoding Technique | Signaling Methods |
|-------|---------------------|--------------------------|-------------------|
| Copper cable | UTP | Manchester encoding | Changes in the electromagnetic field |
| | Coaxial | Nonreturn to zero (NRZ) techniques | |
| | Connectors | | Intensity of the electromagnetic field |
| | NICs | 4B/5B codes used with Multi-Level Transition Level 3 (MLT-3) signaling | |
| | Ports | | Phase of the electromagnetic wave |
| | Interfaces | 8B/10B | |
| | | PAM5 | |
| Fiber-optic cable | Single-mode fiber | Pulses of light | A pulse equals 1 |
| | Multimode fiber | Wavelength multiplexing using different colors | No pulse is 0 |
| | Connectors | | |
| | NICs | | |
| | Interfaces | | |
| | Lasers and LEDs | | |
| | Photoreceptors | | |
| Wireless | Access points | Direct Sequence Spread Spectrum (DSSS) | Radio waves |
| | NICs | | |
| | Radio | Orthogonal frequency division multiplexing (OFDM) | |
| | Antennas | | |

Each media type has its advantages and disadvantages. When choosing the media, consider each of the following:

- **Cable length**: Does the cable need to span a room or run from building to building?

- **Cost**: Does the budget allow for using a more expensive media type?

- **Bandwidth**: Does the technology used with the media provide adequate bandwidth?

- **Ease of installation**: Does the implementation team have the capability to install the cable, or is a vendor required?

- **Susceptibility to EMI/RFI**: Will the local environment interfere with the signal?

Table 19-2 summarizes the media standards for LAN cabling.

**Table 19-2 Media Standard, Cable Length, and Bandwidth**

| Ethernet Type | Bandwidth | Cable Type | Maximum Distance |
|---|---|---|---|
| 10BASE-T | 10Mbps | Cat3/Cat5 UTP | 100 m |
| 100BASE-TX | 100Mbps | Cat5 UTP | 100 m |
| 100BASE-TX | 200Mbps | Cat5 UTP | 100 m |
| 100BASE-FX | 100Mbps | Multimode fiber | 400 m |
| 100BASE-FX | 200Mbps | Multimode fiber | 2 km |
| 1000BASE-T | 1Gbps | Cat5e UTP | 100 m |
| 1000BASE-TX | 1Gbps | Cat6 UTP | 100 m |
| 1000BASE-SX | 1Gbps | Multimode fiber | 550 m |
| 1000BASE-LX | 1Gbps | Single-mode fiber | 2 km |
| 10GBASE-T | 10Gbps | Cat6a/Cat7 UTP | 100 m |
| 10GBASE-SX4 | 10Gbps | Multimode fiber | 550 m |
| 10GBASE-LX4 | 10Gbps | Single-mode fiber | 2 km |

# Copper Cabling

Copper cabling is the most common type of cabling used in networks today because it is inexpensive, easy to install, and has low resistance to electrical current. However, copper media is limited by distance and signal interference. The farther the signal travels, the more it deteriorates (attenuates).

The timing and voltage values of the electrical pulses are also susceptible to interference from two sources:

- **Electromagnetic interference (EMI) or radio frequency interference (RFI)**: EMI and RFI signals from radio waves and electromagnetic devices can distort and corrupt the data signals.

- **Crosstalk**: Crosstalk refers to the interference generated by the electric or magnetic fields in one wire, affecting another wire that is in close proximity.

To counter the negative effects of EMI and RFI, some types of copper cables are wrapped in metallic shielding and require proper grounding connections.

To counter the negative effects of crosstalk, some types of copper cables have opposing circuit wire pairs twisted together, which effectively cancels the crosstalk.

There are three main types of copper media used in networking, as shown in Figure 19-1.

**Figure 19-1  Types of Copper Cabling**

Unshielded Twisted Pair (UTP) Cable                    Shielded Twisted Pair (STP) Cable

Coaxial Cable

# Unshielded Twisted Pair (UTP)

UTP cabling is used for connecting network hosts with networking devices, such as switches and routers. UTP cable consists of four pairs of color-coded wires that have been twisted together and then encased in a flexible plastic sheath that protects from minor physical damage, as shown in Figure 19-2.

**Figure 19-2  UTP Cable**

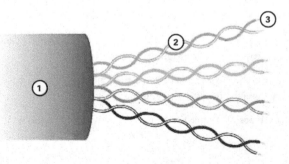

The numbers in Figure 19-2 identify some key features of UTP cable:

1. The outer jacket protects the copper wires from physical damage.

2. The twisted pairs protect the signal from interference.

3. Color-coded plastic insulation electrically isolates wires from each other and identifies each pair.

## Shielded Twisted Pair (STP)

STP cabling provides better noise protection than UTP cabling. However, STP cable is significantly more expensive and difficult to install. STP cables combine the techniques of shielding to counter EMI and RFI and wire twisting to counter crosstalk, as shown in Figure 19-3.

**Figure 19-3   STP Cable**

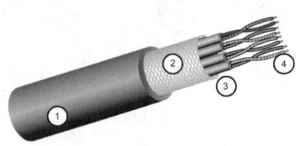

The numbers in Figure 19-3 identify some key features of STP cable:

1. Outer jacket

2. Braided or foil shield

3. Foil shields

4. Twisted pairs

## Coaxial Cable

Coaxial cable, or *coax* for short, gets its name from the fact that there are two conductors that share the same axis. As shown in Figure 19-4, there is a copper conductor (4) and braided copper shielding (2). Also shown in Figure 19-4 are the different types of connectors used with coax cable: Bayonet Neill-Concelman (BNC), N type, and F type connectors.

**Figure 19-4   Coaxial Cable and Connectors**

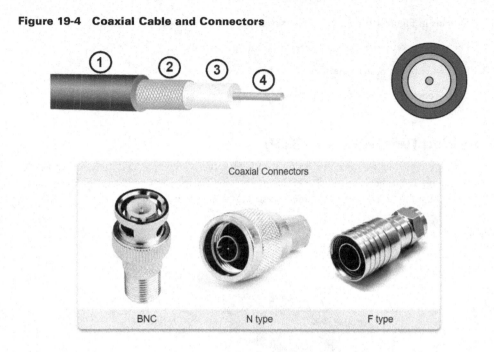

Coaxial Connectors

BNC                    N type                    F type

The numbers in Figure 19-4 identify some key features of coaxial cable:

1. Outer jacket

2. Braided copper shielding

3. Plastic insulation

4. Copper conductor

# UTP Cabling Standards and Connectors

The electrical characteristics of copper cabling are defined by the Institute of Electrical and Electronics Engineers (IEEE). IEEE rates UTP cabling according to its performance.

## UTP Categories

Cables are placed into categories based on their ability to carry higher bandwidth rates. For example, Category 5 cable is used commonly in 100BASE-TX Fast Ethernet installations. Categories of UTP include the following:

- Category 3 was originally used for voice communication over voice lines, but it was later used for data transmission.

- Category 5 and 5e are used for data transmission. Category 5 supports 100Mbps and Category 5e supports 1000Mbps.

- Category 6 has an added separator between each wire pair to support higher speeds. Category 6 supports up to 10Gbps.

- Category 7 also supports 10Gbps.

- Category 8 supports 40Gbps.

## UTP Connectors

UTP cable is usually terminated with an RJ-45 connector, as shown in Figure 19-5. The RJ-45 connector is the male component, crimped at the end of the cable.

**Figure 19-5   RJ-45 UTP Plugs**

The socket, shown in Figure 19-6, is the female component of a network device, wall, cubicle partition outlet, or patch panel.

**Figure 19-6   RJ-45 UTP Sockets**

## Straight-through and Crossover UTP Cables

Different situations may require UTP cables to be wired according to different wiring conventions. This means that the individual wires in the cable have to be connected in different orders to different sets of pins in the RJ-45 connectors.

Table 19-3 shows the UTP cable type, related standards, and the typical application of these cables.

**Table 19-3   Cable Types and Standards**

| Cable Type | Standard | Application |
|---|---|---|
| Ethernet straight-through | Both ends T568A or both ends T568B | Connects a network host to a network device such as a switch or hub |
| Ethernet crossover | One end T568A and the other end T568B | Connects two network hosts or connects two network intermediary devices (switch to switch or router to router) |

Figure 19-7 identifies the individual wire pairs for the T568A and T568B standards.

**Figure 19-7   T568A and T568B Standards**

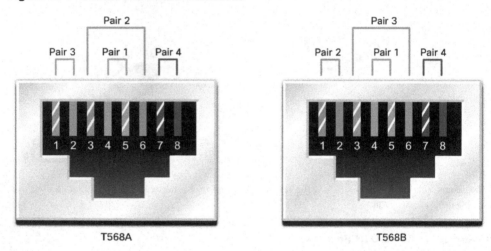

NOTE   Although you are required to know the difference between straight-through and crossover cables, most network interfaces, through a feature called **auto-mdx** on Cisco routers, now autodetect the pinout of the plugged-in cable. With modern devices, you no longer have to ensure you are connecting the correct cable type.

# Fiber-Optic Cabling

Because of its expense, fiber-optic cabling is not as commonly used as the various types of copper cabling. However, fiber-optic cabling has certain properties that make it the best option in certain situations. Fiber-optic cabling transmits data over longer distances, at higher bandwidths, and is completely immune to EMI and RFI.

## Types of Fiber Media

Fiber-optic cables are broadly classified into two types: single-mode fiber and multimode fiber.

# Single-Mode Fiber (SMF)

SMF consists of a very small core and uses expensive laser technology to send a single ray of light, as shown in Figure 19-8. SMF is popular in long-distance situations spanning hundreds of kilometers, such as those required in long-haul telephony and cable TV applications.

**Figure 19-8   Single-Mode Fiber**

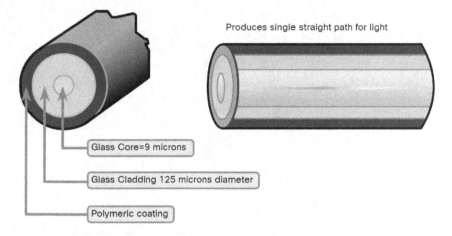

# Multimode Fiber (MMF)

MMF consists of a larger core and uses LED emitters to send light pulses. Specifically, light from an LED enters the multimode fiber at different angles, as shown in Figure 19-9. MMF is popular in local area networks (LANs) because they can be powered by low-cost LEDs. It provides bandwidth up to 10Gbps over link lengths of up to 550 meters.

**Figure 19-9   Multimode Fiber**

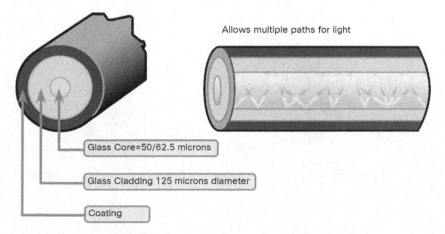

## Fiber-Optic Connectors

Businesses decide on the types of connectors that will be used based on their equipment. The straight-tip (ST) connector, shown in Figure 19-10, was one of the first connector types used. The connector locks securely with a "twist-on/twist-off" bayonet-style mechanism.

**Figure 19-10 Straight-Tip (ST) Connector**

The subscriber connector (SC) type, shown in Figure 19-11, is a widely-adopted LAN and WAN connector that uses a push-pull mechanism to ensure positive insertion. This connector type is used with multimode and single-mode fiber.

**Figure 19-11 Subscriber Connector (SC) Type**

Lucent connector (LC) simplex connector type, shown in Figure 19-12, is a smaller version of the SC connector.

**Figure 19-12   Lucent Connector (LC) Simplex Connectors**

A duplex multimode LC connector, shown in Figure 19-13, is similar to an LC simplex connector but uses a duplex connector.

**Figure 19-13   Duplex Multimode LC Connector**

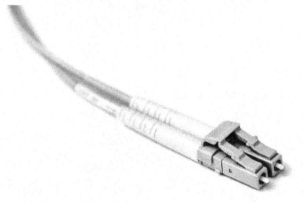

# Fiber Patch Cords

Fiber patch cords are required for interconnecting infrastructure devices. The use of color distinguishes between single-mode and multimode patch cords. A yellow jacket is for single-mode fiber cables, and orange (or aqua) is for multimode fiber cables.

Figures 19-14 through 19-17 show four types of fiber patch cords.

**Figure 19-14   SC-SC Multimode Patch Cord**

**Figure 19-15   LC-LC Single-Mode Patch Cord**

**Figure 19-16   ST-LC Multimode Patch Cord**

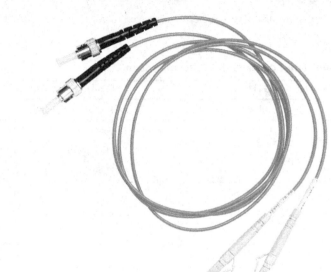

**Figure 19-17   SC-ST Single-Mode Patch Cord**

## Fiber versus Copper

There are many advantages to using fiber-optic cable compared to copper cables. Table 19-4 highlights some of these differences.

**Table 19-4   UTP and Fiber-Optic Cabling Comparison**

| Implementation Issues | UTP Cabling | Fiber-Optic Cabling |
|---|---|---|
| Bandwidth supported | 10Mbps to 10Gbps | 10Mbps to 100Gbps |
| Distance | Relatively short (1–100 meters) | Relatively long (1–100,000 meters) |
| Immunity to EMI and RFI | Low | High (completely immune) |
| Immunity to electrical hazards | Low | High (completely immune) |
| Media and connector costs | Lowest | Highest |
| Installation skills required | Lowest | Highest |
| Safety precautions | Lowest | Highest |

# Study Resources

For today's exam topics, refer to the following resources for more study:

| Resource | Module or Chapter |
|---|---|
| SFA Self Enroll: Networking Basics | 2, 6 |
| SFA Self Enroll: Network Addressing and Basic Troubleshooting | 1 |
| SFA Instructor Led: Networking Essentials | 2, 6, 30 |
| CCST Networking 100-150 Official Cert Guide | 7 |

**NOTE**   SFA: https://skillsforall.com/

# Wireless Technologies

## CCST Networking 100-150 Exam Topic

- 3.2. Differentiate between Wi-Fi, cellular, and wired network technologies.

  - *Copper, including sources of interference; fiber; wireless, including 802.11 (unlicensed, 2.4 GHz, 5 GHz, 6 GHz), cellular (licensed), sources of interference*

## Key Topics

Today we focus on reviewing wireless technologies, including 802.11 and cellular, as well as sources of interference.

## Wi-Fi

The IEEE 802.11 WLAN standards define how radio frequencies (RFs) are used for wireless links. To avoid interference, different channels within an RF spectrum can be used.

### RF Spectrum

The RF spectrum is shown in Figure 18-1. It includes all types of radio communications, including the 2.4 GHz and 5 GHz frequencies used by wireless devices. Not shown in the graphic is the newer 6 GHz band that is also being used by the newest Wi-Fi standards.

### Channels

A frequency range is typically called a band of frequencies. For example, wireless LAN devices with a 2.4 GHz antenna can actually use any frequency from 2.4000 to 2.4835 GHz. The 5 GHz band lies between 5.150 GHz and 5.825 GHz.

These bands are further subdivided into frequency channels. Channels become particularly important when the implementation of wireless devices saturates a specific area. Each channel is known by a channel number and is assigned to a specific frequency. As long as the channels are defined by a national or international standards body, they can be used consistently in all locations. Figures 18-2 and 18-3 show the channel layout for the 2.4 GHz and 5 GHz bands, respectively.

**Figure 18-1   RF Spectrum**

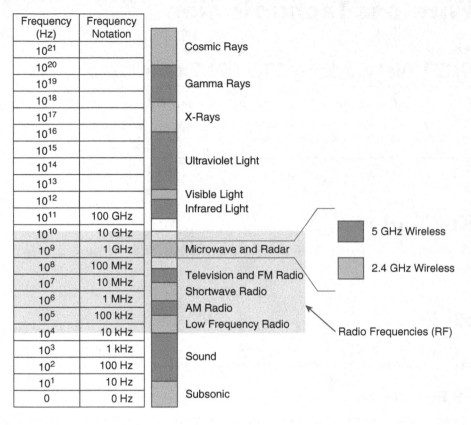

**Figure 18-2   2.4-GHz Channels**

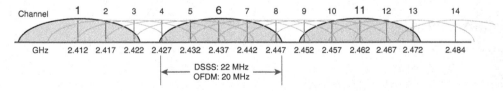

Notice in Figure 18-3 that the 5-GHz band consists of nonoverlapping channels. Each channel is allocated a frequency range that does not encroach on or overlap the frequencies allocated for any other channel.

The same is not true of the 2.4-GHz band in Figure 18-2. The only way to avoid any overlap between adjacent channels is to configure access points (APs) to use only channels 1, 6, and 11.

**Figure 18-3    5-GHz Channels**

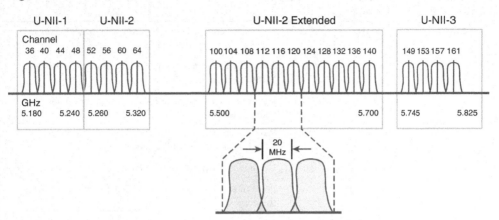

## 802.11 Standards

Most of the standards specify that wireless devices have one antenna to transmit and receive wireless signals on the specified radio frequency (2.4 GHz or 5 GHz). Some of the newer standards that transmit and receive at higher speeds require APs and wireless clients to have multiple antennas using the multiple-input and multiple-output (MIMO) technology. MIMO uses multiple antennas as both the transmitter and receiver to improve communication performance. Up to four antennas can be supported.

Various implementations of the IEEE 802.11 standard have been developed over the years. Table 18-1 highlights these standards.

**Table 18-1    Summary of 802.11 Standards**

| IEEE WLAN Standard | Radio Frequency | Description |
|---|---|---|
| 802.11 | 2.4 GHz | ■ Speeds of up to 2Mbps |
| | | ■ No longer in use |
| 802.11a | 5 GHz | ■ Speeds of up to 54Mbps |
| | | ■ Small coverage area |
| | | ■ Less effective at penetrating building structures |
| | | ■ Not interoperable with the 802.11b and 802.11g |
| 802.11b | 2.4 GHz | ■ Speeds of up to 11Mbps |
| | | ■ Longer range than 802.11a |
| | | ■ Better able to penetrate building structures |
| 802.11g | 2.4 GHz | ■ Speeds of up to 54Mbps |
| | | ■ Backward compatible with 802.11b with reduced bandwidth capacity |

| IEEE WLAN Standard | Radio Frequency | Description |
|---|---|---|
| 802.11n | 2.4 GHz<br><br>5 GHz | ▪ Data rates range from 150Mbps to 600Mbps with a distance range of up to 70 m (.5 mile)<br><br>▪ APs and wireless clients require multiple antennas using MIMO technology<br><br>▪ Backward compatible with 802.11a/b/g devices with limiting data rates |
| 802.11ac | 5 GHz | ▪ Provides data rates ranging from 450Mbps to 1.3Gbps (1300Mbps) using MIMO technology<br><br>▪ Up to eight antennas can be supported<br><br>▪ Backward compatible with 802.11a/n devices with limiting data rates |
| 802.11ax | 2.4 GHz<br><br>5 GHz<br><br>6 GHz | ▪ Released in 2019 (latest standard)<br><br>▪ Marketing name is Wi-Fi 6 or Wi-Fi 6e; also known as High-Efficiency Wireless (HEW)<br><br>▪ Higher data rates and increased capacity<br><br>▪ Handles many connected devices<br><br>▪ Improved power efficiency<br><br>▪ 1GHz and 7GHz capable when those frequencies become available |

# Wireless Interference

Wireless interference occurs when signals from different sources mix with a transmitted signal, deteriorating its quality. This interference can emerge from various sources, including other transmissions and environmental noise, especially when those sources are either close to the same frequency or extremely powerful.

Common sources of powerful signals that can cause interference include electrical wires, amateur radio sets, fluorescent lights, some LED bulbs, lightning storms, automobile engines, television sets, and generators. These high-power electronics can emit signals that interfere with wireless data transmission.

Wi-Fi, which operates in an unlicensed frequency range shared by many other devices, is notably susceptible to this kind of interference. For example, microwave ovens, baby monitors, handheld radios, and Bluetooth devices all operate in the 2.4-GHz frequency range, which overlaps with one band of Wi-Fi and can therefore cause interference.

Electromagnetic waves also lose power when passing through materials other than air. For example, approximately

- 20% of a Wi-Fi signal can pass through a brick or concrete wall,
- 30% of a Wi-Fi signal can pass through a sheet of metal,

- 50% of a Wi-Fi signal can pass through an empty metal rack, and

- 70% of a Wi-Fi signal can pass through a clear window, sheet of drywall, or wooden door.

These figures are estimates, and certain large metal appliances, such as refrigerators or washing machines, can block almost 100% of a Wi-Fi signal.

## Wi-Fi Networks

Wi-Fi networks consist of wireless adapters, access points (APs), and repeaters, as shown in Figure 18-4. Devices connected to a Wi-Fi network, like laptops, printers, desktop computers, and handheld devices, require a Wi-Fi modem. The AP bridges the Wi-Fi and wired networks, while repeaters extend the wireless signal to devices that are out of reach from the AP. In smaller networks, the AP and router are often combined into a single wireless router.

**Figure 18-4   Wi-Fi Components**

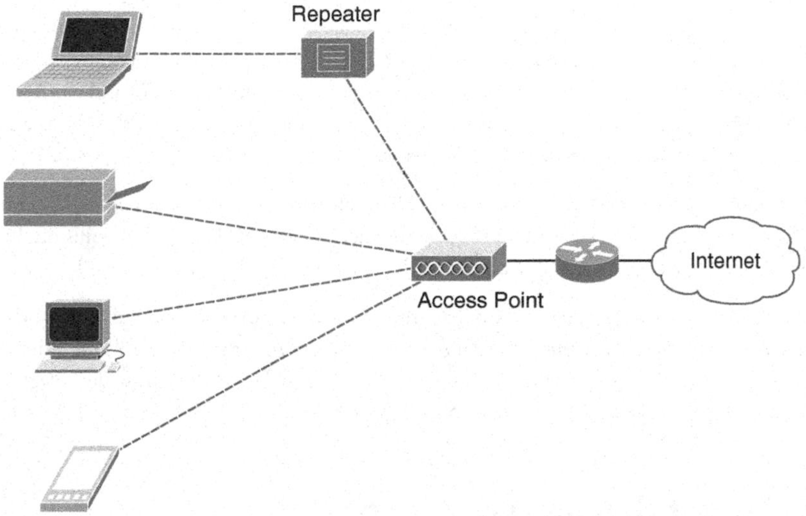

Standard Wi-Fi signals have a limited range, which can be problematic in large houses or buildings. Repeaters can be used to extend signal coverage, but they may not provide the best Wi-Fi performance. An alternative is a Wi-Fi mesh system, where two or more APs are connected via a backhaul, as shown in Figure 18-5, creating a larger Wi-Fi network. The backhaul can be a wired or wireless connection. In the figure, users can seamlessly switch between AP A and AP B within the mesh network without losing connection.

**Figure 18-5   Wireless Mesh Example**

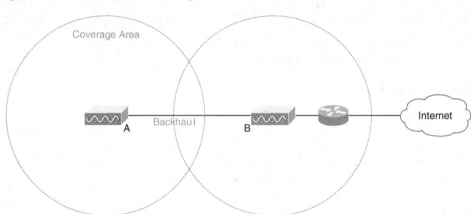

Wi-Fi's primary advantages include operation in unlicensed spectrum and minimal infrastructure requirements. However, these advantages also bring disadvantages. The use of unlicensed spectrum limits transmission power, making it challenging to cover large outdoor spaces and causing potential interference from other devices operating in the same frequency range. The lack of a data limit can lead to network overload and degraded performance.

All hosts connected to a single AP through one channel share the same bandwidth. Wi-Fi uses Carrier Sense Multiple Access with Collision Avoidance (CSMA/CA) to avoid collisions, with some APs using beam forming to separate transmissions.

Choosing Wi-Fi channels can be done by detecting current electromagnetic radiation and choosing a channel with minimal interference. For large-scale deployments, this is done using radio receivers. Smaller installations may require trial and error. Many newer APs can automatically select the optimal channel using Dynamic Frequency Selection (DFS).

# Cellular Networks

Cellular networks are a type of wireless network designed and operated by large-scale dedicated organizations. They are designed to support a global scale, including roaming between wireless connections and networks. They provide end-user billing, maintain defined quality-of-service guarantees, and control device connection with strong authentication and authorization mechanisms. Cellular networks have evolved over many generations, from 2G to the current 5G.

## 5G Cellular Network Components

5G cellular networks are composed of three main components, as shown in Figure 18-6:

- **Radio access network (RAN):** This includes a group of towers and a local network that connects these towers. Each tower has a base station that controls the function of the radio and its communication with other network elements.

- **Mobile core**: This is a set of servers and software that handle tasks such as user authentication, de-encapsulation of user data, tracking user location, and enabling billing.

- **Backhaul network**: This carries data from the RAN to and from the mobile core. It is usually some form of fiber network, which can be leased from other providers or carried over the Internet.

**Figure 18-6   5G Cellular Network Components**

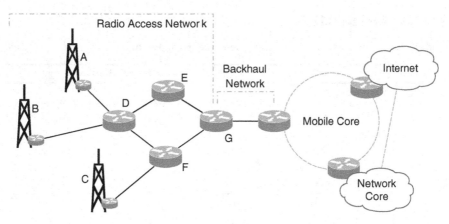

## Radio Access Network (RAN)

The RAN connects the mobile devices to the mobile core. Each RAN tower has a base station, also known as a gNodeB, which is responsible for establishing the wireless channel used for communication with the end user's device. This wireless channel is called a bearer service. The base station reclaims channels when a device has been idle for too long and establishes a control plane connection to the device for signaling services. It also establishes a tunnel for each service from the device to a termination point in the mobile core.

## Mobile Core

The mobile core is a set of servers and software that handle various tasks, such as the following:

- Authenticating users based on a subscriber identity module (SIM) card. Each SIM card contains a 64-bit International Mobile Subscriber Identity (ISMI) as well as a private key for building encrypted tunnels.

- De-encapsulating user data and forwarding this traffic on to the Internet or other services.

- Tracking the user's location and handing off users to other mobile cores when necessary.

- Tracking usage and enabling billing.

## Advantages and Disadvantages of Cellular Networks

Cellular networks offer a wide reach and scale, providing users with service in most moderately dense population areas, and maintain consistent connection quality for connected devices. However, they require an extensive infrastructure, including specialized hardware and software for cellular physical transmitters, base stations, and the mobile core. This complexity can be a disadvantage when considering the cost and specialized knowledge required for setup and maintenance. Despite these challenges, organizations can deploy private 5G networks for large physical facilities, such as factories and campuses, to supplement local coverage from cellular telephone towers in large office buildings and apartment complexes.

# Study Resources

For today's exam topics, refer to the following resources for more study:

| Resource | Module or Chapter |
| --- | --- |
| SFA Self Enroll: Networking Basic | 4 |
| SFA Instructor Led: Networking Essentials | 4 |
| CCST Networking 100-150 Official Cert Guide | 8 |

**NOTE**   SFA: https://skillsforall.com/

# Endpoint Devices

## CCST Networking 100-150 Exam Topic

- 3.3. Identify types of endpoint devices.
  - *Internet of Things (IoT) devices, computers, mobile devices*

## Key Topics

Today we focus on endpoint devices and their operations, including hosts, mobile devices, and IoT devices.

## Hosts

The term *host* typically refers to one of the following main categories of endpoints:

- **Desktop computers:** These include all-in-one computers, separate processor units with monitors, gaming systems, point-of-sale systems, and graphics workstations.

- **Laptop computers:** These devices can connect via either a wired or wireless interface, but they typically use a wireless connection.

- **Servers:** These are the powerhouses behind websites, cloud services, and on-premises computing services. They are typically housed in data centers and are not usually visible to the general user.

A host, in computing, consists of software and hardware components. Its operating system can be divided into the kernel and user space, as shown in Figure 17-1, where applications in user space appear to each other to have dedicated resources, but in reality, these resources are shared. In general, kernel applications share the same memory and processor space.

**Figure 17-1   Host Networking Stack**

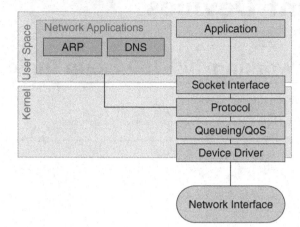

# Sending a Packet

An application sends a packet by placing it into a socket queue. The protocol application inside the kernel will take the packet off the socket queue, process the packet through any queueing, and then hand off the packet to the device driver.

The device driver will then pass the packet to the physical interface chipset, which will convert the packet from the internal computer system representation to the external network representation and send the packet.

The process of sending a packet from the user space to the kernel for network transmission involves the following steps, as numbered in Figure 17-1:

**1.** The application places the packet into a socket queue.

**2.** The kernel's protocol application retrieves the packet from the socket queue and processes it.

**3.** The packet is processed through any queuing necessary and then is passed to the device driver.

**4.** The device driver hands the packet over to the network interface chipset.

**5.** The network interface chipset converts the packet from the internal computer system format to the external network format and sends it out.

During this process of sending the packet out, if the protocol stack is missing information such as the destination IP address or the gateway MAC address, it will call the appropriate network application residing in the user space, such as ARP or DNS, to discover the missing information.

Everything you do on a computer today touches the network somehow, so the protocol stack running through the user space into the kernel tends to be very busy.

# Virtual Hosts

Virtual hosts add another layer of complexity, as shown in Figure 17-2.

**Figure 17-2    Virtual Namespaces in Linux**

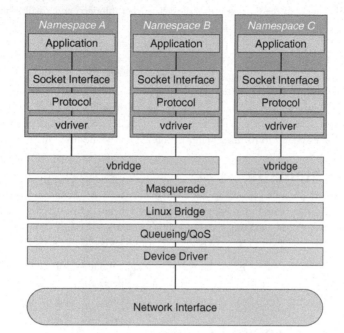

In a Linux system, multiple virtual hosts (or containers) can be configured using several namespaces. Each namespace has its own socket interface, protocol stack, and virtual driver (vdriver). The vdriver, acting as a hardware abstraction layer (HAL), behaves like a network interface from the protocol stack's perspective.

The vdriver differs from the external network driver in that processed packets are sent to an internal virtual bridge (vbridge). Much like a physical switch, every namespace connected to the same vbridge can receive and process packets. For example, if a packet is sent from namespace A to namespace B, it crosses the vbridge between them in the same way it would cross a physical network connection, but without going through an external network interface.

A Linux host can have multiple virtual bridges, and various namespaces can connect to different vbridges. If a packet is sent from namespace A to namespace C, it would traverse through the vbridge, the masquerade, the Linux bridge, back up through the masquerade to the second vbridge, and finally through the vdriver and protocol stack in namespace C. Thus, multiple virtual hosts can create an entire network behind the Linux bridge.

The masquerade is a virtual switch that performs network address translation (NAT), allowing each virtual host to have a separate IP address space. Packets intended for other hosts connected through an external network go through a queuing process, then a device driver, and finally onto a network interface.

When a packet is received at the network interface, it undergoes the same process as a conventional host. The received packet is inspected and queued for processing by the masquerade. The masquerade translates the external interface address and port number into their internal equivalents, and then it passes the packets across the correct vbridge into the appropriate vdriver queue. The vdriver then hands off the packet to the correct protocol stack, socket interface, and, finally, the application.

# Mobile Devices

Mobile devices are small, handheld, battery-powered apparatuses designed for general communications and running lightweight applications. The evolution of these devices can be traced back to the early 1900s with the advent of analog radio communications. Telecommunication has progressed from wired telephone systems to handheld radios, mobile phones, and now smartphones and tablets.

## Early Developments

In the initial stages, telephone services were used like mail systems. An executive would dictate information to a secretary, who would then contact the intended recipient through a phone call, and the message would be transcribed and delivered. Over time, telephones became a common household item and were directly installed in offices, where secretaries screened calls for their managers.

Amateur radio operators, popularly known as "hams," brought about a significant shift in the 1920s. They developed smaller radios and demonstrated the effectiveness of person-to-person communication.

## The Advent of Mobile Phones

Recognizing the potential, telephone companies started developing similar systems for cars in the mid-1940s, with the first car phone calls made in Chicago in 1946. Sweden launched the first commercial service for car telephones in 1956. These initial attempts at creating a commercially successful mobile (car) phone network were not very successful due to limited frequencies and inefficient frequency usage.

In 1987, the technical specifications for Europe's first large-scale mobile-phone network were standardized. The first text message was sent in 1992, and the first downloadable content, a ringtone, was made available in 1998.

## The Smartphone Era

The earlier mobile phones were modeled on the desk phones, equipped with a small keypad for making calls and sending messages through the Simple Messaging Service (SMS). The concept of a mobile phone changed dramatically with the launch of the iPhone by Apple in 2007. The iPhone, with its single large screen, transformed the mobile phone from a small desk phone to a small handheld computer.

The success of the iPhone and commercial cellular mobile networks can be attributed to the significant improvement in bandwidth usage brought about by Voice over IP (VoIP). It allowed the conversion of analog voice signals into a digital format that could be carried over packet-switched networks like the Internet.

## Tablets and Phablets

The mobile device market further expanded into tablets in the mid-2000s, followed by phablets, which bridged the gap between cellular phones and tablets. Mobile devices are now a prominent source of traffic on computer networks. Interestingly, they are seldom connected via a wired interface and, instead, use Wi-Fi or cellular networks to connect to the Internet.

## Operating Systems

Two operating systems now dominate the mobile device market: Apple's iOS and Android. Apple's iOS is proprietary, with limited information available about its interaction with computer networks. Android, on the other hand, is open source and based on a standard Linux kernel. This makes it easier for developers to adapt new processors and interfaces to Android devices. However, many components above the hardware abstraction layer are Android-specific, such as the native libraries and runtime, as shown in Figure 17-3. Most principles of networking in the Linux kernel apply to the Android operating system as well.

**Figure 17-3   Android System Architecture**

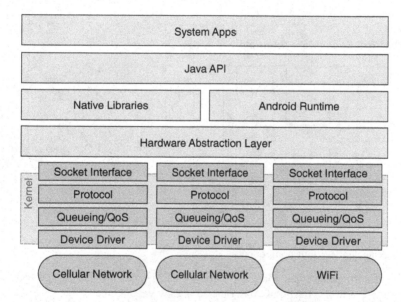

# Internet of Things

The concept of "things" in the context of the Internet refers to any device that can monitor or control real-world systems and is connected to a network, thus contributing to the Internet of Things (IoT).

According to statista.com, in 2023 there were over 15 billion IoT devices connected to the Internet. The number of IoT devices is projected to rise to close to 30 billion by 2030. These "things" can be any electronic device that can be tracked or provide environmental information. Examples include the following:

- **Vehicles**: They can be connected as a single entity. But within each car, hundreds of components can be connected to a car area network (CAN), providing internal and external telemetry.

- **Homes**: IoT can be useful in various home appliances. For instance, refrigerators can monitor internal temperatures, and thermostats can learn usage habits.

- **Medical care**: Hearing devices, insulin pumps, and fitness trackers can be connected to the Internet for better monitoring and improved results.

- **Farms**: IoT devices can monitor soil moisture and nutrients, making irrigation and fertilization more effective and efficient.

- **Industrial manufacturing**: IoT can enable close environmental control, with sensors tracking physical changes in manufactured devices.

The IoT ecosystem generally consists of a hub or IoT gateway, an analysis process, user interfaces, and a user profile, as shown in Figure 17-4.

**Figure 17-4  IoT Ecosystem Example**

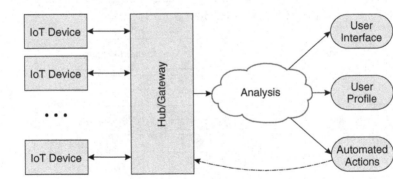

IoT devices generally have four components:

- **Means of communication**: Many IoT devices use low-power wireless systems such as personal area networks (PANs), CANs, Bluetooth, Z-Wave, and others.

- **Processing and memory**: These support gathering and formatting information, and they might also be used to take actions, such as changing the temperature setting on a thermostat.

- **Sensors**: These detect temperature, movement, humidity level, and other environmental conditions.

- **Power supply**: Some IoT devices capture power from the environment, others draw power from the larger system, while others have batteries.

An interesting variant of IoT is fog computing, which distributes processing among local devices rather than relying on a centralized processing facility. This provides for a more decentralized and efficient mode of operation. Fog computing allows for quicker responses and less reliance on long-distance communication with central servers.

# Study Resources

For today's exam topics, refer to the following resources for more study:

| Resource | Module or Chapter |
| --- | --- |
| SFA Self Enroll: Networking Basics | 1, 2 |
| SFA Instructor Led: Networking Essentials | 1, 2 |
| CCST Networking 100-150 Official Cert Guide | 5 |

**NOTE**   SFA: https://skillsforall.com/

# Configure PC and Mobile Access

## CCST Networking 100-150 Exam Topic

- 3.4. Demonstrate how to set up and check network connectivity on Windows, Linux, Mac, Android, and Apple mobile OS.

  - *Networking utilities on Windows, Linux, Android, and Apple operating systems; how to run troubleshooting commands; wireless client settings (SSID, authentication, WPA mode)*

## Key Topics

Today we review how to configure and verify network connectivity on all the most popular endpoints, including both PC and mobile operating systems.

## Windows

In Windows 11, the network interface configuration can be examined, verified, and configured via three different methods:

- The Settings app

- The Control Panel

- The command line

### The Settings App

The Settings app provides a graphical user interface (GUI) for managing network configurations. To access them, open the **Settings** app and navigate to the **Network & internet** section. As shown in Figure 16-1, in this section, you can view and modify information such as the following:

- Manual or automatic IP address and DNS server address assignment

- Wireless information such as SSID, protocol, and security type

- Link speed

- Link-local IPv6 address

- IPv4 address and DNS servers

- Physical address (MAC)

You can also manually assign an IP address or DNS server address by clicking the **Edit** button.

**Figure 16-1   Verifying Addressing Through the Settings App in Windows 11**

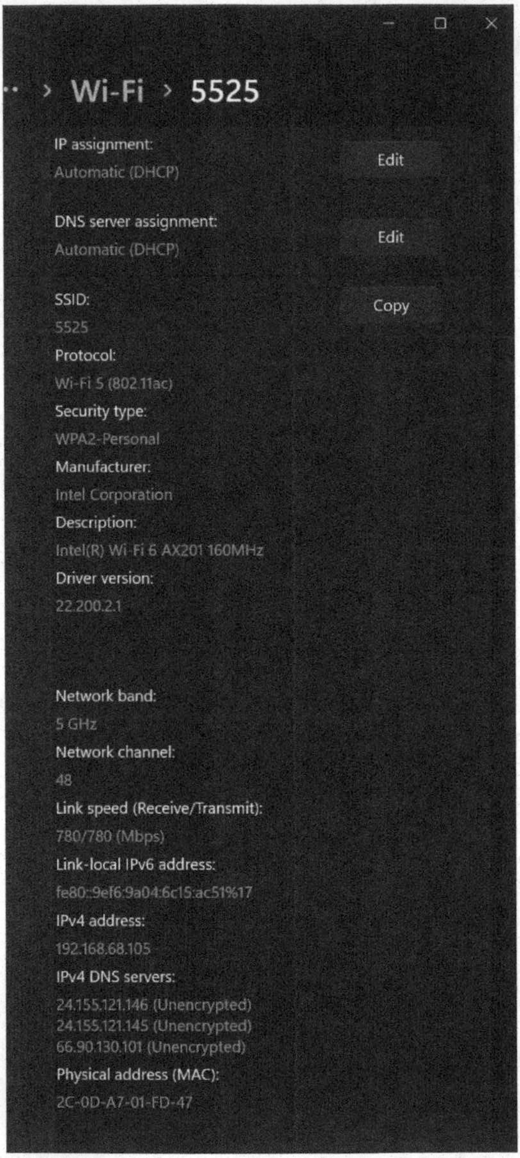

## The Control Panel

The Control Panel is another method to view and modify network configurations. Open the Control Panel, navigate to **Network & internet**, and then select **View network status and**

**tasks**. Select the active port to view the wired or wireless interface information, as shown in Figure 16-2.

**Figure 16-2   Verifying Addressing Through the Control Panel in Windows 11**

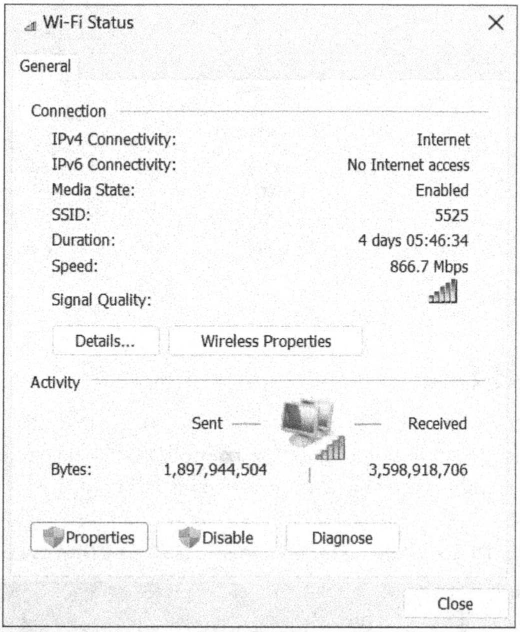

Here, you can view:

- IPv4/IPv6 connectivity

- Media state

- SSID (if a wireless interface)

- Duration

- Speed

- Bytes sent and received

There are also options to disable the interface, diagnose network issues, and modify properties.

To change the IP configuration, click **Properties** and then **Internet Protocol Version 4 (TCP/IPv4)**. Here, you can toggle the IP address and DNS configurations to set them manually, as shown in Figure 16-3.

**Figure 16-3   Manually Configuring IP Addressing Using the Control Panel in Windows 11**

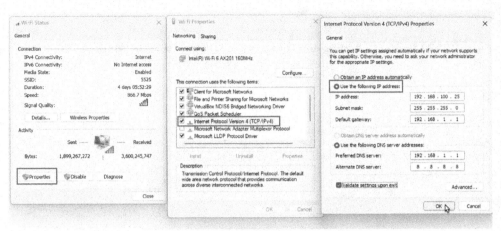

# The Command Line

Windows 11 includes PowerShell, a command-line interface (CLI) tool that provides a fast and resource-efficient alternative to GUIs. Using the **getmac /v** command, you can retrieve information about the physical interfaces on your devices, as shown in Figure 16-4.

**Figure 16-4   Viewing Physical Interface Information in Windows 11**

```
PS C:\> getmac /v

Connection Name  Network Adapter  Physical Address  Transport Name
===============  ===============  ================  ==============
Ethernet 3       Cisco AnyConnec  00-05-9A-3C-7A-00  \Device\Tcpip_{1DC9EC9A-02A0-48F4-9ED9-7F627D066775F}
Wi-Fi            Intel(R) Wi-Fi   2C-0D-A7-01-FD-47  \Device\Tcpip_{9D519EA5-0687-4FFF-9CD1-545A9545AF30}
Bluetooth Netwo  Bluetooth Devic  2C-0D-A7-01-FD-4B  Media disconnected
Ethernet         VirtualBox Host  0A-00-27-00-00-13  \Device\Tcpip_{F43E7683-55DB-4226-BEBF-075814014D86}
PS C:\>
```

Use the **ipconfig /all** command for more detailed information, such as the physical interface address, the default gateway, and the DHCPv6 Client DUID, as shown in the truncated output in Example 16-1.

**Example 16-1   Viewing Detailed IP Configuration Information in Windows 11**

```
PS C:\> ipconfig /all


Windows IP Configuration


    Host Name . . . . . . . . . . . . : DESKTOP-AV6N3RS

    Primary Dns Suffix  . . . . . . . :

    Node Type . . . . . . . . . . . . : Hybrid

    IP Routing Enabled. . . . . . . . : No

    WINS Proxy Enabled. . . . . . . . : No


<output omitted>
```

```
Wireless LAN adapter Wi-Fi:


   Connection-specific DNS Suffix  . :
   Description . . . . . . . . . . . : Killer(R) Wi-Fi 6 AX1650i
   Physical Address. . . . . . . . . : A4-B1-C1-11-F7-E2
   DHCP Enabled. . . . . . . . . . . : Yes
   Autoconfiguration Enabled . . . . : Yes
   Link-local IPv6 Address . . . . . : fe80::154a:653:931a:5619%23(Preferred)
   IPv4 Address. . . . . . . . . . . : 192.168.68.106(Preferred)
   Subnet Mask . . . . . . . . . . . : 255.255.255.0
   Lease Obtained. . . . . . . . . . : Wednesday, November 15, 2023 10:55:34 PM
   Lease Expires . . . . . . . . . . : Saturday, November 18, 2023 5:26:14 PM
   Default Gateway . . . . . . . . . : fe80::86d8:1bff:fedf:8704%23
                                       192.168.68.1
   DHCP Server . . . . . . . . . . . : 192.168.68.1
   DHCPv6 IAID . . . . . . . . . . . : 178565569
   DHCPv6 Client DUID. . . . . . . . : 00-01-00-01-26-FB-66-5A-A4-BB-6D-58-94-5C
   DNS Servers . . . . . . . . . . . : 24.155.121.146
                                       24.155.121.145
                                       66.90.130.101
   NetBIOS over Tcpip. . . . . . . . : Enabled

<output omitted>

PS C:\>
```

Other useful switches for the **ipconfig** command include the following:

- **/release**: Releases DHCP-learned IPv4 addresses

- **/renew**: Renews the DHCP-learned IPv4 addresses

- **/release6**: Releases DHCP-learned IPv6 addresses

- **/renew6**: Renews DHCP-learned IPv6 addresses

- **/flushdns**: Flushes the local DNS cache

To view the ARP cache, use the **arp -a** command, as shown in Example 16-2.

**Example 16-2   Viewing the ARP Cache in Windows 11**

```
PS C:\> arp -a


Interface: 192.168.56.1 --- 0x7
  Internet Address        Physical Address        Type
  192.168.56.255          ff-ff-ff-ff-ff-ff       static
  224.0.0.22              01-00-5e-00-00-16       static
  224.0.0.251             01-00-5e-00-00-fb       static
  224.0.0.252             01-00-5e-00-00-fc       static
```

```
   239.255.255.250       01-00-5e-7f-ff-fa     static
   255.255.255.255       ff-ff-ff-ff-ff-ff     static

Interface: 192.168.68.106 --- 0x17
   Internet Address      Physical Address      Type
   192.168.68.1          84-d8-1b-df-87-04     dynamic
   192.168.68.102        dc-98-40-ea-7b-65     dynamic
   192.168.68.105        2c-0d-a7-01-fd-47     dynamic
   192.168.68.110        94-57-a5-9a-cb-0b     dynamic
   192.168.68.120        c4-b3-01-a0-64-98     dynamic
   192.168.68.255        ff-ff-ff-ff-ff-ff     static
   224.0.0.22            01-00-5e-00-00-16     static
   224.0.0.251           01-00-5e-00-00-fb     static
   224.0.0.252           01-00-5e-00-00-fc     static
   239.255.255.250       01-00-5e-7f-ff-fa     static
   255.255.255.255       ff-ff-ff-ff-ff-ff     static
PS C:\>
```

Each IP address is shown with its matching physical address in the table. Addresses marked dynamic were learned using ARP. Addresses marked static are embedded in the operating system software; for instance, the IP broadcast address (255.255.255.255) is always mapped to the physical interface broadcast address (ff-ff-ff-ff-ff-ff).

To view the host routing table, enter the command **Get-NetRoute**, as shown in the truncated screenshot in Figure 16-5.

**Figure 16-5 Viewing the Host Routing Table in Windows 11**

```
PS C:\> Get-NetRoute

ifIndex DestinationPrefix                                NextHop                              RouteMetric ifMetric PolicyStore
------- -----------------                                -------                              ----------- -------- -----------
7       255.255.255.255/32                               0.0.0.0                                      256 1        ActiveStore
13      255.255.255.255/32                               0.0.0.0                                      256 25       ActiveStore
15      255.255.255.255/32                               0.0.0.0                                      256 25       ActiveStore
17      255.255.255.255/32                               0.0.0.0                                      256 35       ActiveStore
2       255.255.255.255/32                               0.0.0.0                                      256 65       ActiveStore
19      255.255.255.255/32                               0.0.0.0                                      256 25       ActiveStore
1       255.255.255.255/32                               0.0.0.0                                      256 75       ActiveStore
7       224.0.0.0/4                                      0.0.0.0                                      256 1        ActiveStore
13      224.0.0.0/4                                      0.0.0.0                                      256 25       ActiveStore
15      224.0.0.0/4                                      0.0.0.0                                      256 25       ActiveStore
17      224.0.0.0/4                                      0.0.0.0                                      256 35       ActiveStore
2       224.0.0.0/4                                      0.0.0.0                                      256 65       ActiveStore
19      224.0.0.0/4                                      0.0.0.0                                      256 25       ActiveStore
1       224.0.0.0/4                                      0.0.0.0                                      256 75       ActiveStore
17      216.223.38.0/24                                  192.168.68.1                                   0 35       ActiveStore
17      216.151.128.0/19                                 192.168.68.1                                   0 35       ActiveStore
17      216.147.0.0/18                                   192.168.68.1                                   0 35       ActiveStore
17      216.17.8.0/24                                    192.168.68.1                                   0 35       ActiveStore
17      216.9.196.0/22                                   192.168.68.1                                   0 35       ActiveStore
17      210.4.192.0/20                                   192.168.68.1                                   0 35       ActiveStore
17      209.197.192.0/19                                 192.168.68.1                                   0 35       ActiveStore
17      207.182.160.0/19                                 192.168.68.1                                   0 35       ActiveStore
17      199.59.64.0/21                                   192.168.68.1                                   0 35       ActiveStore
17      199.19.199.0/24                                  192.168.68.1                                   0 35       ActiveStore
17      199.19.196.0/23                                  192.168.68.1                                   0 35       ActiveStore
```

Figure 16-5 contains the following fields:

- **ifIndex**: Indicates which interface to send packets through when following this route.
- **DestinationPrefix**: Indicates the destination network.

- **NextHop**: Identifies where to send packets to reach this destination; 0.0.0.0 means "this device" or the local host.

- **RouteMetric**: Indicates the metric, or cost, to reach this destination. Windows hosts use the hop count as a metric.

- **ifMetric**: Indicates the default metric for routes reachable through this interface.

You may also come across the **route print** command in older documentation. The **route print** command and **Get-NetRoute** command are both used to display the routing table in Windows, but they are part of different command-line interfaces and provide different levels of detail and formatting. The **route print** command is a traditional command-line tool available in the Command Prompt (**cmd.exe**) and is part of the suite of networking tools that have been included in Windows for many years. However, the output is textual and is designed to be human-readable but can be difficult to parse programmatically.

The **Get-NetRoute** command is part of the PowerShell interface and is included in the NetTCPIP module, which provides a suite of cmdlets for managing TCP/IP networking settings. **Get-NetRoute** returns objects rather than text. This means you can easily filter, sort, and manipulate the output using other PowerShell cmdlets. For example, to filter the output in PowerShell to show the default route (which isn't easily possible with **route print**), you might enter the following:

```
Get-NetRoute | Where-Object { $_.DestinationPrefix -eq '0.0.0.0/0' }
```

**NOTE**  PowerShell supports the **route print** command. However, you cannot execute **Get-NetRoute** in the Command Prompt utility.

# Verifying Connectivity

Beyond simply opening a web page to see if you can access a website, there are two popular commands for testing connectivity in Windows 11: **ping** and **traceroute**.

The **ping** command is an effective way to quickly test Layer 3 connectivity between a source and destination IP address, as shown in Example 16-3.

**Example 16-3  Verifying Connectivity in Windows 11**

```
PS C:\> ping 192.168.68.1

Pinging 192.168.68.1 with 32 bytes of data:
Reply from 192.168.68.1: bytes=32 time<1ms TTL=64
Reply from 192.168.68.1: bytes=32 time=1ms TTL=64
Reply from 192.168.68.1: bytes=32 time=1ms TTL=64
Reply from 192.168.68.1: bytes=32 time=1ms TTL=64

Ping statistics for 192.168.68.1:
    Packets: Sent = 4, Received = 4, Lost = 0 (0% loss),
Approximate round trip times in milli-seconds:
    Minimum = 0ms, Maximum = 1ms, Average = 0ms
PS C:\>
```

If a ping fails but the device can still access the default gateway, network administrators will often use a traceroute command, which is **tracert** in Windows 11, to find where the path fails. This may work nicely within a corporate network. However, tracing the path on the Internet is often blocked by firewall configurations that restrict replying to traces, which is probably what happened at the hops that timed out in Example 16-4.

**Example 16-4   Tracing the Path in Windows 11**

```
PS C:\> tracert www.google.com


Tracing route to www.google.com [142.251.116.103]
over a maximum of 30 hops:


  1     1 ms     <1 ms     1 ms   192.168.68.1
  2     *         *         *      Request timed out.
  3     8 ms      7 ms     17 ms   24-155-250-86.dyn.grandenetworks.net
  [24.155.250.86]
  4    14 ms     13 ms     12 ms   ae3.0.core02.smrctx.grandecom.net
  [24.155.121.163]
  5    24 ms     24 ms     24 ms   24-155-121-22.static.grandenetworks.net
  [24.155.121.22]
  6    25 ms     23 ms     25 ms   24-155-121-238.static.grandenetworks.net
  [24.155.121.238]
  7    25 ms     24 ms     24 ms   142.250.167.112
  8    23 ms     24 ms     24 ms   108.170.231.48
  9    24 ms     24 ms     25 ms   108.170.252.131
 10    26 ms     31 ms     30 ms   108.170.228.103
 11   100 ms     25 ms     29 ms   142.250.233.171
 12    45 ms     25 ms     29 ms   142.250.236.158
 13    27 ms     26 ms     29 ms   142.250.234.117
 14     *         *         *      Request timed out.
 15     *         *         *      Request timed out.
 16     *         *         *      Request timed out.
 17     *         *         *      Request timed out.
 18     *         *         *      Request timed out.
 19     *         *         *      Request timed out.
 20     *         *         *      Request timed out.
 21     *         *         *      Request timed out.
 22     *         *         *      Request timed out.
 23     *         *         *      Request timed out.
 24     *         *         *      Request timed out.
 25    28 ms     49 ms     25 ms   rt-in-f103.1e100.net [142.251.116.103]


Trace complete.
PS C:\>
```

# Linux

Verifying IP settings using the GUI on a Linux machine will differ depending on the Linux distribution (distro) and desktop interface. Figure 16-6 shows the **Connection Information** dialog box on the Ubuntu distro running the Gnome desktop.

**Figure 16-6   Verifying a Wired Connection in Linux**

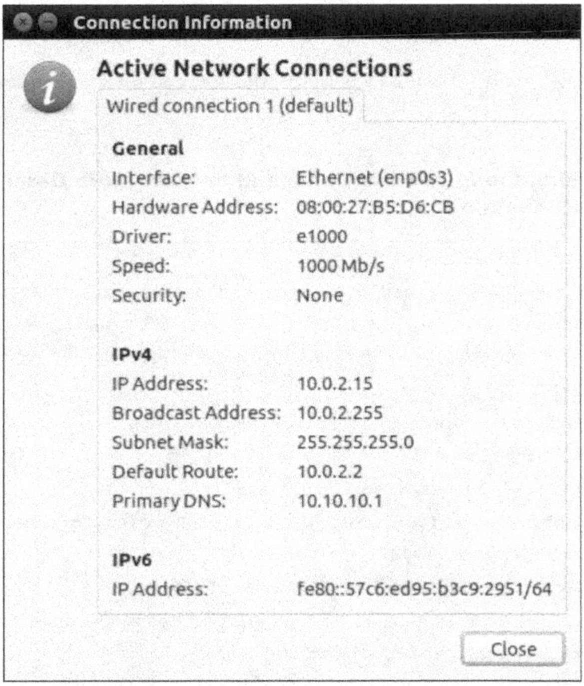

As with Windows, network administrators prefer to use the **ifconfig** command to display the status of the currently active interfaces and their IP configuration, as shown in Example 16-5.

**Example 16-5   Using the *ifconfig* Command to Verify Addressing in Linux**

```
ubuntu@ubuntu2004:~$ ifconfig
enp0s3    Link encap:Ethernet  HWaddr 08:00:27:b5:d6:cb
          inet addr: 10.0.2.15   Bcast:10.0.2.255   Mask: 255.255.255.0
          inet6 addr: fe80::57c6:ed95:b3c9:2951/64 Scope:Link
          UP BROADCAST RUNNING MULTICAST   MTU:1500 Metric:1
          RX packets:1332239 errors:0 dropped:0 overruns:0 frame:0
          TX packets:105910 errors:0 dropped:0 overruns:0 carrier:0
          collisions:0 txqueuelen:1000
          RX bytes:1855455014 (1.8 GB)   TX bytes:13140139 (13.1 MB)
```

```
lo: flags=73 mtu 65536
            inet 127.0.0.1   netmask 255.0.0.0
            inet6 ::1   prefixlen 128   scopeid 0x10
            loop   txqueuelen 1000   (Local Loopback)
            RX packets 0   bytes 0 (0.0 B)
            RX errors 0   dropped 0   overruns 0   frame 0
            TX packets 0   bytes 0 (0.0 B)
            TX errors 0   dropped 0 overruns 0   carrier 0   collisions 0
```

The Linux **ip address** command is used to display addresses and their properties, as shown in
Example 16-6.

**Example 16-6   Using the *ip address* Command to View More Detailed Addressing
Information**

```
ubuntu@ubuntu2004:~$ ip address
1: lo: <LOOPBACK,UP,LOWER_UP> mtu 65536 qdisc noqueue state UNKNOWN group
default qlen 1000
    link/loopback 00:00:00:00:00:00 brd 00:00:00:00:00:00
    inet 127.0.0.1/8 scope host lo
       valid_lft forever preferred_lft forever
    inet6 ::1/128 scope host
       valid_lft forever preferred_lft forever
2: eth0: <BROADCAST,MULTICAST,UP,LOWER_UP> mtu 1500 qdisc fq_codel
state UP group default qlen 1000
    link/ether 08:00:27:e1:b0:44 brd ff:ff:ff:ff:ff:ff
    inet 10.0.2.15/24 brd 10.0.2.255 scope global dynamic noprefixroute eth0
       valid_lft 59234sec preferred_lft 59234sec
    inet6 fe80::a00:27ff:fee1:b044/64 scope link noprefixroute
       valid_lft forever preferred_lft forever
<output omitted>
```

Notice that this command also shows DHCP lease information. For example, **valid_lft forever
preferred_lft forever** means the DHCP lease lifetime is forever. The **ip address** command can
also be used to add or delete IP addresses.

# Verifying Connectivity

The **ping** command in Linux has several options that allow you to customize its behavior. Here are
some of the most commonly used options:

- **-c count**: This stops the **ping** command after sending a specific number of requests.

- **-i interval**: This allows you to set the interval between ping requests in seconds. The default is
  1 second.

- **-w deadline**: The **ping** command will stop after the specified deadline (in seconds) has passed.

- **-W timeout:** This sets the amount of time, in seconds, that the **ping** command will wait for a response before it times out.

- **-q:** This option turns on quiet output. Only the summary lines at startup time and the end of output are displayed.

- **-b:** This allows you to ping a broadcast address.

- **-v:** Verbose output. It shows ICMP packets that were received other than replies.

Note that some of these options might require superuser (root) privileges to run, depending on your system setup.

In Example 16-7, the command will ping the host www.google.com a total of four times and then stop.

**Example 16-7   Modifying the *ping* Command in Linux**

```
ubuntu@ubuntu2004:~$ ping -c 4 www.google.com
PING www.google.com (142.251.116.106) 56(84) bytes of data.
64 bytes from rt-in-f106.1e100.net (142.251.116.106): icmp_seq=1 ttl=105
time=20.6 ms
64 bytes from rt-in-f106.1e100.net (142.251.116.106): icmp_seq=2 ttl=105
time=21.2 ms
64 bytes from rt-in-f106.1e100.net (142.251.116.106): icmp_seq=3 ttl=105
time=21.8 ms
64 bytes from rt-in-f106.1e100.net (142.251.116.106): icmp_seq=4 ttl=105
time=19.5 ms

--- www.google.com ping statistics ---
4 packets transmitted, 4 received, 0% packet loss, time 3004ms
rtt min/avg/max/mdev = 19.528/20.761/21.788/0.833 ms
```

**NOTE**   In Linux, you use the **traceroute** command instead of the **tracert** command to trace the path to the destination.

Several other Linux command-line tools are available for most Linux distributions, including the following:

- **speedtest:** This is a tool that tests the bandwidth of your connectivity with your Internet provider.

- **ncat:** Ncat is a networking utility that is part of the nmap suite of networking tools. Ncat, or nc, has many uses, including verifying connectivity to a device using a specific port. In Example 16-8, the network technician is using ncat to test HTTPS (port 443) connectivity to two different devices.

**Example 16-8   Using the *nc* Command to Test HTTPS Connectivity in Linux**

```
ubuntu@ubuntu2004:~$ nc -z -v www.google.com 443
 Connection to www.google.com (142.250.138.105) 443 port [tcp/https] succeeded!
 ubuntu@ubuntu2004:~$
 ubuntu@ubuntu2004:~$ nc -z -v 10.0.0.122 443
 nc: connect to 10.0.0.122 port 443 (tcp) failed: Connection refused
 ubuntu@ubuntu2004:~$
```

To view the routing table in Linux, use the **netstat -rn** command, as shown in Example 16-9.

**Example 16-9   Viewing the Routing Table in Linux**

```
ubuntu@ubuntu2004:~$ netstat -rn
Kernel IP routing table
Destination     Gateway       Genmask         Flags   MSS Window  irtt Iface
0.0.0.0         10.0.2.2      0.0.0.0         UG        0 0         0 eth0
10.0.2.0        0.0.0.0       255.255.255.0   U         0 0         0 eth0
10.6.6.0        0.0.0.0       255.255.255.0   U         0 0         0 br-internal
172.17.0.0      0.0.0.0       255.255.0.0     U         0 0         0 docker0
```

---

**NOTE**   The Linux verification commands reviewed in this section are also available in macOS.

---

# Finding Your Public IP Address

The simplest way to discover your public IP address is to open a web browser and search for "what is my IP address." Your search engine will then display your public IP address. You can also navigate to https://checkip.amazonaws.com or https://tnx.nl/ip to display your public IP address. These sites can be used with the **curl** command to display your public IP address, as shown in Example 16-10. This is particularly helpful if your Linux host, such as a remote server or router, does not have a web browser installed.

**Example 16-10   Using *curl* to View the Public IP Address of a Browser-less Linus Host**

```
$ curl https://checkip.amazonaws.com
130.45.1.184
$ curl https://tnx.nl/ip
<130.45.1.184>
```

# macOS

In the GUI of a Mac host, open **Network Preferences > Advanced** to get the IP addressing information, as shown in Figure 16-7.

However, the **ifconfig** command can also be used in the terminal command line to verify the interface IP configuration, as shown in Example 16-11.

**Figure 16-7    Verifying IP Addressing in macOS GUI**

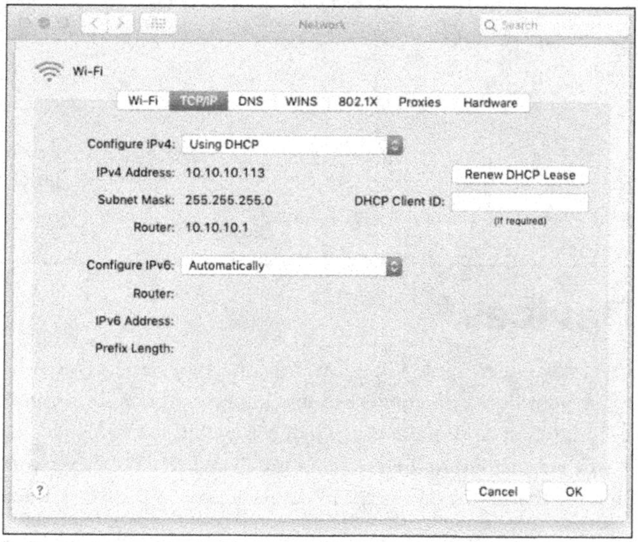

**Example 16-11    Verifying IP Addressing in the macOS Terminal Command Line**

```
MacBook-Air:~ Admin$ ifconfig en0
en0: flags=8863 mtu 1500
        ether c4:b3:01:a0:64:98
        inet6 fe80::c0f:1bf4:60b1:3adb%en0 prefixlen 64 secured scopeid 0x5
        inet 10.10.10.113 netmask 0xffffff00 broadcast 10.10.10.255
        nd6 options=201
        media: autoselect
        status: active
MacBook-Air:~ Admin$
```

Other useful macOS commands to verify the host IP settings include **networksetup -listallnet-workservices** and **networksetup -getinfo <network service>**, as shown in Example 16-12.

**Example 16-12    Verifying Available Network Services in the macOS Terminal Command Line**

```
MacBook-Air:~ Admin$ networksetup -listallnetworkservices
An asterisk (*) denotes that a network service is disabled.
iPhone USB
Wi-Fi
Bluetooth PAN
Thunderbolt Bridge
MacBook-Air:~ Admin$
MacBook-Air:~ Admin$ networksetup -getinfo Wi-Fi
DHCP Configuration
```

```
IP address: 10.10.10.113
Subnet mask: 255.255.255.0
Router: 10.10.10.1
Client ID:
IPv6: Automatic
IPv6 IP address: none
IPv6 Router: none
Wi-Fi ID: c4:b3:01:a0:64:98
MacBook-Air:~ Admin$
```

# Mobile Devices

Mobile devices are typically either Apple iOS or Android. Each operating system has settings that enable you to configure your device to connect to wireless networks, as shown in Figures 16-8 and 16-9. To connect an iOS or Android device when it is within the coverage range of a Wi-Fi network, turn on Wi-Fi and the device then searches for all available Wi-Fi networks and displays them in a list. Touch a Wi-Fi network in the list to connect. Enter a password if needed.

**Figure 16-8   Activating Wireless and Choosing a Wi-Fi Network on iOS**

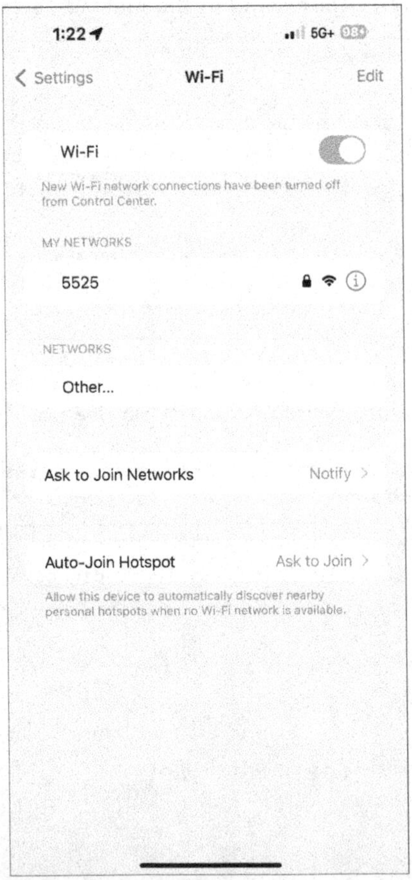

**Figure 16-9    Activating Wireless and Choosing a Wi-Fi Network on Android**

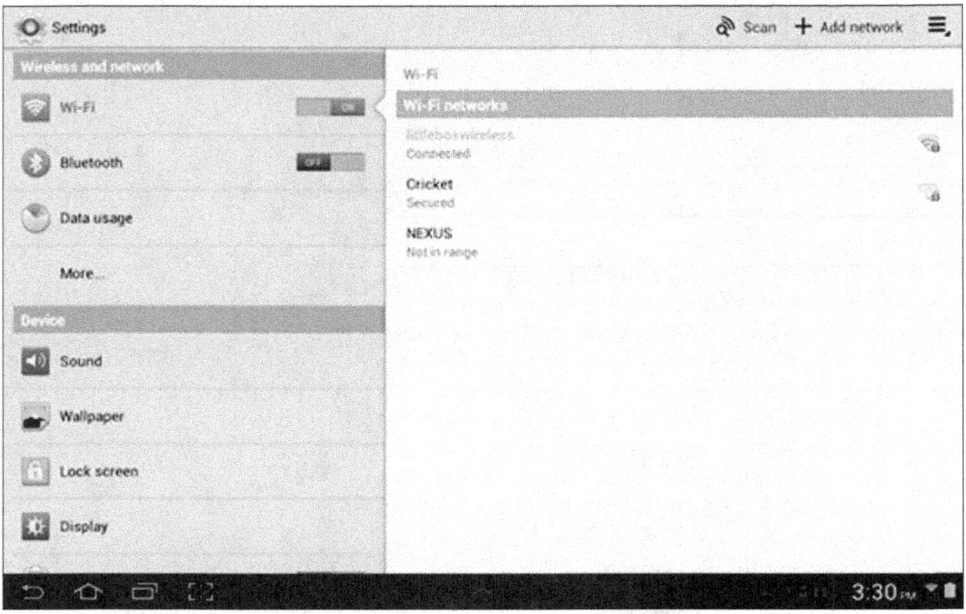

## Verify Connectivity

Apple iOS and Android have different methods for verifying connectivity.

## iOS

Like any other device with a browser, network connectivity on an Apple iOS device can be easily verified by attempting to reach a website or an online application.

You can also verify the IPv4 and IPv6 addressing information, including the default gateway (router) on an Apple IOS device. To do so, go to **Settings** > **Wi-Fi**. Tap the Wi-Fi network you are connected to and scroll down to see the IP address configuration, as shown in Figure 16-10.

## Android

Like Apple iOS, network connectivity on an Android device can be verified by attempting to reach a website or an online application.

The Android interface can vary significantly depending on the Android version and the device manufacturer. Therefore, the process for checking network connections may differ slightly between devices.

**Figure 16-10   Verifying the IP Addressing on an iOS Mobile Device**

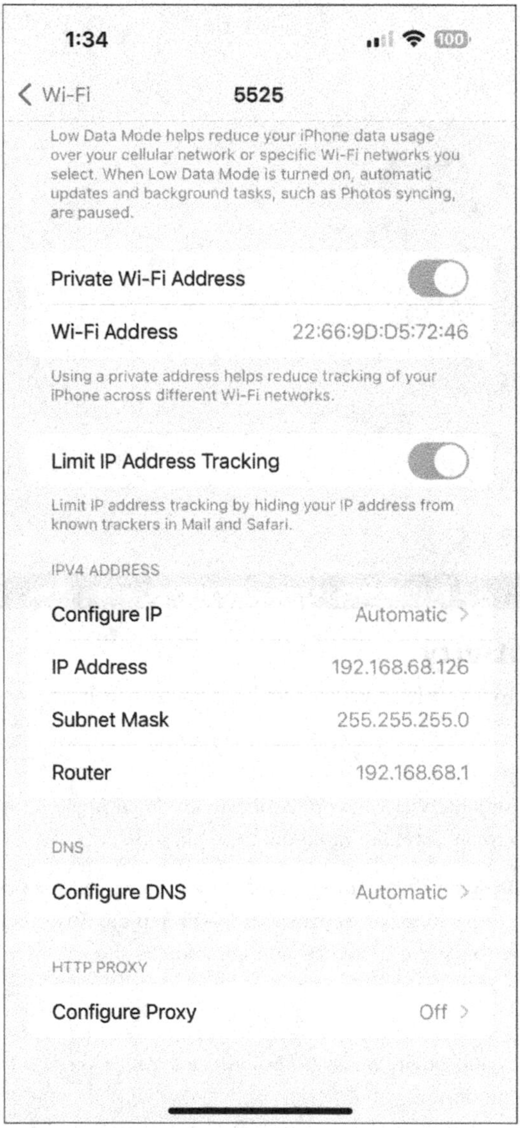

To access your network settings, open the Settings app on your phone and touch **Connections** or **Network and Internet**. Do the following:

1. If you're using Wi-Fi, verify that Wi-Fi is active on your phone.

2. Touch Wi-Fi and verify that you are connected to a network that you can authenticate to. Check **Available Networks** to see if other networks may be more suitable.

**3.** If you're using a mobile cellular data network, verify that you have connectivity to that net-work in the device status bar. Check the swipe-down settings menu to ensure that mobile data is active on your device.

IPv4 and IPv6 addressing information, including the default gateway (router), can be verified by going to **Settings > About phone > Status**, as shown in Figure 16-11.

**Figure 16-11   Verifying the IP Addressing on an Android Mobile Device**

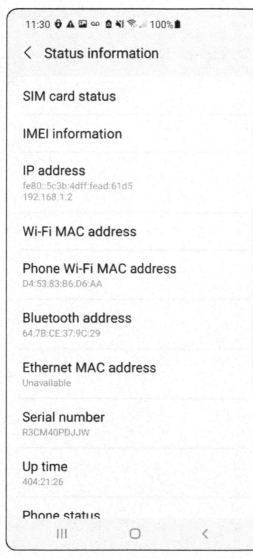

# Study Resources

For today's exam topics, refer to the following resources for more study:

| Resource | Module or Chapter |
|---|---|
| SFA Self Enroll: Networking Basics | 3 |
| SFA Self Enroll: Network Support and Security | 1 |
| SFA Instructor Led: Networking Essentials | 3, 37 |
| CCST Networking 100–150 Official Cert Guide | 4, 11 |

**NOTE**   SFA: https://skillsforall.com/

# Device Status Lights

## CCST Networking 100-150 Exam Topic

- 4.1. Identify the status lights on a Cisco device when given instruction by an engineer.
  - Link light color and status (blinking or solid)

## Key Topics

Today's exam topic is a quick review of what is most common about link lights on Cisco devices.

## Cisco Device Link Lights

There is a wide variety of Cisco devices, as shown in Figure 15-1. Each of these devices has link lights to indicate various statuses.

**Figure 15-1  A Collection of Cisco Networking Devices**

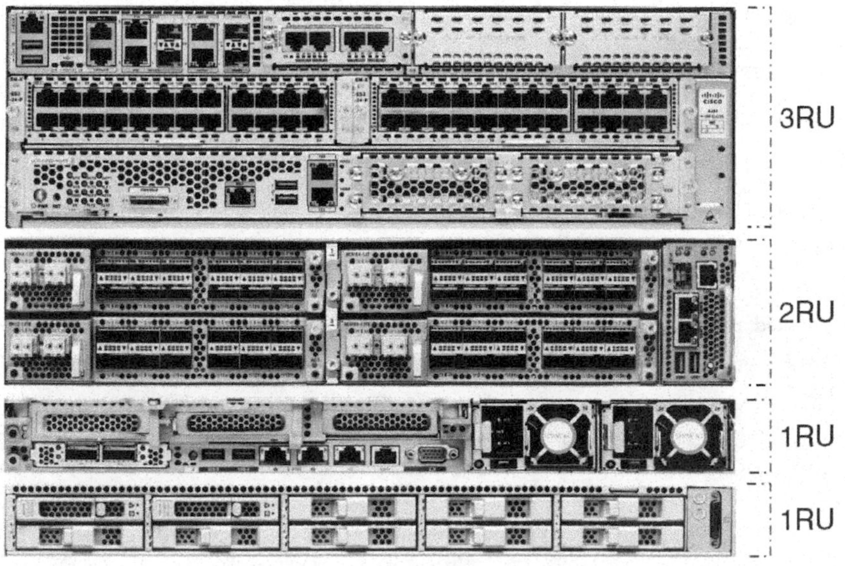

RU in Figure 15-1 stands for rack units and is used to determine how much space a particular device will require. In Figure 15-1, the Cisco devices are as follows:

- A Cisco 4000 series integrated services router (ISR)

- A Cisco 1004 series optical networking convergence system

- A Cisco UCS C220 rack server

- A Cisco email security appliance

Almost every port you encounter in computer networks will have an associated light. These lights, or light-emitting diodes (LEDs), are an important diagnostic tool. However, you must know what the color and condition of the light mean. Some lights, such as the following, are generally assumed to be common among all networking hardware:

- A solid green status light means the port is operating correctly.

- A flashing green status light means the port is connected and data is being transmitted.

- A yellow status light means the port is connecting or has malfunctioned.

- A red status light means the port has malfunctioned.

Unfortunately, however, these lights do not always mean the same thing on every piece of networking hardware. For instance, on the Cisco 1120 Connected Grid Router, the pluggable Ethernet 1/1 and 1/2 ports have two lights—one for port speed and another for port status:

- If the port speed light blinks green twice and then pauses, the port is connected at 100Mbps.

- If the port speed light blinks green three times and then pauses, the port is connected at 1Gbps.

- If the port status light is solid green, the port is connected and active.

- If the port status light is yellow, the port is connected, but there is an error condition.

- If the port status light is flashing green, the pluggable interface can be safely removed.

If you believe a flashing green light means data is being transmitted on a Cisco 1120 Connected Grid, you could be misled.

To add confusion, you can program the lights on many systems to use any color combination you like. You should always check the equipment manual if you are unsure about the different states of the port lights.

For the rest of today's review time, practice searching for each of the models listed under Figure 15-1 to view their documentation. Just enter a search such as "Cisco 4000 series link lights." Feel free to search for other Cisco devices to see how these link lights can indicate a variety of different statuses.

# Study Resources

For today's exam topics, refer to the following resources for more study:

| Resource | Module or Chapter |
|---|---|
| SFA Self Enroll: Network Addressing and Basic Troubleshooting | 7 |
| SFA Instructor Led: Networking Essentials | 35 |
| CCST Networking 100-150 Official Cert Guide | 10 |

**NOTE**    SFA: https://skillsforall.com/

# Connecting Cables

## CCST Networking 100-150 Exam Topic

- 4.2. Use a network diagram provided by an engineer to attach the appropriate cables.
  - *Patch cables, switches and routers, small topologies*

## Key Topics

Today's review includes common networking icons that represent devices and media in diagrams, a brief discussion of switches and how they are used in a hierarchical network layer, using patch or cross-over cables, physical and logical topologies, and cable management.

## Networking Icons

Before you can interpret networking diagrams or topologies, you must understand the symbols or icons used to represent different networking devices and media. The icons in Figure 14-1 are the most common networking symbols for networking studies.

## Switches

In today's wired networks, switches are almost exclusively used to connect end devices to a single local area network (LAN). Occasionally, you might see a hub connecting end devices, but hubs are really legacy devices. The following differences exist between a hub and a switch:

- Hubs were typically chosen as an intermediary device within a very small LAN, in which bandwidth usage was not an issue or cost limitations a factor. In today's networks, switches have replaced hubs.

- Switches replaced hubs as the LAN intermediary device because a switch can segment collision domains and provide enhanced security.

When you're choosing a switch, these are the main factors to consider:

- **Cost:** The cost is determined by the number and type of ports, network management capabilities, embedded security technologies, and optional advanced switching technologies.

- **Interface characteristics:** The number of ports must be sufficient both for now and for future expansion. Other characteristics include uplink speeds, a mixture of unshielded twisted pair (UTP) and fiber cabling, and modularity.

- **Hierarchical network layer:** Switches at the access layer have different requirements than switches at the distribution or core layers.

**Figure 14-1   Networking Icons**

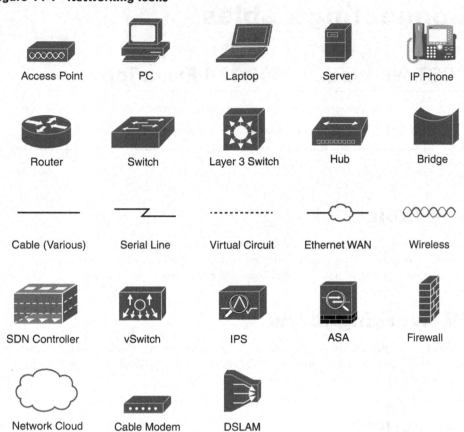

## Access Layer Switches

Access layer switches facilitate the connection of end devices to the network. Features of access layer switches include the following:

- Port security

- VLANs

- Fast Ethernet/Gigabit Ethernet

- Power over Ethernet (PoE)

- Link aggregation

- Quality of service (QoS)

## Distribution Layer Switches

Distribution layer switches receive the data from the access layer switches and forward it to the core layer switches. Features of distribution layer switches include the following:

- Layer 3 support
- High forwarding rate
- Gigabit Ethernet/10 Gigabit Ethernet
- Redundant components
- Security policies/access control lists
- Link aggregation
- QoS

## Core Layer Switches

Core layer switches make up the backbone and are responsible for handling the majority of data on a switched LAN. Features of core layer switches include the following:

- Layer 3 support
- Very high forwarding rate
- Gigabit Ethernet/10 Gigabit Ethernet
- Redundant components
- Link aggregation
- QoS

# LAN Device Connection Guidelines

End devices are pieces of equipment that are either the original source or the final destination of a message. Intermediary devices connect end devices to the network, to assist in getting a message from the source end device to the destination end device.

Connecting devices in a LAN is usually done with UTP cabling. Although many newer devices have an automatic crossover feature that enables you to connect either a straight-through (patch) or a crossover cable, you still need to know the following basic rules:

- Use straight-through cables for the following connections:
  - Switch-to-router Ethernet port
  - Computer to switch
  - Computer to hub

- Use crossover cables for the following connections:

  - Switch to switch

  - Switch to hub

  - Hub to hub

  - Router to router (Ethernet ports)

  - Computer to computer

  - Computer to router Ethernet port

---

**NOTE**   Although you are required to know the difference between straight-through and crossover cables, most network interfaces, through a feature called auto-mdx on Cisco routers, now autodetect the pin out of the plugged-in cable. With modern devices, you no longer have to ensure you are connecting the correct cable type.

---

# Physical and Logical Topologies

Network diagrams are usually referred to as *topologies*. A topology graphically displays the interconnection methods used between devices.

Physical topologies refer to the physical layout of devices and how they are cabled. Seven basic physical topologies exist, as shown in Figure 14-2.

**Figure 14-2   Physical Topologies**

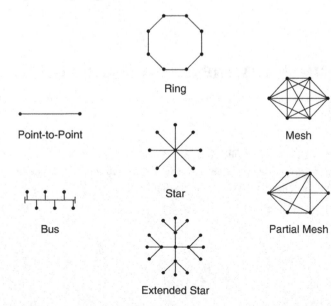

Logical topologies refer to the way that a signal travels from one point on the network to another and are largely determined by the access method—deterministic or nondeterministic. Ethernet is a nondeterministic access method. Logically, Ethernet operates as a bus topology. However, Ethernet networks are almost always physically designed as a star or extended star.

Other access methods use a deterministic access method. Token Ring and Fiber Distributed Data Interface (FDDI) both logically operate as a ring, passing data from one station to the next. Although these networks can be designed as a physical ring, like Ethernet, they are often designed as a star or extended star. Logically, however, they operate like a ring.

# Topology Examples

In his book *Cisco Certified Support Technician CCST Networking 100-150 Official Cert Guide*, Russ White provides two excellent real-world examples of what a physical and logical topology might look like for a small network.

## Physical Topology Example

Figure 14-3 shows a physical topology. Note how this would guide an engineer on where to slot the devices in the rack and how they should be connected.

**Figure 14-3    Physical Topology Example**

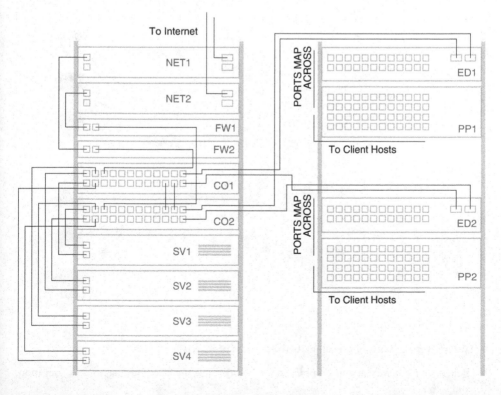

Note the following in Figure 14-3:

- **CO**: Core router

- **ED**: Edge router

- **FW**: Firewall

- **SV**: Server

- **PP**: Patch panel

- **NET**: Internet connection router

## Logical Topology Example

Figure 14-4 shows a logical version of the physical topology shown in Figure 14-3. In Figure 14-4, we see the way in which data is actually transferred around a network. Unlike the physical topology, the logical topology is more about the path that the data takes when moving from one device to another.

**Figure 14-4   Logical Topology Example**

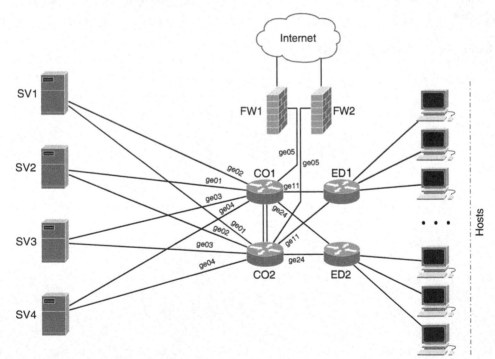

Logical diagrams can also contain the following:

- Which routing protocol is running between pairs of routers

- Policies implemented at a given point in a network, such as packet filtering, route aggregation, and so on

- Where links are connected, such as the Gigabit Ethernet (GE) labels given in Figure 14-3

- IP addresses

- Where services are running or located in the network

# Cable Management

Cable management is an important aspect of a network engineer's job. Figure 14-5 shows the difference between improper and proper cable management.

**Figure 14-5   Improper and Proper Cable Management Examples**

Proper cable management adds a bit of time upfront designing the system and then implementing it every time new devices are added to the network. However, the time invested pays off in the long run. Here are some reasons why cable management is important:

- **Organization:** When cables are tidy and organized, it is easier to trace them, identify problems, make changes, and add/remove cables. Without cable management, cables can become a tangled mess, as shown in the left side of Figure 14-5.

- **Accessibility:** Engineers can more easily access devices and patch panels to make changes and conduct maintenance.

- **Airflow**: Bundles of messy cables can block airflow, which can cause overheating of networking equipment. Good cable management helps maximize airflow.

- **Safety**: Neat cable management reduces trip risks and creates a safer working environment.

- **Reliability**: Good cable management reduces cable stress and damage to maximize reliability.

- **Capacity**: Cable management helps maximize space and capacity. This leaves room to add, remove, or route cables efficiently, as needed.

- **Aesthetics**: Nobody likes looking at a tangled web of cables. Effective cable management just makes the overall networking setup look cleaner and more professional.

# Study Resources

For today's exam topics, refer to the following resources for more study:

| Resource | Module or Chapter |
|---|---|
| SFA Self Enroll: Networking Basics | 4 |
| SFA Instructor Led: Networking Essentials | 4 |
| CCST Networking 100-150 Official Cert Guide | 10 |

**NOTE**   SFA: https://skillsforall.com/

# Device Ports

## CCST Networking 100-150 Exam Topic

- 4.3. Identify the various ports on network devices.
  - Console port, serial port, fiber port, Ethernet ports, SFPs, USB port, PoE

## Key Topics

Today we review the types of ports you typically find on network devices. To do this, we will focus on the Cisco 4461 Integrated Services Router (ISR). As its name implies, the ISR integrates many features of other devices, including the ports used.

## Cisco 4461 ISR Ports

The back panel of the Cisco 4461 ISR chassis is shown in Figure 13-1. We are using this router because it has all the ports listed in the exam topic. The Cisco 4461 ISR is classified as a branch router, meaning that you would typically see this router in a small office where it is connected to the corporate network. The Cisco 4461 ISR is modular, meaning you can purchase different modules for the chassis, depending on your needs. The Cisco 4461 ISR comes with three network interface module (NIM) slots and three Enhanced Service Module (SM-X) slots.

**Figure 13-1   Cisco 4461 Back Panel**

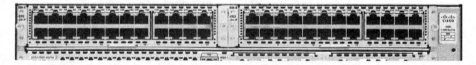

### Fixed Ports and NIMs

Let's review each section of the Cisco 4461 ISR back panel, beginning with the top-left corner in Figure 13-2. The ports on the left up to the 10 Gigabit Ethernet ports are fixed and come with every Cisco 4461 ISR.

**Figure 13-2  Top-Left Ports of the Cisco 4461 ISR**

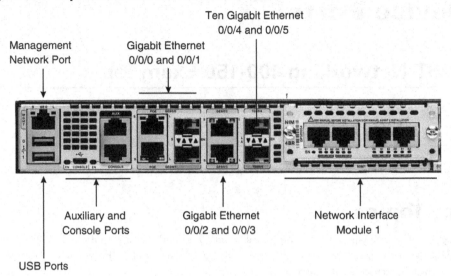

In Figure 13-2, the following ports are labeled:

- **Management network port:** This port provides out-of-band management so that engineers can access the router's command-line interface (CLI) and management features without impacting data ports.

- **USB ports:** These ports are typically used for configuring the router or uploading and downloading the router's operating system, among other purposes.

- **Auxiliary port:** This port is used with a modem for out-of-band remote management of a router.

- **Console ports:** These ports are used for local, direct access to the router for configuration. Two are shown in Figure 13-2. The one on the left for a USB connection. The one on the right is for an RJ-45 connection to support older DB-9 serial connectors on PCs.

- **Gigabit Ethernet 0/0/0 and 0/0/1:** Power over Ethernet (PoE) ports supply DC power over the Ethernet cable, eliminating the need for separate power cables on devices such as IP phones, wireless access points, and other network-connected devices.

- **Gigabit Ethernet 0/0/2 and 0/0/3:** These ports are standard GE ports that provide additional connections for devices.

- **Ten Gigabit Ethernet 0/0/4 and 0/0/5:** These provide 10 Gigabit connections using small form-factor pluggable (SFP) modules to convert to the appropriate media type, such as the Cat6A/Cat7 or better SFPs, as shown in Figure 13-3. Note that SFP slots are also available for GE0 0/0/0 and 0/0/1. SFPs provide the flexibility to switch between CatX and fiber connections, depending on your infrastructure.

- **NIM 1:** These allow various interface cards to be inserted to add a connectivity option such as Ethernet, Serial, T1/E1, and the Integrated Services Digital Network (ISDN) NIM shown in Figure 13-2. NIM 2 and NIM 3 are also available.

**Figure 13-3   Cisco SFP-10G-T-X Module**

## SM-X Slots

Figure 13-4 shows the center-right module, which is identical to the center-left module. These two modules are installed in SM-X slots 1 and 2. Together, these modules add 48 switch ports to the Cisco 4461 ISR.

**Figure 13-4   Center-Right Ports of the Cisco 4461 ISR**

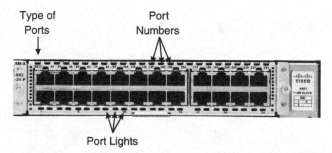

Figure 13-5 shows the bottom of the Cisco 4461 ISR. A double-wide Cisco Unified Computing System (UCS) E-series M3 server has been installed in SM-X slot 3. This UCS server provides virtualization and supports mission-critical, on-premises business applications in the branch office.

**Figure 13-5  Bottom of the Cisco 4461 ISR**

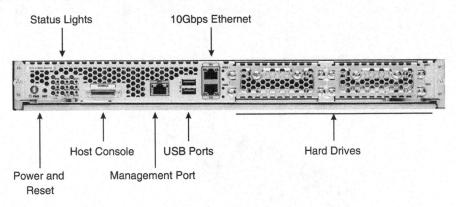

This UCS module has its own power indicator, reset button, status lights, and console port. There is also a management port for the out-of-band management network described earlier.

This host (server) module has two 10Gbps Ethernet ports. These ports would be configured through the host console rather than the router CLI. Four hard drives are also included on this module's right side; each pair has its own cover plate.

For the rest of today's review time, practice searching for different models from Cisco and other manufacturers to view their documentation. You will quickly see that there are a variety of differences. The skill you need to develop is the ability to read and interpret device documentation so that you can easily identify ports on networking devices.

# Study Resources

For today's exam topics, refer to the following resources for more study:

| Resource | Module or Chapter |
| --- | --- |
| SFA Self Enroll: Networking Basics | 4 |
| SFA Instructor Led: Networking Essentials | 4 |
| CCST Networking 100-150 Official Cert Guide | 10 |

**NOTE**  SFA: https://skillsforall.com/

# Routing Concepts

## CCST Networking 100-150 Exam Topic

- 4.4. Explain basic routing concepts.
  - *Default gateway, Layer 2 vs. Layer 3 switches, local network vs. remote network*

## Key Topics

Today we review basic routing concepts, including exactly how a packet is processed by intermediary devices (routers) on its way from source to destination. We then review the basic routing methods, including connected, static, and dynamic routes. We conclude the day's review with a deep dive into the operation of dynamic routing protocols.

## Packet Forwarding

Packet forwarding by routers is accomplished through path determination and switching functions. The path determination function is the process of how the router determines which path to use when forwarding a packet.

---

**NOTE** We are using the term *router* here to explicitly indicate that a Layer 3 device determines the best path to a remote network. Although these devices are traditionally a router, multilayer switches, which operate at Layers 2 and 3, also perform the routing function.

---

To determine the best path, the router searches its routing table for a network address that matches the packet's destination IP address.

This search results in one of three path determinations:

- **Directly connected network**: If the destination IP address of the packet belongs to a device on a network that is directly connected to one of the router's interfaces, that packet is forwarded directly to that device. This means that the destination IP address of the packet is a host address on the same network as this router's interface.

- **Remote network**: If the destination IP address of the packet belongs to a remote network, the packet is forwarded to another router. Remote networks can be reached only by forwarding packets to another router.

- **No route determined**: If the destination IP address of the packet does not belong to a connected or remote network and the router does not have a default route, the packet is discarded. The router sends an Internet Control Message Protocol (ICMP) Unreachable message to the source IP address of the packet.

In the first two results, the router completes the process by switching the packet out the correct interface. It does this by re-encapsulating the IP packet into the appropriate Layer 2 data-link frame format for the exit interface. The type of interface determines the type of Layer 2 encapsulation. For example, if the exit interface is Fast Ethernet, the packet is encapsulated in an Ethernet frame.

## Path Determination and Switching Function Example

Let's review the process of path determination and switching functions that routers perform as a packet travels from source to destination. This scenario uses the topology in Figure 12-1.

**Figure 12-1   Packet Forwarding Sample Topology**

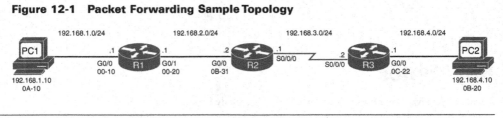

---

**NOTE**   For brevity, Figure 12-1 shows only the last two octets of the MAC address.

---

1. PC1 has a packet to send to PC2.

   Using the AND operation on the destination's IP address and PC1's subnet mask, PC1 has determined that the IP source and IP destination addresses are on different networks. Therefore, PC1 checks its Address Resolution Protocol (ARP) table for the IP address of the default gateway and its associated MAC address. It then encapsulates the packet in an Ethernet header and forwards it to R1.

2. Router R1 receives the Ethernet frame.

   Router R1 examines the destination MAC address, which matches the MAC address of the receiving interface, G0/0. R1 will therefore copy the frame into its buffer to be processed.

   R1 decapsulates the Ethernet frame and reads the destination IP address. Because it does not match any of R1's directly connected networks, the router consults its routing table to route this packet.

   R1 searches the routing table for a network address and subnet mask that include this packet's destination IP address as a host address on that network. It selects the entry with the longest match (longest prefix). R1 encapsulates the packet in the appropriate frame format for the exit interface and switches the frame to the interface (G0/1 in this example). The interface then forwards it to the next hop.

3. Packet arrives at Router R2.

   R2 performs the same functions as R1, but this time, the exit interface is a serial interface—not Ethernet. Therefore, R2 encapsulates the packet in the appropriate frame format for the serial interface and sends it to R3. For this example, assume that the interface is using High-Level Data Link Control (HDLC), which uses the data-link address 0x8F. Remember, serial interfaces do not use MAC addresses.

**4.** Packet arrives at R3.

R3 decapsulates the data-link HDLC frame. The search of the routing table results in a network that is one of R3's directly connected networks. Because the exit interface is a directly connected Ethernet network, R3 needs to resolve the destination IP address of the packet with a destination MAC address.

R3 searches for the packet's destination IP address of 192.168.4.10 in its ARP cache. If the entry is not in the ARP cache, R3 sends an ARP request out its G0/0 interface.

PC2 sends back an ARP reply with its MAC address. R3 updates its ARP cache with an entry for 192.168.4.10 and the MAC address returned in the ARP reply.

The IP packet is encapsulated into a new data-link Ethernet frame and sent out R3's G0/0 interface.

**5.** The Ethernet frame with the encapsulated IP packet arrives at PC2.

PC2 examines the destination MAC address, which matches the MAC address of the receiving interface—that is, its own Ethernet NIC. PC2 will therefore copy the rest of the frame. PC2 sees that the Ethernet Type field is 0x800, which means that the Ethernet frame contains an IP packet in the data portion of the frame. PC2 decapsulates the Ethernet frame and passes the IP packet to its operating system's IP process.

# Routing Methods

A router can learn routes from three basic sources:

- **Directly connected routes**: Automatically entered in the routing table when an interface is activated with an IP address

- **Static routes**: Manually configured by the network administrator and entered in the routing table if the exit interface for the static route is active

- **Dynamic routes**: Learned by the routers through sharing routes with other routers that use the same routing protocol

In many cases, the complexity of the network topology, the number of networks, and the need for the network to automatically adjust to changes require the use of a dynamic routing protocol. Dynamic routing certainly has several advantages over static routing; however, networks still use static routing. In fact, networks typically use a combination of both static and dynamic routing.

Table 12-1 compares dynamic and static routing features. From this comparison, you can list the advantages of each routing method. The advantages of one method are the disadvantages of the other.

**Table 12-1   Dynamic Versus Static Routing**

| Feature | Dynamic Routing | Static Routing |
|---|---|---|
| Configuration complexity | Generally stays independent of the network size | Increases with network size |
| Required administrator knowledge | Requires advanced knowledge | Requires no extra knowledge |
| Topology changes | Automatically adapts to topology changes | Requires administrator intervention |
| Scaling | Suitable for simple and complex topologies | Suitable for simple topologies |
| Security | Less secure | More secure |
| Resource usage | Uses CPU, memory, and link bandwidth | Requires no extra resources |
| Predictability | Uses a route that depends on the current topology | Always uses the same route to the destination |

# Classifying Dynamic Routing Protocols

Figure 12-2 shows a timeline of IP routing protocols, along with a chart to help you memorize the various ways to classify routing protocols.

**Figure 12-2   Routing Protocols' Evolution and Classification**

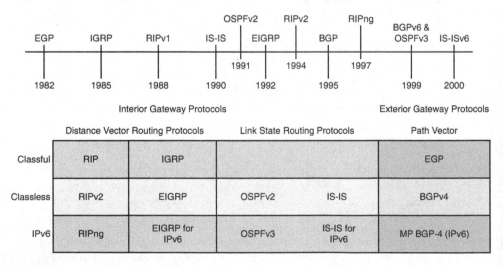

Routing protocols are classified into different groups according to their characteristics:

- IGP or EGP

- Distance vector or link state

- Classful or classless

# IGP and EGP

An autonomous system (AS) is a collection of routers under a common administration that presents a common, clearly defined routing policy to the Internet. Typical examples are a large company's internal network and an ISP's network. Most company networks are not autonomous systems; they are a network within their own ISP's autonomous system. Because the Internet is based on the autonomous system concept, two types of routing protocols are required:

- **Interior gateway protocols (IGP)**: Used for intra-AS routing—that is, routing inside an AS

- **Exterior gateway protocols (EGP)**: Used for inter-AS routing—that is, routing between autonomous systems

# Distance Vector Routing Protocols

*Distance vector* means that routes are advertised as vectors of distance and direction. Distance is defined in terms of a metric such as hop count, and direction is the next-hop router or exit interface. Distance vector protocols typically use the Bellman-Ford algorithm for the best-path route determination.

Some distance vector protocols periodically send complete routing tables to all connected neighbors. In large networks, these routing updates can become enormous, causing significant traffic on the links.

Although the Bellman-Ford algorithm eventually accumulates enough knowledge to maintain a database of reachable networks, the algorithm does not allow a router to know the exact topology of an internetwork. The router knows only the routing information received from its neighbors.

Distance vector protocols use routers as signposts along the path to the final destination. The only information a router knows about a remote network is the distance or metric to reach that network and which path or interface to use to get there. Distance vector routing protocols do not have an actual map of the network topology.

Distance vector protocols work best in these situations:

- The network is simple and flat and does not require a hierarchical design.

- The administrators do not have enough knowledge to configure and troubleshoot link-state protocols.

- Specific types of networks, such as hub-and-spoke networks, are being implemented.

- Worst-case convergence times in a network are not a concern.

# Link-State Routing Protocols

In contrast to distance vector routing protocol operation, a router configured with a link-state routing protocol can create a complete view, or topology, of the network by gathering information from all the other routers. Think of a link-state routing protocol as having a complete map of the network topology. The signposts along the way from source to destination are not necessary because all link-state routers are using an identical map of the network. A link-state router uses the link-state information to create a topology map and to select the best path to all destination networks in the topology.

With some distance vector routing protocols, routers send periodic updates of their routing information to their neighbors. Link-state routing protocols do not use periodic updates. After the network has converged, a link-state update is sent only when the topology changes.

Link-state protocols work best in these situations:

- The network design is hierarchical, usually occurring in large networks.

- The administrators have a good knowledge of the implemented link-state routing protocol.

- Fast convergence of the network is crucial.

## Classful Routing Protocols

Classful routing protocols do not send subnet mask information in routing updates. The first routing protocols, such as Routing Information Protocol (RIP), were classful. This was at a time when network addresses were allocated based on classes: Class A, B, or C. A routing protocol did not need to include the subnet mask in the routing update because the network mask could be determined based on the first octet of the network address.

Classful routing protocols can still be used in some of today's networks, but because they do not include the subnet mask, they cannot be used in all situations. Classful routing protocols cannot be used when a network is subnetted using more than one subnet mask. In other words, classful routing protocols do not support variable-length subnet masking (VLSM).

Other limitations are a factor with classful routing protocols, including their inability to support noncontiguous networks and supernets. Classful routing protocols include Routing Information Protocol version 1 (RIPv1) and Interior Gateway Routing Protocol (IGRP). CCNA exam topics do not include either RIPv1 or IGRP.

## Classless Routing Protocols

Classless routing protocols include the subnet mask with the network address in routing updates. Today's networks are no longer allocated based on classes, and the subnet mask cannot be determined by the value of the first octet. Classless routing protocols are required in most networks today because of their support for VLSM and noncontiguous networks and supernets. Classless routing protocols are Routing Information Protocol version 2 (RIPv2), Enhanced IGRP (EIGRP), Open Shortest Path First (OSPF), Intermediate System-to-Intermediate System (IS-IS), and Border Gateway Protocol (BGP).

# Dynamic Routing Metrics

In some cases, a routing protocol learns of more than one route to the same destination from the same routing source. To select the best path, the routing protocol must be capable of evaluating and differentiating among the available paths. A *metric* is used for this purpose. Two different routing protocols might choose different paths to the same destination because they use different metrics. Metrics used in IP routing protocols include the following:

- **RIP—hop count:** The best path is chosen by the route with the lowest hop count.

- **IGRP and EIGRP—bandwidth, delay, reliability, and load:** The best path is chosen by the route with the smallest composite metric value calculated from these multiple parameters. By default, only bandwidth and delay are used.

- **IS-IS and OSPF—cost:** The best path is chosen by the route with the lowest cost. The Cisco implementation of OSPF uses bandwidth to determine the cost.

The metric associated with a certain route can be best viewed using the **show ip route** command. The metric value is the second value in the brackets for a routing table entry. In Example 12-1, R2 has a route to the 192.168.8.0/24 network that is two hops away.

**Example 12-1    Routing Table for R2**

```
R2# show ip route

<output omitted>

Gateway of last resort is not set

R    192.168.1.0/24 [120/1] via 192.168.2.1, 00:00:20, Serial0/0/0
     192.168.2.0/24 is variably subnetted, 2 subnets, 2 masks
C       192.168.2.0/24 is directly connected, Serial0/0/0
L       192.168.2.2/32 is directly connected, Serial0/0/0
     192.168.3.0/24 is variably subnetted, 2 subnets, 2 masks
C       192.168.3.0/24 is directly connected, GigabitEthernet0/0
L       192.168.3.1/32 is directly connected, GigabitEthernet0/0
     192.168.4.0/24 is variably subnetted, 2 subnets, 2 masks
C       192.168.4.0/24 is directly connected, Serial0/0/1
L       192.168.4.2/32 is directly connected, Serial0/0/1
R    192.168.5.0/24 [120/1] via 192.168.4.1, 00:00:25, Serial0/0/1
R    192.168.6.0/24 [120/1] via 192.168.2.1, 00:00:20, Serial0/0/0
                    [120/1] via 192.168.4.1, 00:00:25, Serial0/0/1
R    192.168.7.0/24 [120/1] via 192.168.4.1, 00:00:25, Serial0/0/1
R    192.168.8.0/24 [120/2] via 192.168.4.1, 00:00:25, Serial0/0/1
```

Notice in the output that one network, 192.168.6.0/24, has two routes. RIP will load-balance between these equal-cost routes. All the other routing protocols are capable of automatically load-balancing traffic for up to four equal-cost routes, by default. EIGRP is also capable of load balancing across unequal-cost paths.

# Administrative Distance

Sometimes a router learns a route to a remote network from more than one routing source. For example, a static route might have been configured for the same network/subnet mask that was learned dynamically by a dynamic routing protocol, such as RIP. The router must choose which route to install.

Although less common, more than one dynamic routing protocol can be deployed in the same network. In some situations, it might be necessary to route the same network address using multiple routing protocols, such as RIP and OSPF. Because different routing protocols use different metrics—RIP uses hop count and OSPF uses bandwidth—it is not possible to compare metrics to determine the best path.

Administrative distance (AD) defines the preference of a routing source. Each routing source—including specific routing protocols, static routes, and even directly connected networks—is prioritized in order of most preferable to least preferable using an AD value. Cisco routers use the AD feature to select the best path when they learn about the same destination network from two or more different routing sources.

The AD value is an integer value from 0 to 255. The lower the value, the more preferred the route source. An administrative distance of 0 is the most preferred. Only a directly connected network has an AD of 0, which cannot be changed. An AD of 255 means the router will not believe the source of that route, and it will not be installed in the routing table.

In the routing table in Example 12-1, the AD value is the first value listed in the brackets. You can see that the AD value for RIP routes is 120. You can also verify the AD value with the **show ip protocols** command, as Example 12-2 demonstrates.

**Example 12-2   Verifying the AD Value with the show ip protocols Command**

```
R2# show ip protocols

Routing Protocol is "rip"
    Outgoing update filter list for all interfaces is not set
    Incoming update filter list for all interfaces is not set
    Sending updates every 30 seconds, next due in 21 seconds
    Invalid after 180 seconds, hold down 180, flushed after 240
    Redistributing: rip
    Default version control: send version 1, receive any version
        Interface             Send Recv Triggered RIP Key-chain
        GigabitEthernet0/0  1     1 2
        Serial0/0/0         1     1 2
        Serial0/0/1         1     1 2
    Automatic network summarization is in effect
    Maximum path: 4
    Routing for Networks:
        192.168.2.0
        192.168.3.0
        192.168.4.0
    Routing Information Sources:
        Gateway         Distance   Last Update
        192.168.2.1        120     00:00:01
        192.168.4.1        120     00:00:01
    Distance: (default is 120)

R2#
```

Table 12-2 shows a chart of the different administrative distance values for various routing protocols.

**Table 12-2    Default Administrative Distances**

| Route Source | AD |
|---|---|
| Connected | 0 |
| Static | 1 |
| EIGRP summary route | 5 |
| External BGP | 20 |
| Internal EIGRP | 90 |
| IGRP | 100 |
| OSPF | 110 |
| IS-IS | 115 |
| RIP | 120 |
| External EIGRP | 170 |
| Internal BGP | 200 |

# IGP Comparison Summary

Table 12-3 compares several features of the currently most popular IGPs: RIPv2, OSPF, and EIGRP.

**Table 12-3    Comparing Features of IGPs: RIPv2, OSPF, and EIGRP**

| Feature | RIPv2 | OSPF | EIGRP |
|---|---|---|---|
| Metric | Hop count | Bandwidth | Function of bandwidth, delay |
| Sends periodic updates | Yes (30 seconds) | No | No |
| Full or partial routing updates | Full | Partial | Partial |
| Where updates are sent | (224.0.0.9) | (224.0.0.5, 224.0.0.6) | (224.0.0.10) |
| Route considered unreachable | 16 hops | Depends on MaxAge of LSA, which is never incremented past 3600 seconds | A delay of all 1s |
| Supports unequal-cost load balancing | No | No | Yes |

# Routing Loop Prevention

Without preventive measures, distance vector routing protocols can cause severe routing loops in the network. A routing loop is a condition in which a packet is continuously transmitted within a series of routers without ever reaching its intended destination network. A routing loop can occur when two or more routers have inaccurate routing information to a destination network.

Several mechanisms are available to eliminate routing loops, primarily with distance vector routing protocols. These mechanisms include the following:

- **A maximum metric to prevent count to infinity**: To eventually stop the incrementing of a metric during a routing loop, infinity is defined by setting a maximum metric value. For example, RIP defines infinity as 16 hops, an unreachable metric. When the routers "count to infinity," they mark the route as unreachable.

- **Hold-down timers**: Routers are instructed to hold any changes that might affect routes for a specified period of time. If a route is identified as down or possibly down, any other information for that route containing the same status, or worse, is ignored for a predetermined amount of time (the hold-down period) so that the network has time to converge.

- **Split horizon**: A routing loop is prevented by not allowing advertisements to be sent back through the interface where they originated. The split horizon rule stops a router from incrementing a metric and then sending the route back to its source.

- **Route poisoning or poison reverse**: The route is marked as unreachable in a routing update that is sent to other routers. *Unreachable* is interpreted as a metric that is set to the maximum.

- **Triggered updates**: A routing table update is sent immediately in response to a routing change. Triggered updates do not wait for update timers to expire. The detecting router immediately sends an update message to adjacent routers.

- **TTL field in the IP header**: The Time To Live (TTL) field avoids a situation in which an undeliverable packet circulates endlessly on the network. With TTL, the source device of the packet sets the 8-bit field with a value. This TTL value is decreased by 1 by every router in the path until the packet reaches its destination. If the TTL value reaches 0 before the packet arrives at its destination, the packet is discarded and the router sends an ICMP error message back to the source of the IP packet.

# Link-State Routing Protocol Features

Just as distance vector protocols send routing updates to their neighbors, link-state protocols send link-state updates to neighboring routers, which then forward that information to their neighbors, and so on. Also similar to distance vector protocols, at the end of the process, routers that use link-state protocols add the best routes to their routing tables, based on metrics. However, beyond this level of explanation, these two types of routing protocol algorithms have little in common.

## Building the Link-State Database

Link-state routers flood detailed information about the internetwork to all the other routers so that every router has the same information about the internetwork. Routers use this link-state database (LSDB) to calculate the current best routes to each subnet.

OSPF, the most popular link-state IP routing protocol, advertises information in routing update messages of various types. The updates contain information called link-state advertisements (LSAs).

Figure 12-3 shows the general idea of the flooding process. R8 is creating and flooding its router LSA. Note that Figure 12-3 shows only a subset of the information in R8's router LSA.

**Figure 12-3   Flooding LSAs Using a Link-State Routing Protocol**

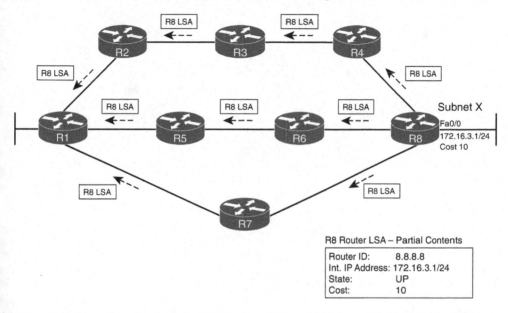

Figure 12-3 shows the rather basic flooding process. R8 is sending the original LSA for itself, and the other routers are flooding the LSA by forwarding it until every router has a copy.

After the LSA has been flooded, even if the LSAs do not change, link-state protocols require periodic reflooding of the LSAs by default every 30 minutes. However, if an LSA changes, the router immediately floods the changed LSA. For example, if Router R8's LAN interface failed, R8 would need to reflood the R8 LSA, stating that the interface is now down.

## Calculating the Dijkstra Algorithm

The flooding process alone does not cause a router to learn what routes to add to the IP routing table. Link-state protocols must then find and add routes to the IP routing table using the Dijkstra Shortest Path First (SPF) algorithm.

The SPF algorithm is run on the LSDB to create the SPF tree. The LSDB holds all the information about all the possible routers and links. Each router must view itself as the starting point, view each subnet as the destination, and use the SPF algorithm to build its own SPF tree to pick the best route to each subnet.

Figure 12-4 shows a graphical view of route possibilities from the results of the SPF algorithm run by router R1 when trying to find the best route to reach subnet 172.16.3.0/24 (based on Figure 12-3).

**Figure 12-4   SPF Tree to Find R1's Route to 172.16.3.0/24**

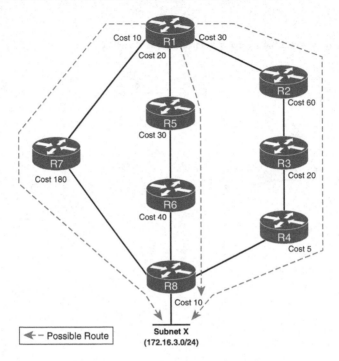

To pick the best route, a router's SPF algorithm adds the cost associated with each link between itself and the destination subnet, over each possible route. Figure 12-4 shows the costs associated with each route beside the links. The dashed lines show the three routes R1 finds between itself and subnet X (172.16.3.0/24).

Table 12-4 lists the three routes shown in Figure 12-4, with their cumulative costs. You can see that R1's best route to 172.16.3.0/24 starts by going through R5.

**Table 12-4   Comparing R1's Three Alternatives for the Route to 172.16.3.0/24**

| Route | Location in Figure 12-2 | Cumulative Cost |
|---|---|---|
| R1–R7–R8 | Left | 10 + 180 + 10 = 200 |
| R1–R5–R6–R8 | Middle | 20 + 30 + 40 + 10 = 100 |
| R1–R2–R3–R4–R8 | Right | 30 + 60 + 20 + 5 + 10 = 125 |

As a result of the SPF algorithm's analysis of the LSDB, R1 adds a route to subnet 172.16.3.0/24 to its routing table, with the next-hop router of R5.

## Convergence with Link-State Protocols

Remember, when an LSA changes, link-state protocols react swiftly, converging the network and using the currently best routes as quickly as possible. For example, imagine that the link between

R5 and R6 fails in the internetwork of Figures 12-3 and 12-4. R1 then uses the following process to switch to a different route:

1. R5 and R6 flood LSAs, stating that their interfaces are now in a down state.

2. All routers run the SPF algorithm again to see if any routes have changed.

3. All routers replace routes, as needed, based on the results of SPF. For example, R1 changes its route for subnet X (172.16.3.0/24) to use R2 as the next-hop router.

These steps allow the link-state routing protocol to converge quickly—much more quickly than distance vector routing protocols.

# Study Resources

For today's exam topics, refer to the following resources for more study:

| Resource | Module or Chapter |
| --- | --- |
| SFA Self Enroll: Networking Basics | 12, 14 |
| SFA Self Enroll: Network Addressing and Basic Troubleshooting | 3, 6 |
| SFA Instructor Led: Networking Essentials | 12, 14, 32, 34 |
| CCST Networking 100-150 Official Cert Guide | 3 |

**NOTE**   SFA: https://skillsforall.com/

# Switching Concepts

## CCST Networking 100-150 Exam Topic

- 4.5. Explain basic switching concepts.

  - *MAC address tables, MAC address filtering, VLAN (Layer 2 network segment)*

## Key Topics

Today we review the concepts behind how switching works and how virtual LANs (VLANs) can improve switching performance.

## Evolution to Switching

Today's LANs almost exclusively use switches to interconnect end devices; however, this was not always the case. Initially, devices were connected to a physical bus, a long run of coaxial backbone cabling. With the introduction of 10BASE-T and UTP cabling, the hub gained popularity as a cheaper, easier way to connect devices. But even 10BASE-T with hubs had the following limitations:

- A frame sent from one device can collide with a frame sent by another device attached to that LAN segment. Devices were in the same collision domain sharing the bandwidth.

- Broadcasts sent by one device were heard and processed by all other devices on the LAN. Devices were in the same broadcast domain. Similar to hubs, switches forward broadcast frames out all ports except for the incoming port.

Ethernet bridges were soon developed to solve some of the inherent problems in a shared LAN. A bridge basically segmented a LAN into two collision domains, which reduced the number of collisions in a LAN segment. This increased the performance of the network by decreasing unnecessary traffic from another segment.

When switches arrived on the scene, these devices provided the same benefits of bridges, in addition to the following:

- A larger number of interfaces to break up the collision domain into more segments

- Hardware-based switching instead of using software to make the decision

In a LAN where all nodes are connected directly to the switch, the throughput of the network increases dramatically. With each computer connected to a separate port on the switch, each is in a separate collision domain and has its own dedicated segment. The three primary reasons for this increase are:

- Dedicated bandwidth to each port
- Collision-free environment
- Full-duplex operation

# Switching Logic

Ethernet switches selectively forward individual frames from a receiving port to the port where the destination node is connected. During this time, the switch creates a full-bandwidth, logical, point-to-point connection between the two nodes.

Switches create this logical connection based on the source and destination Media Access Control (MAC) addresses in the Ethernet header. Specifically, the primary job of a LAN switch is to receive Ethernet frames and then make a decision to either forward each frame or ignore the frame. To accomplish this, the switch performs three actions:

1. It decides when to forward a frame or when to filter (not forward) a frame, based on the destination MAC address.

2. It learns MAC addresses by examining the source MAC address of each frame the switch receives.

3. It creates a (Layer 2) loop-free environment with other switches by using Spanning Tree Protocol (STP).

To make the decision to forward or filter, the switch uses a dynamically built MAC address table stored in RAM. By comparing the frame's destination MAC address with the fields in the table, the switch decides how to forward and/or filter the frame.

For example, in Figure 11-1, the switch receives a frame from Host A with the destination MAC address OC. The switch looks in its MAC table, finds an entry for the MAC address, and forwards the frame out port 6. The switch also filters the frame by not forwarding it out any other port, including the port on which the frame was received.

In addition to forwarding and filtering frames, the switch refreshes the timestamp for the source MAC address of the frame. In Figure 11-1, the MAC address for Host A, OA, is already in the MAC table, so the switch refreshes the entry. Entries that are not refreshed eventually are removed (after the default 300 seconds in Cisco IOS).

Continuing the example in Figure 11-1, assume that another device, Host E, is attached to port 10. Host B then sends a frame to the new Host E. The switch does not yet know where Host E is located, so it forwards the frame out all active ports except for the port on which the frame was received. The new Host E receives the frame. When it replies to Host B, the switch learns Host E's MAC address and port for the first time and stores this information in the MAC address table. Subsequent frames destined for Host E then are sent out only port 10.

**Figure 11-1   Switch Forwarding Based on MAC Address**

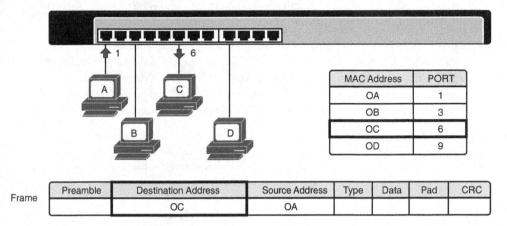

| MAC Address | PORT |
|---|---|
| OA | 1 |
| OB | 3 |
| OC | 6 |
| OD | 9 |

Frame

| Preamble | Destination Address | Source Address | Type | Data | Pad | CRC |
|---|---|---|---|---|---|---|
|  | OC | OA |  |  |  |  |

Finally, LAN switches must have a method for creating a loop-free path for frames to take within the LAN. STP provides loop prevention in Ethernet networks where redundant physical links exist.

# Collision and Broadcast Domains

A collision domain is the set of LAN interfaces whose frames could collide with each other. All shared media environments, such as those created by using hubs, are collision domains. When one host is attached to a switch port, the switch creates a dedicated connection, thereby eliminating the potential for a collision. Switches reduce collisions and improve bandwidth use on network segments because they provide dedicated bandwidth to each network segment.

Out of the box, however, a switch cannot provide relief from broadcast traffic. A collection of connected switches forms one large broadcast domain. If a frame with the destination address FFFF. FFFF.FFFF crosses a switch port, that switch must flood the frame out all other active ports. Each attached device must then process the broadcast frame at least up to the network layer. Routers and VLANs are used to segment broadcast domains.

# Frame Forwarding

Switches operate in several ways to forward frames. They can differ in forwarding methods, port speeds, memory buffering, and the OSI layers used to make the forwarding decision. The following sections discuss these concepts in greater detail.

## Switch Forwarding Methods

Switches use one of the following forwarding methods to switch data between network ports:

- **Store-and-forward switching:** The switch stores received frames in its buffers, analyzes each frame for information about the destination, and evaluates the data integrity using the cyclic redundancy check (CRC) in the frame trailer. The entire frame is stored and the CRC is calculated before any of the frame is forwarded. If the CRC passes, the frame is forwarded to the destination.

- **Cut-through switching**: The switch buffers just enough of the frame to read the destination MAC address so that it can determine to which port to forward the data. When the switch determines a match between the destination MAC address and an entry in the MAC address table, the frame is forwarded out the appropriate port(s). This happens as the rest of the initial frame is still being received. The switch does not perform any error checking on the frame.

- **Fragment-free**: The switch waits for the collision window (64 bytes) to pass before forwarding the frame. This means that each frame is checked into the data field to make sure that no fragmentation has occurred. Fragment-free mode provides better error checking than cut-through, with practically no increase in latency.

## Symmetric and Asymmetric Switching

Symmetric switching provides switched connections between ports with the same bandwidth, such as all 100Mbps ports or all 1000Mbps ports. An asymmetric LAN switch provides switched connections between ports of unlike bandwidth, such as a combination of 10Mbps, 100Mbps, and 1000Mbps ports. For example, in Figure 11-1, even if host A was connected at 100Mbps and host B was connected at 1000Mbps, the switch would buffer traffic to allow both devices to communicate.

## Memory Buffering

Switches store frames for a brief time in a memory buffer. Two methods of memory buffering exist:

- **Port-based memory**: Frames are stored in queues that are linked to specific incoming ports.

- **Shared memory**: Frames are deposited into a common memory buffer that all ports on the switch share.

## Layer 2 and Layer 3 Switching

A Layer 2 LAN switch performs switching and filtering based only on MAC addresses. A Layer 2 switch is completely transparent to network protocols and user applications. A Layer 3 switch functions similarly to a Layer 2 switch. However, instead of using only the Layer 2 MAC address information for forwarding decisions, a Layer 3 switch can also use IP address information. Layer 3 switches are also capable of performing Layer 3 routing functions, reducing the need for dedicated routers on a LAN. Because Layer 3 switches have specialized switching hardware, they can typically route data as quickly as they can switch data.

# VLAN Concepts

Although a switch comes out of the box with only one VLAN, normally a switch is configured to have two or more VLANs. Doing so creates multiple broadcast domains by putting some interfaces into one VLAN and other interfaces into other VLANs.

Consider these reasons for using VLANs:

- Grouping users by department instead of by physical location

- Segmenting devices into smaller LANs to reduce processing overhead for all devices on the LAN

- Reducing the workload of STP by limiting a VLAN to a single access switch

- Enforcing better security by isolating sensitive data to separate VLANs

- Separating IP voice traffic from data traffic

- Assisting troubleshooting by reducing the size of the failure domain (the number of devices that can cause a failure or be affected by one)

Benefits of using VLANs include the following:

- **Security**: Sensitive data can be isolated to one VLAN, separating it from the rest of the network.

- **Cost reduction**: Cost savings result from less need for expensive network upgrades and more efficient use of existing bandwidth and uplinks.

- **Higher performance**: Dividing flat Layer 2 networks into multiple logical broadcast domains reduces unnecessary traffic on the network and boosts performance.

- **Broadcast storm mitigation**: VLAN segmentation prevents a broadcast storm from propagating throughout the entire network.

- **Ease of management and troubleshooting**: A hierarchical addressing scheme groups network addresses contiguously. Because a hierarchical IP addressing scheme makes problem components easier to locate, network management and troubleshooting are more efficient.

# Traffic Types

The key to successful VLAN deployment is understanding the traffic patterns and the various traffic types in the organization. Table 11-1 lists the common types of network traffic to evaluate before placing devices and configuring VLANs.

**Table 11-1   Traffic Types**

| Traffic Type | Description |
|---|---|
| Network management | Many types of network management traffic can be present on the network. To make network troubleshooting easier, some designers assign a separate VLAN to carry certain types of network management traffic. |
| IP telephony | Two types of IP telephony traffic exist: signaling information between end devices and the data packets of the voice conversation. Designers often configure the data to and from the IP phones on a separate VLAN designated for voice traffic so that they can apply quality-of-service measures to give high priority to voice traffic. |

| Traffic Type | Description |
|---|---|
| IP multicast | Multicast traffic can produce a large amount of data streaming across the network. Switches must be configured to keep this traffic from flooding to devices that have not requested it, and routers must be configured to ensure that multicast traffic is forwarded to the network areas where it is requested. |
| Normal data | Normal data traffic is typical application traffic that is related to file and print services, email, Internet browsing, database access, and other shared network applications. |
| Scavenger class | Scavenger class includes all traffic with protocols or patterns that exceed their normal data flows. Applications assigned to this class have little or no contribution to the organizational objectives of the enterprise and are typically entertainment-oriented. |

# Types of VLANs

Some VLAN types are defined by the type of traffic they support; others are defined by the specific functions they perform. The principal VLAN types and their descriptions follow:

- **Data VLAN**: Configured to carry only user-generated traffic, ensuring that voice and management traffic is separated from data traffic.

- **Default VLAN**: All the ports on a switch are members of the default VLAN when the switch is reset to factory defaults. The default VLAN for Cisco switches is VLAN 1. VLAN 1 has all the features of any VLAN, except that you cannot rename it and you cannot delete it. It is a security best practice to restrict VLAN 1 to serve as a conduit only for Layer 2 control traffic (for example, CDP), supporting no other traffic.

- **Black hole VLAN**: A security best practice is to define a black hole VLAN to be a dummy VLAN distinct from all other VLANs defined in the switched LAN. All unused switch ports are assigned to the black hole VLAN so that any unauthorized device connecting to an unused switch port is prevented from communicating beyond the switch to which it is connected.

- **Native VLAN**: This VLAN type serves as a common identifier on opposing ends of a trunk link. A security best practice is to define a native VLAN to be a dummy VLAN distinct from all other VLANs defined in the switched LAN. The native VLAN is not used for any traffic in the switched network unless legacy bridging devices happen to be present in the network or a multi-access interconnection exists between switches joined by a hub.

- **Management VLAN**: The network administrator defines this VLAN as a means to access the management capabilities of a switch. By default, VLAN 1 is the management VLAN. It is a security best practice to define the management VLAN to be a VLAN distinct from all other VLANs defined in the switched LAN. You do this by configuring and activating a new VLAN interface.

- **Voice VLANs**: The voice VLAN feature enables switch ports to carry IP voice traffic from an IP phone. The network administrator configures a voice VLAN and assigns it to access ports. Then when an IP phone is connected to the switch port, the switch sends CDP messages that instruct the attached IP phone to send voice traffic tagged with the voice VLAN ID.

# Voice VLAN Example

Figure 11-2 shows an example of using one port on a switch to connect a user's IP phone and PC. The switch port is configured to carry data traffic on VLAN 20 and voice traffic on VLAN 150. The Cisco IP Phone contains an integrated three-port 10/100 switch to provide the following dedicated connections:

- Port 1 connects to the switch or other VoIP device.

- Port 2 is an internal 10/100 interface that carries the IP Phone traffic.

- Port 3 (access port) connects to a PC or other device.

**Figure 11-2    Cisco IP Phone Switching Voice and Data Traffic**

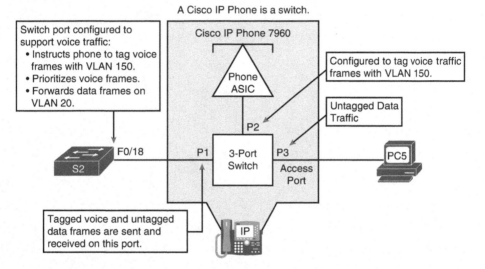

The traffic from the PC5 attached to the IP Phone passes through the IP Phone untagged. The link between S2 and the IP Phone acts as a modified trunk to carry both the tagged voice traffic and the untagged data traffic.

# Study Resources

For today's exam topics, refer to the following resources for more study:

| Resource | Module or Chapter |
| --- | --- |
| SFA Self Enroll: Networking Basics | 13 |
| SFA Self Enroll: Networking Devices and Initial Configuration | 4, 7 |
| SFA Instructor Led: Networking Essentials | 13, 21, 24 |
| CCST Networking 100-150 Official Cert Guide | 3 |

**NOTE**    SFA: https://skillsforall.com/

# Troubleshooting and Help Desks

## CCST Networking 100-150 Exam Topic

- 5.1. Demonstrate effective troubleshooting methodologies and help desk best practices, including ticketing, documentation, and information gathering.
  - *Policies and procedures, accurate and complete documentation, prioritization*

## Key Topics

Today we review troubleshooting in a network environment and managing or working in a help desk. These require an understanding of various methodologies and best practices, such as ticketing, documentation, and information gathering.

## Troubleshooting Methodology Overview

To maintain and improve network performance, it's essential to quickly and efficiently identify and resolve issues. This is where troubleshooting methodologies come in. These systematic approaches help IT professionals trace and fix problems, minimizing network downtime and improving quality of service.

There are several commonly used troubleshooting methodologies in the IT industry. All of them will have variations on the following steps:

**Step 1.** **Identify the problem**: Begin by understanding the issue. This can involve speaking to users, re-creating the problem, and gathering data.

**Step 2.** **Establish a theory of probable cause**: Based on the problem, establish a theory of what could be causing it. This can involve researching similar issues and their solutions as well as applying that knowledge to the current problem.

**Step 3.** **Test the theory**: Implement the steps necessary to test your theory. If it's correct, you can move to the next step. If not, you'll need to establish a new theory or escalate the issue.

**Step 4.** **Plan and implement a solution**: Once the problem's cause is known, plan a solution, implement it, and verify its effectiveness.

**Step 5.** **Verify full system functionality**: After implementing the solution, ensure the entire system is functioning as expected.

**Step 6.** **Document findings**: Most help desk systems have a documentation process established. Once the problem is resolved, document everything. This includes the problem, the troubleshooting steps taken, the solution, and any other relevant information.

## Structured Troubleshooting Methods

The type of problem and the level of experience of the technician can dictate the type of trouble-shooting method to use. A structured, methodical approach should be used to effectively identify and resolve problems. Table 10-1 lists several structured troubleshooting methods as well as their advantages, disadvantages, and best-use scenarios. The first three methods focus on what layer of the OSI model the technician starts troubleshooting.

**Table 10-1   Structured Troubleshooting Methods**

| Method | Description | Advantages | Disadvantages |
|---|---|---|---|
| Bottom-up troubleshooting | This approach begins with the physical components of the network, gradually moving up through the layers of the OSI model until the problem's cause is identified. | ▪ Effective when the problem is suspected to be physical.<br><br>▪ Most networking problems reside at the lower levels, making this approach often effective. | ▪ Requires checking every device and interface on the portion of the network impacted.<br><br>▪ Can create a lot of paperwork due to necessary documentation of each conclusion and possibility. |
| Top-down troubleshooting | Top-down troubleshooting starts with end-user applications and moves down through the OSI model layers until the problem's cause is identified. | Useful for simpler problems or when the problem is suspected to be with the software. | ▪ May require checking multiple network applications.<br><br>▪ Like the bottom-up approach, it can create a lot of paperwork due to necessary documentation. |
| Divide-and-conquer troubleshooting | In this approach, you collect user experiences and document symptoms. Based on this information, you make an informed guess about which OSI layer to start your investigation from and then test in both directions from there. | Allows for systematic elimination of potential sources of the problem. | Requires a good understanding of and experience with network operations to make an informed guess. |
| Follow-the-path troubleshooting | This approach involves discovering the traffic path from source to destination, reducing the scope of troubleshooting to just the links and devices in the forwarding path. | Helps to eliminate irrelevant links and devices from the troubleshooting process. | Often needs to be complemented with another troubleshooting approach for comprehensive problem resolution. |

| Method | Description | Advantages | Disadvantages |
|---|---|---|---|
| Substitution troubleshooting | Also known as swap-the-component troubleshooting, this approach involves replacing the problematic device with a known, working one. | Ideal for quick problem resolution in specific situations, such as with a critical single point of failure. | If multiple devices are causing the problem, it may not be possible to correctly isolate the problem. |
| Comparison troubleshooting | Also known as the spot-the-differences approach, this method attempts to resolve the problem by changing the nonoperational elements to be consistent with the working ones. | Useful in identifying discrepancies between working and nonworking configurations, software versions, hardware, or other properties. | May lead to a working solution without revealing the root cause of the problem. |
| Educated guess troubleshooting | This least-structured method uses an educated guess based on the symptoms of the problem. | Can be effective for seasoned technicians who can draw on their extensive knowledge and experience. | For less-experienced network administrators, this method can be too random to be effective. |

Figure 10-1 can be helpful in selecting which OSI model troubleshooting method to use based on the type of problem.

**Figure 10-1   Selecting a Troubleshooting Method**

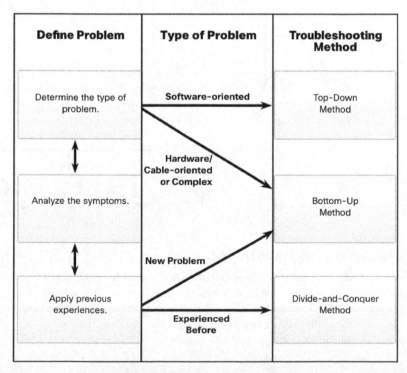

# Help Desks

A help desk is a specialized team in an IT department that is the central point of contact for employees or customers. Help desks are the first line of support in any organization, providing assistance for various technical issues. By adhering to best practices, help desks can resolve issues efficiently, maintain excellent customer service, and contribute positively to the overall IT operations.

## Policies and Procedures

Policies and procedures need to be clearly documented and easily accessible. This allows staff to reference them when needed and reduces the chance of errors or inconsistencies. In addition, regular reviews and updates should be performed to ensure that these documents reflect current best practices and regulatory requirements.

Organizations have several categories of policies. Most will have classifications for corporate, employee, and security policies. Policies and procedures are the backbone of any help desk or IT department. They provide a framework to guide actions, ensure consistency, and maintain quality. They cover a wide range of topics, from how to handle confidential information to the steps for troubleshooting a specific problem. Many of the policies and procedures followed by help desk technicians fall under the larger security policy of the organization, as shown in Figure 10-2.

**Figure 10-2   Example of How Security Documentation Fits in with the Larger Organizational Policies**

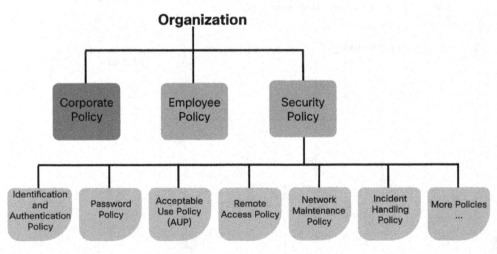

## Prioritization and Escalation

Prioritization in a help desk context involves determining the order in which tickets or tasks should be addressed. This is often based on factors such as the severity of the issue, the impact on the business, and the resources available. Effective prioritization is key to efficient troubleshooting. By focusing on the most critical issues first, IT teams can minimize downtime, reduce the impact on users, and maintain the overall performance of the network.

When users require support, they must contact the IT help desk. This may be done by using an online reporting tool, live chat, telephone, or email (for example, IT-support@email.com). Often, the help desk technician may be able to quickly answer or solve user issues. However, the technician will create a "trouble ticket" if the issue is new and unknown. The technician would then analyze the collected data and then take one of the following actions:

- **Solve the problem**: Once the user problem has been addressed, the technician would update and close the trouble ticket, storing it in the system for reference later if the same problem is reported by another user. In addition, administrators can analyze the tickets to identify common issues and their causes in order to globally eliminate the problem, if possible.

- **Escalate the trouble ticket**: Some problems are more complex or require access to devices the technician has no credentials for. In these cases, the technician must escalate the trouble ticket to a more experienced technician.

Figure 10-3 summarizes a typical trouble ticket process that a help desk technician would have to perform.

**Figure 10-3   Typical Trouble Ticket Process**

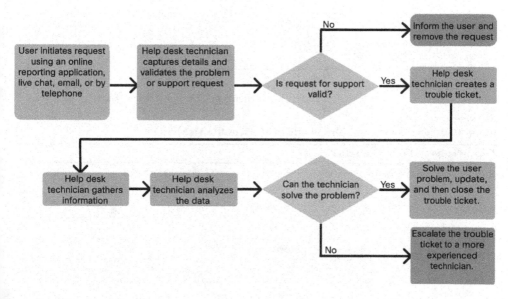

## Ticketing Systems

Ticketing systems are key tools for managing and tracking user issues. They provide a method for gathering information and documenting the problem and its resolution. When a problem is reported, a ticket is created that details the problem, who is handling it, and what steps are being taken to resolve it. This provides a clear and organized way to manage and prioritize problems. Figure 10-4 shows a generic trouble ticket.

---

**NOTE**    A quick Internet search for "help desk software" reveals many different software vendors, including Zendesk, HaloITSM, ConnectWise, and more.

**Figure 10-4   A Sample Trouble Ticket**

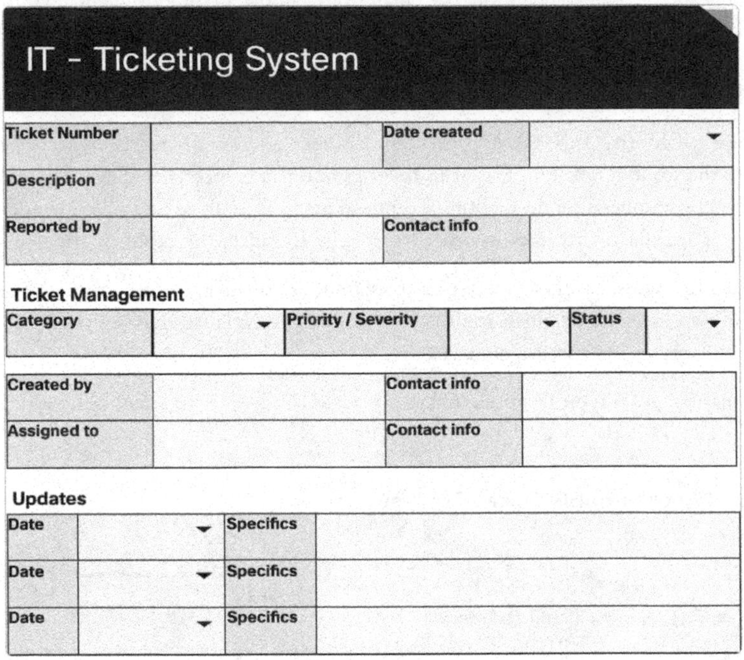

Table 37-2 describes the fields that could be used when a trouble ticket is created.

**Table 10-2   Explanation of the Fields in the Trouble Ticket**

| Field Name | Field Contains ... |
| --- | --- |
| Ticket Number | A unique number automatically generated by the ticketing system to keep track of the request. Note that the ticket number never changes. |
| Date created | A drop-down list that displays the date the ticket was created. |
| Description | A free-form field that describes the request. |
| Reported by | Free-form fields that identify who requested the support. |
| Category | A drop-down list for selecting pre-determined categories. This is useful to group related tickets together (for example, New Device / App Request, Employee Onboarding / Termination, Support, Report a Problem, and Security Incident). |
| Priority / Severity | A drop-down list for selecting pre-determined priority levels (for example, high, medium, low, or critical, major, and minor). |
| Status | A drop-down list for selecting predetermined status levels (for example, not started, opened, in progress, and completed). |
| Created by and Assigned to | Free-form fields that identify the technician who created the ticket and to whom the ticket was assigned if escalation was required. |
| Date and Specifics | A drop-down list that displays the date the ticket was updated and a free-form field for updating the ticket, respectively. |

# Study Resources

For today's exam topics, refer to the following resources for more study:

| Resource | Module or Chapter |
| --- | --- |
| SFA Self Enroll: Network Addressing and Basic Troubleshooting | 8 |
| SFA Self Enroll: Network Support and Security | 1 |
| SFA Instructor Led: Networking Essentials | 36, 37 |
| CCST Networking 100–150 Official Cert Guide | 21 |

**NOTE**   SFA: https://skillsforall.com/

# Wireshark

## CCST Networking 100-150 Exam Topic

- 5.2. Perform a packet capture with Wireshark and save it to a file.
  - *Purpose of using a packet analyzer, saving and opening a .pcap file*

## Key Topics

Today we review how to use Wireshark to monitor network traffic.

## Wireshark Overview

Wireshark is one of the world's foremost and most widely used network protocol analyzers. It lets you see what's happening on your network at a microscopic level and is the de facto standard across many commercial and nonprofit enterprises, government agencies, and educational institutions. Third-party packet viewers almost always support opening Wireshark's .pcap files.

## Features

Wireshark features include the following:

- **Live capture**: Wireshark can capture live packet data from a network interface.

- **Deep inspection**: Wireshark can read hundreds of different network protocol types.

- **Offline analysis**: Captured network data can be browsed via a GUI or via the terminal (TShark) utility.

- **Rich VoIP analysis**: Wireshark provides detailed information about Voice over Internet Protocol (VoIP) calls when captured data includes VoIP traffic.

- **Read and write many different capture file formats**: Wireshark can read and write a large number of different capture file formats.

- **Multiplatform**: Wireshark runs on most types of computers and operating systems, including Windows, macOS, and Linux.

## Who Uses Wireshark?

Wireshark is used by network professionals around the world for network troubleshooting, analysis, software and communications protocol development, and education. Here are some specific roles:

- **Network administrators**: They use Wireshark to troubleshoot network problems.

- **Security professionals**: They use Wireshark to examine security problems, check for malicious network traffic, and for forensic analysis.

- **Developers**: Developers use Wireshark to debug protocol implementations. It helps them to see what's happening on the network layer when developing applications for that environment.

- **Educators and students**: In educational institutions, Wireshark is often used for teaching purposes, as it provides detailed visibility into network protocols and communications.

# Wireshark Packet Capture

Wireshark is a useful tool for anyone working with networks and can be used with most equipment-based labs for data analysis and troubleshooting. If you haven't installed and played with Wireshark, you should definitely do it now because you will likely be getting questions about the program on the CCST Networking exam.

## Download and Install Wireshark

If you don't already have Wireshark installed, you should do so now by following these generic steps:

**Step 1.**   Go to www.wireshark.org and choose the software version based on your computer's architecture and operating system.

**Step 2.**   Install Wireshark, accept the licensing agreement, and keep all the default settings.

**Step 3.**   Click **Install Npcap.*x.x.x*** (where *x.x.x* is the version number). Npcap must be installed to capture live network traffic.

**Step 4.**   After Wireshark installs, the Npcap install window will open. Accept the licensing agreement to install Npcap.

**Step 5.**   Follow the remaining steps by clicking **Next** until you get to the **Finish** button. Wireshark should now be installed and ready to use.

---

**NOTE**   If you have difficulty installing Wireshark, search the Internet for a more detailed step-by-step guide.

---

# Save a Packet Capture

Let's use Wireshark to capture some packets on your network and save the capture to a .pcap file. Follow these steps:

**Step 1.**    Document the IP address of your PC's default gateway. On Windows, use the **ipconfig** command. On macOS and Linux, use the **netstat -rn** command.

**Step 2.**    Open Wireshark, select the interface you want to capture, and then click the shark fin icon on the toolbar or select the **Capture > Start** menu, as shown in Figure 9-1.

**Step 3.**    Use the filter feature to filter only ICMP traffic. In the **Apply a display filter...** field, enter **icmp**, as shown in Figure 9-2.

**Figure 9-1    Start a Packet Capture**

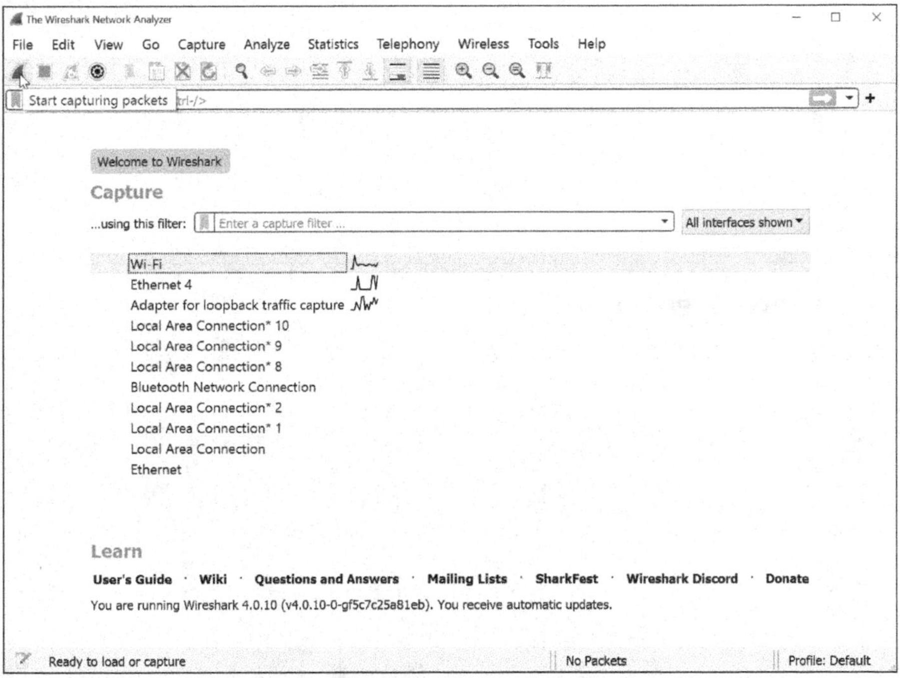

**Step 4.**    Return to your command prompt and ping your default gateway.

**Step 5.**    Return to Wireshark and click the **Stop Capturing Packets** icon (the red square), as shown in Figure 9-3.

**Figure 9-2    Filter Captured Packets**

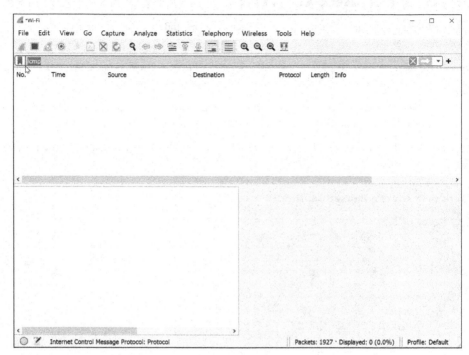

**Figure 9-3    Stop the Packet Capture**

**Step 6.**   Click **File** > **Save** and save your .pcap file with a name and location of your choosing.

---

**NOTE**   You can choose the .pcap or .pcapng file format. Your installation may default to the latest .pcapng format. The "ng" stands for next generation. The .pcapng format retains all the capabilities of the original .pcap format but adds several new features, including support for multiple interfaces and other additional information, such as packet comments.

---

**Step 7.**   Close Wireshark.

# Open a Packet Capture

Now, let's open the .pcap file you saved in the previous section.

**Step 1.**   Navigate to where you stored your .pcap file and double-click it to open Wireshark and display your packet.

**Step 2.**   Enter **icmp** in the **Apply a display filter…** field to filter for just the ICMP packets you captured.

**Step 3.**   Examine the details of the ICMP packets. Can you find the IP addresses, MAC addresses, and the type of ICMP packet?

Practice capturing and viewing different packet types. Do this enough so that you are comfortable navigating a packet capture and asking basic questions about its contents.

# Study Resources

For today's exam topics, refer to the following resources for more study:

| Resource | Module or Chapter |
| --- | --- |
| SFA Self Enroll: Networking Devices and Initial Configuration | 4 |
| SFA Instructor Led: Networking Essentials | 21 |
| CCST Networking 100-150 Official Cert Guide | 22 |

---

**NOTE**   SFA: https://skillsforall.com/

---

# Diagnostic Commands

## CCST Networking 100-150 Exam Topic

- 5.3. Run basic diagnostic commands and interpret the results.

  - *ping, ipconfig/ifconfig/ip, tracert/traceroute, nslookup; recognize how firewalls can influence the result*

## Key Topics

Today, we review the fundamental diagnostic utilities used in networking. Most of these utilities are commands provided by the operating system as command-line interface (CLI) commands. The syntax for the commands may vary between operating systems.

## IP Diagnostic Commands

Commands used to view the IP configuration information of a device vary based on the operating system. For Windows, we use the **ipconfig** command. For macOS and Linux, we use the **ifconfig** and the newer **ip** commands.

### The ipconfig Command

If a device does not have a correct IP address configuration, it will have problems with network communication and Internet access. For Windows devices, the IP configuration can be checked using the **ipconfig** command at the command line. This command displays all current TCP/IP network configuration values, as shown in Example 8-1.

**Example 8-1   Viewing the IP Settings on a Windows Device**

```
C:\> ipconfig

Windows IP Configuration


Ethernet adapter Ethernet:

   Media State . . . . . . . . . . . : Media disconnected
   Connection-specific DNS Suffix  . :
```

```
Wireless LAN adapter Wi-Fi:


   Connection-specific DNS Suffix   .   :  lan
   Link-local IPv6 Address . . . . . :  fe80::a1cc:4239:d3ab:2675%6
   IPv4 Address. . . . . . . . . . . :  10.10.10.130
   Subnet Mask . . . . . . . . . . . :  255.255.255.0
   Default Gateway . . . . . . . . . :  10.10.10.1


C:\>
```

The **/all** option displays additional information, including the MAC address, IP addresses of the default gateway, and the DNS servers, as shown in Example 8-2. It also indicates whether Dynamic Host Configuration Protocol (DHCP) is enabled, the DHCP server address, and lease information. This level of detail is instrumental in diagnosing network issues. For example, without a proper IP configuration, a host cannot communicate on the network, and if it lacks knowledge of the Domain Name System (DNS) server locations, it cannot convert domain names into IP addresses.

**Example 8-2   Viewing Detailed IP Setting Information on a Windows Device**

```
C:\> ipconfig/all

Windows IP Configuration


   Host Name . . . . . . . . . . . . : your-a9270112e3
   Primary Dns Suffix  . . . . . . . :
   Node Type . . . . . . . . . . . . : Hybrid
   IP Routing Enabled. . . . . . . . : No
   WINS Proxy Enabled. . . . . . . . : No
   DNS Suffix Search List. . . . . . : lan


Ethernet adapter Ethernet:


   Media State . . . . . . . . . . . : Media disconnected
   Connection-specific DNS Suffix .  :
   Description . . . . . . . . . . . : Realtek PCIe GBE Family Controller
   Physical Address. . . . . . . . . : 00-16-D4-02-5A-EC
   DHCP Enabled. . . . . . . . . . . : Yes
   Autoconfiguration Enabled . . . . : Yes


Wireless LAN adapter Wi-Fi:


   Connection-specific DNS Suffix .  : lan
   Description . . . . . . . . . . . : Intel(R) Dual Band Wireless-AC 3165
   Physical Address. . . . . . . . . : 00-13-02-47-8C-6A
```

```
DHCP Enabled. . . . . . . . . . . : Yes
Autoconfiguration Enabled . . . . : Yes
Link-local IPv6 Address . . . . . : fe80::a1cc:4239:d3ab:2675%6(Preferred)
IPv4 Address. . . . . . . . . . . : 10.10.10.130(Preferred)
Subnet Mask . . . . . . . . . . . : 255.255.255.0
Lease Obtained. . . . . . . . . . : Wednesday, September 2, 2020 10:03:43 PM
Lease Expires . . . . . . . . . . : Friday, September 11, 2020 10:23:36 AM
Default Gateway . . . . . . . . . : 10.10.10.1
DHCP Server . . . . . . . . . . . : 10.10.10.1
DHCPv6 IAID . . . . . . . . . . . : 98604135
DHCPv6 Client DUID. . . . . . . . : 00-01-00-01-1E-21-A5-84-44-A8-42-FC-0D-6F
DNS Servers . . . . . . . . . . . : 10.10.10.1
NetBIOS over Tcpip. . . . . . . . : Enabled

C:\>
```

The **ipconfig** command has options for refreshing the DHCP and DNS settings. The **/release** option is used to release the current DHCP bindings, essentially clearing the current IP configuration. Then, the **/renew** option is used to request new configuration information from the DHCP server. This process can resolve issues with faulty or outdated IP configuration, often restoring network connectivity. Both **ipconfig** options are shown in Example 8-3.

**Example 8-3    Releasing and Renewing the IP Settings on a Windows Device**

```
C:\> ipconfig/release

Windows IP Configuration


No operation can be performed on Ethernet while it has its media disconnected.


Ethernet adapter Ethernet:

   Media State . . . . . . . . . . : Media disconnected
   Connection-specific DNS Suffix .  :


Wireless LAN adapter Wi-Fi:

   Connection-specific DNS Suffix .  :
   Link-local IPv6 Address . . . . . : fe80::a1cc:4239:d3ab:2675%6
   Default Gateway . . . . . . . .  :

C:\> ipconfig/renew

Windows IP Configuration


No operation can be performed on Ethernet while it has its media disconnected.
```

```
Ethernet adapter Ethernet:


   Media State . . . . . . . . . . . : Media disconnected
   Connection-specific DNS Suffix .   :

Wireless LAN adapter Wi-Fi:


   Connection-specific DNS Suffix .   : lan
   Link-local IPv6 Address . . . . . : fe80::a1cc:4239:d3ab:2675%6
   IPv4 Address. . . . . . . . . . . : 10.10.10.130
   Subnet Mask . . . . . . . . . . . : 255.255.255.0
   Default Gateway . . . . . . . . . : 10.10.10.1

C:\>
```

If a host fails to obtain new IP information after releasing its configuration, check the network interface card (NIC) for an illuminated link light, which confirms a physical network connection. If this doesn't resolve the issue, the problem might lie with the DHCP server itself or with the network connections to the DHCP server, thus requiring further investigation.

## The ifconfig Command

Similar to **ipconfig**, the **ifconfig** command (shown in Example 8-4) is a legacy command used on macOS and Linux systems to configure, control, and query TCP/IP network interface parameters from a CLI.

**Example 8-4   Viewing the IP Settings on a macOS or Linux Device**

```
$ ifconfig
eth0: flags=4163<UP,BROADCAST,RUNNING,MULTICAST>  mtu 1500
        inet 10.0.2.15  netmask 255.255.255.0  broadcast 10.0.2.255
        inet6 fe80::a00:27ff:fee1:b044  prefixlen 64  scopeid 0x20<link>
        ether 08:00:27:e1:b0:44  txqueuelen 1000  (Ethernet)
        RX packets 251  bytes 304295 (297.1 KiB)
        RX errors 0  dropped 0  overruns 0  frame 0
        TX packets 116  bytes 11281 (11.0 KiB)
        TX errors 0  dropped 0 overruns 0  carrier 0  collisions 0


lo: flags=73<UP,LOOPBACK,RUNNING>  mtu 65536
        inet 127.0.0.1  netmask 255.0.0.0
        inet6 ::1  prefixlen 128  scopeid 0x10<host>
        loop  txqueuelen 1000  (Local Loopback)
        RX packets 40  bytes 2584 (2.5 KiB)
        RX errors 0  dropped 0  overruns 0  frame 0
        TX packets 40  bytes 2584 (2.5 KiB)
        TX errors 0  dropped 0 overruns 0  carrier 0  collisions 0
```

> **NOTE** The **ifconfig** command has been deprecated in favor of the **ip** command in many Linux distributions.

# The ip Command

The **ip** command offers a more consistent and unified interface for managing all aspects of the network stack, compared to **ifconfig**, which has a more limited scope. The **ip** command is a powerful and essential tool for managing macOS and Linux network settings. Its comprehensive functionality and detailed output make it the ideal choice for Linux networking tasks. The **ip** options are shown in Example 8-5.

**Example 8-5    Options for the macOS and Linux ip Command**

```
$ ip
Usage: ip [ OPTIONS ] OBJECT { COMMAND | help }
       ip [ -force ]  -batch filename
where  OBJECT := {  address | addrlabel | amt | fou | help | ila | ioam | l2tp |
                    link | macsec | maddress | monitor | mptcp | mroute | mrule |
                    neighbor | neighbour | netconf | netns | nexthop | ntable |
                    ntbl | route | rule | sr | tap | tcpmetrics |
                    token | tunnel | tuntap | vrf | xfrm }
       OPTIONS := {  -V[ersion] | -s[tatistics] | -d[etails] | -r[esolve] |
                     -h[uman-readable] | -iec | -j[son] | -p[retty] |
                     -f[amily] { inet | inet6 | mpls | bridge | link } |
                     -4 | -6 | -M | -B | -0 |
                     -l[oops] { maximum-addr-flush-attempts } | -br[ief] |
                     -o[neline] | -t[imestamp] | -ts[hort] | -b[atch] [filename] |
                     -rc[vbuf] [size] | -n[etns] name | -N[umeric] | -a[ll] |
                     -c[olor] }
```

Some of the more important options for the network technician include the following:

- **ip addr**: Display all network interfaces and their IP addresses.

- **ip addr add [IP address] dev [interface]**: Assign a new IP address to an interface.

- **ip route**: List the routing table entries.

- **ip neigh**: Show the Address Resolution Protocol (ARP) table for IPv4 or the neighbor table for IPv6.

## The ip addr Command

The **ip addr** command can be used instead of the **ifconfig** command. While **ifconfig** offers a simpler and more concise output suitable for basic network interface checks, **ip addr**, shown in Example 8-6, provides a more detailed and structured view, which is particularly useful for advanced network management and troubleshooting.

**Example 8-6   Output for the *ip addr* Command**

```
$ ip addr
1: lo: <LOOPBACK,UP,LOWER_UP> mtu 65536 qdisc noqueue state UNKNOWN
group default qlen 1000
    link/loopback 00:00:00:00:00:00 brd 00:00:00:00:00:00
    inet 127.0.0.1/8 scope host lo
        valid_lft forever preferred_lft forever
    inet6 ::1/128 scope host
        valid_lft forever preferred_lft forever
2: eth0: <BROADCAST,MULTICAST,UP,LOWER_UP> mtu 1500 qdisc fq_codel state UP
group default qlen 1000
    link/ether 08:00:27:e1:b0:44 brd ff:ff:ff:ff:ff:ff
    inet 10.0.2.15/24 brd 10.0.2.255 scope global dynamic noprefixroute eth0
        valid_lft 75973sec preferred_lft 75973sec
    inet6 fe80::a00:27ff:fee1:b044/64 scope link noprefixroute
        valid_lft forever preferred_lft forever
```

**NOTE**   In the command output above, line breaks were added to both the **lo** and **eth0** interfaces. Similar line breaks would happen if your terminal had word or text wrapping enabled and the display width is set to a low character count.

## The ip addr add Command

To add the IP address 192.168.1.50 with a subnet mask of 255.255.255.0 (which is equivalent to a /24 prefix) to the network interface **eth0**, you would use the following command:

```
$ sudo ip addr add 192.168.1.50/24 dev eth0
```

Note the following points in this command:

- **sudo** is used because changing network configurations typically requires administrative rights.

- **ip addr add** is the command to add a new address.

- **192.168.1.50/24** specifies the IP address and the subnet mask.

- **dev eth0** specifies the network interface.

After you run this command, the eth0 interface will have the new IP address assigned to it, in addition to any other IP addresses it already had. You can verify this by entering **ip addr show eth0**, as shown in Example 8-7, or simply **ip addr**.

**Example 8-7   Verifying a New IP Address Was Added to the Interface**

```
$ ip addr show eth0
2: eth0: <BROADCAST,MULTICAST,UP,LOWER_UP> mtu 1500 qdisc fq_codel state UP
group default qlen 1000
    link/ether 08:00:27:e1:b0:44 brd ff:ff:ff:ff:ff:ff
    inet 10.0.2.15/24 brd 10.0.2.255 scope global dynamic noprefixroute eth0
```

```
      valid_lft 74332sec preferred_lft 74332sec
   inet 192.168.1.50/24 scope global eth0
      valid_lft forever preferred_lft forever
   inet6 fe80::a00:27ff:fee1:b044/64 scope link noprefixroute
      valid_lft forever preferred_lft forever
```

---

**NOTE**   In the command output above, line breaks were added to the **eth0** interface.
A similar line break would happen if your terminal had word or text wrapping enabled
and the display width is set to a low character count.

---

Remember, this change is temporary and will be lost after a system reboot. To make the change
permanent, you would need to modify the network configuration files, which varies depending on
your Linux distribution.

## The ip route Command

The **ip route** command (shown in Example 8-8) shows the IP routing table, which indicates how
packets are routed through the network.

**Example 8-8   Displaying the Routing Table**

```
$ ip route
default via 10.0.2.2 dev eth0 proto dhcp src 10.0.2.15 metric 100
10.0.2.0/24 dev eth0 proto kernel scope link src 10.0.2.15 metric 100
```

## The ip neigh Command

The **ip neigh** command (shown in Example 8-9) displays the ARP table, showing mappings
between network layer addresses and link layer addresses (IP and MAC addresses).

**Example 8-9   Displaying the ARP Table**

```
$ ip neigh
10.0.2.2 dev eth0 lladdr 52:54:00:12:35:02 REACHABLE
```

# The ping Command

If the IP configuration appears to be correctly configured on the local host, next, test network
connectivity by using **ping**. The **ping** command is one of the most basic yet vital tools for network
troubleshooting. It tests the connectivity between the host (your computer or device) and another
networked device. Ping uses the Internet Control Message Protocol (ICMP) to send echo request
messages to the target host and waits for an echo reply.

As shown in Example 8-10 on a Windows device, the **ping** command can be followed by either an
IP address or the name of a destination host. In the example, the user pings the default gateway at
10.10.10.1 and then pings www.cisco.com.

**Example 8-10   Pinging an IP Address and Hostname on a Windows Device**

```
C:\> ping 10.10.10.1


Pinging 10.10.10.1 with 32 bytes of data:
Reply from 10.10.10.1: bytes=32 time=1ms TTL=64
Reply from 10.10.10.1: bytes=32 time=1ms TTL=64
Reply from 10.10.10.1: bytes=32 time=1ms TTL=64
Reply from 10.10.10.1: bytes=32 time=1ms TTL=64


Ping statistics for 10.10.10.1:
    Packets: Sent = 4, Received = 4, Lost = 0 (0% loss),
Approximate round trip times in milli-seconds:
    Minimum = 1ms, Maximum = 1ms, Average = 1ms


C:\> ping www.cisco.com


Pinging e2867.dsca.akamaiedge.net [104.112.72.241] with 32 bytes of data:
Reply from 104.112.72.241: bytes=32 time=25ms TTL=53
Reply from 104.112.72.241: bytes=32 time=25ms TTL=53
Reply from 104.112.72.241: bytes=32 time=27ms TTL=53
Reply from 104.112.72.241: bytes=32 time=24ms TTL=53


Ping statistics for 104.112.72.241:
    Packets: Sent = 4, Received = 4, Lost = 0 (0% loss),
Approximate round trip times in milli-seconds:
    Minimum = 24ms, Maximum = 27ms, Average = 25ms


C:\>
```

By default, on a macOS or Linux device, the **ping** command will be sending echo requests continuously until you stop it with **Ctrl+C**. However, you can use the **- c** option to specify how many pings to send, as shown in Example 8-11.

**Example 8-11   Pinging an IP Address and Hostname on a macOS or Linux Device**

```
$ ping -c 4 10.0.2.2
PING 10.0.2.2 (10.0.2.2) 56(84) bytes of data.
64 bytes from 10.0.2.2: icmp_seq=1 ttl=64 time=0.125 ms
64 bytes from 10.0.2.2: icmp_seq=2 ttl=64 time=0.078 ms
64 bytes from 10.0.2.2: icmp_seq=3 ttl=64 time=0.085 ms
64 bytes from 10.0.2.2: icmp_seq=4 ttl=64 time=0.070 ms


--- 10.0.2.2 ping statistics ---
4 packets transmitted, 4 received, 0% packet loss, time 3075ms
rtt min/avg/max/mdev = 0.070/0.089/0.125/0.021 ms
```

```
$ ping -c 4 www.cisco.com
PING e2867.dsca.akamaiedge.net (23.60.105.39) 56(84) bytes of data.
64 bytes from a23-60-105-39.deploy.static.akamaitechnologies.com (23.60.105.39):
   icmp_seq=1 ttl=54 time=23.0 ms
64 bytes from a23-60-105-39.deploy.static.akamaitechnologies.com (23.60.105.39):
   icmp_seq=2 ttl=54 time=24.8 ms
64 bytes from a23-60-105-39.deploy.static.akamaitechnologies.com (23.60.105.39):
   icmp_seq=3 ttl=54 time=21.0 ms
64 bytes from a23-60-105-39.deploy.static.akamaitechnologies.com (23.60.105.39):
   icmp_seq=4 ttl=54 time=25.0 ms


--- e2867.dsca.akamaiedge.net ping statistics ---
4 packets transmitted, 4 received, 0% packet loss, time 3006ms
rtt min/avg/max/mdev = 21.022/23.460/25.040/1.621 ms
```

When the **ping** command is used to contact a domain like www.cisco.com, the system initially consults a DNS server to translate the domain name into an IP address. Once this address is acquired, the ping sends an echo request to it. A successful ping to the IP address but not to the domain name typically indicates a DNS issue.

On the other hand, if pinging both the domain name and the IP address works, but accessing the specific application fails, the issue likely lies within the application on the target server. This could be due to the service you are trying to access not being active.

In situations where both pings are unsuccessful, the problem is likely related to network connectivity to the destination. A common diagnostic step is to ping the default gateway. If this ping succeeds, the issue is likely beyond the local network; if it fails, the problem exists within the local network.

It's important to note that failed pings don't always signify a connectivity issue. They could be the result of firewalls on the sender or receiver's end, or on a router in the pathway, blocking ICMP packets used by ping.

The standard **ping** command typically sends four echo requests, awaiting responses for each. However, its functionality can be expanded through using the options shown in Example 8-12.

### Example 8-12  Ping Options on Windows Devices

```
C:\> ping

Usage: ping [-t] [-a] [-n count] [-l size] [-f] [-i TTL] [-v TOS]
            [-r count] [-s count] [[-j host-list] | [-k host-list]]
            [-w timeout] [-R] [-S srcaddr] [-c compartment] [-p]
            [-4] [-6] target_name

Options:
    -t              Ping the specified host until stopped.
                    To see statistics and continue - type Control-Break;
```

```
                      To stop - type Control-C.
    -a                Resolve addresses to hostnames.
    -n count          Number of echo requests to send.
    -l size           Send buffer size.
    -f                Set Don't Fragment flag in packet (IPv4-only).
    -i TTL            Time To Live.
    -v TOS            Type Of Service (IPv4-only. This setting has been deprecated
                      and has no effect on the type of service field in the IP
                      Header).
    -r count          Record route for count hops (IPv4-only).
    -s count          Timestamp for count hops (IPv4-only).
    -j host-list      Loose source route along host-list (IPv4-only).
    -k host-list      Strict source route along host-list (IPv4-only).
    -w timeout        Timeout in milliseconds to wait for each reply.
    -R                Use routing header to test reverse route also (IPv6-only).
                      Per RFC 5095 the use of this routing header has been
                      deprecated. Some systems may drop echo requests if
                      this header is used.
    -S srcaddr        Source address to use.
    -c compartment    Routing compartment identifier.
    -p                Ping a Hyper-V Network Virtualization provider address.
    -4                Force using IPv4.
    -6                Force using IPv6.


C:\>
```

On a macOS or Linux device, the ping options are different, as shown in Example 8-13.

**Example 8-13  Ping Options on macOS and Linux Devices**

```
$ ping -h

Usage
  ping [options] <destination>

Options:
  <destination>      dns name or ip address
  -a                 use audible ping
  -A                 use adaptive ping
  -B                 sticky source address
  -c <count>         stop after <count> replies
  -C                 call connect() syscall on socket creation
  -D                 print timestamps
```

```
  -d                      use SO_DEBUG socket option
  -e <identifier>         define identifier for ping session, default is random for
                          SOCK_RAW and kernel defined for SOCK_DGRAM
                          Imply using SOCK_RAW (for IPv4 only for identifier 0)
  -f                      flood ping
  -h                      print help and exit
  -I <interface>          either interface name or address
  -i <interval>           seconds between sending each packet
  -L                      suppress loopback of multicast packets
  -l <preload>            send <preload> number of packages while waiting replies
  -m <mark>               tag the packets going out
  -M <pmtud opt>          define mtu discovery, can be one of <do|dont|want>
  -n                      no dns name resolution
  -O                      report outstanding replies
  -p <pattern>            contents of padding byte
  -q                      quiet output
  -Q <tclass>             use quality of service <tclass> bits
  -s <size>               use <size> as number of data bytes to be sent
  -S <size>               use <size> as SO_SNDBUF socket option value
  -t <ttl>                define time to live
  -U                      print user-to-user latency
  -v                      verbose output
  -V                      print version and exit
  -w <deadline>           reply wait <deadline> in seconds
  -W <timeout>            time to wait for response

IPv4 options:
  -4                      use IPv4
  -b                      allow pinging broadcast
  -R                      record route
  -T <timestamp>          define timestamp, can be one of <tsonly|tsandaddr|tsprespec>

IPv6 options:
  -6                      use IPv6
  -F <flowlabel>          define flow label, default is random
  -N <nodeinfo opt>       use icmp6 node info query, try <help> as argument

For more details see ping(8).
```

# The tracert Command

The **ping** command effectively checks for end-to-end connectivity to a target destination. However, it doesn't pinpoint where a connection failure occurs if the destination cannot be reached. In such cases, tracing the route becomes essential.

The **tracert** command in Windows and **traceroute** in macOS and Linux trace the path a packet takes to its destination. They provide detailed information about each router or hop the packet encounters along its journey. Crucially, these utilities measure the round-trip time, which is the time it takes for a packet to travel from the source to each hop and back. This feature can be particularly useful for identifying points in the network where packets are lost or delayed, which might be causing bottlenecks or slowdowns.

Example 8-14 shows output for the Windows **tracert** command. The output is similar on macOS and Linux devices. The path is unique to this user. Your path will have a different listing of hops and may be shorter or longer (number of hops).

**Example 8-14   Using the *tracert* Command on a Windows Device**

```
C:\> tracert www.cisco.com

Tracing route to e2867.dsca.someispedge.net [104.95.63.78]
over a maximum of 30 hops:


    1     1 ms     1 ms     <1 ms     10.10.10.1
    2     *        *        *         Request timed out.
    3     8 ms     8 ms     8 ms      24-155-250-94.dyn.yourisp.net
    [172.30.250.94]
    4     22 ms    23 ms    23 ms     24-155-121-218.static.yourisp.net
    [172.30.121.218]
    5     23 ms    24 ms    25 ms     dls-b22-link.anotherisp.net
    [64.0.70.170]
    6     25 ms    24 ms    25 ms     dls-b23-link.anotherisp.net
    [192.168.137.106]
    7     24 ms    23 ms    21 ms     someisp-ic-341035-dls-b1.c.anotherisp.
    net [192.168.169.47]
    8     25 ms    24 ms    23 ms     ae3.databank-dfw5.netarch.someisp.com
    [10.250.230.195]
    9     25 ms    24 ms    24 ms     a104-95-63-78.deploy.static.
    someisptechnologies.com [104.95.63.78]

Trace complete.

C:>
```

**NOTE** The output in Example 8-14 is anonymized. Also, notice that the second hop failed. This is most likely due to a firewall configuration on that device that does not permit responding packets from the **tracert** command. However, the device does forward the packets to the next hop.

The basic **tracert** command will only allow up to 30 hops between a source and destination device before it assumes that the destination is unreachable. This number is adjustable by using the **-h** parameter. All the **tracert** options are shown in Example 8-15.

**Example 8-15   The *tracert* Options on a Windows Device**

```
C:\> tracert


Usage: tracert [-d] [-h maximum_hops] [-j host-list] [-w timeout]
               [-R] [-S srcaddr] [-4] [-6] target_name


Options:
    -d                      Do not resolve addresses to hostnames.
    -h maximum_hops         Maximum number of hops to search for target.
    -j host-list            Loose source route along host-list (IPv4-only).
    -w timeout              Wait timeout milliseconds for each reply.
    -R                      Trace round-trip path (IPv6-only).
    -S srcaddr              Source address to use (IPv6-only).
    -4                      Force using IPv4.
    -6                      Force using IPv6.


C:\>
```

# The nslookup Command

During the setup of a network device, it's common to specify one or more DNS server addresses for the device's DNS client to use in resolving domain names to IP addresses. These DNS server addresses are often provided by the Internet service provider (ISP). When a user's application needs to connect to a remote device using its domain name, the DNS client reaches out to these DNS servers to convert the domain name into an IP address.

Operating systems include a utility called **nslookup** that allows users to manually query DNS servers to resolve hostnames. This tool is particularly useful for diagnosing issues related to domain name resolution and for checking the operational status of the DNS servers.

On a Windows device, when you run the **nslookup** command, it initially shows the default DNS server that your system is configured to use, as shown in Example 8-16. At the **nslookup** prompt, you can then input a hostname or domain to resolve. The **nslookup** tool is equipped with a variety of options for comprehensive testing and confirmation of the DNS resolution process.

**Example 8-16   Using the *netstat* Command on a Windows Device**

```
C:\Users> nslookup
Default Server:  24-155-121-146.static.grandenetworks.net
Address:  24.155.121.146


> www.cisco.com
Server:  24-155-121-146.static.grandenetworks.net
Address:  24.155.121.146
```

```
Non-authoritative answer:
Name:      e2867.dsca.akamaiedge.net
Addresses:   2600:1404:ec00:1195::b33
             2600:1404:ec00:1197::b33
             23.60.105.39
Aliases:   www.cisco.com
           www.cisco.com.akadns.net
           wwwds.cisco.com.edgekey.net
           wwwds.cisco.com.edgekey.net.globalredir.akadns.net
```

# Study Resources

For today's exam topics, refer to the following resources for more study:

| Resource | Module or Chapter |
|---|---|
| SFA Self Enroll: Networking Basics | 17 |
| SFA Self Enroll: Networking Devices and Initial Configuration | 12 |
| SFA Self Enroll: Network Addressing and Basic Troubleshooting | 8 |
| SFA Self Enroll: Network Support and Security | 1 |
| SFA Instructor Led: Networking Essentials | 17, 29, 36, 37 |
| CCST Networking 100-150 Official Cert Guide | 4 |

**NOTE** SFA: https://skillsforall.com/

# Device Management

## CCST Networking 100-150 Exam Topic

- 5.4. Differentiate between different ways to access and collect data about network devices.

    - *Remote access (RDP, SSH, Telnet), VPN, terminal emulators, consoles, network management systems, network cloud management (Meraki), scripts*

## Key Topics

Today, we review various remote access methods and tools used in networking, focusing on how these tools and protocols operate, their common uses, security considerations, and configuration.

## Remote Access

The CCST-N exam covers three main remote access methods: Remote Desktop Protocol (RDP), Secure Shell (SSH), and Telnet.

### RDP

RDP is a proprietary protocol that Microsoft developed. Its primary role is to allow users to connect to another computer over a network connection and gain full desktop access. On a Windows device, search for "Remote Desktop Connection" for the graphical interface shown in Figure 7-1.

At the command line, use a command like **mstsc /v:*servername*** to establish this connection. While RDP is generally considered secure, it's worth noting that it's often a target for brute force attacks, so it's crucial to implement strong passwords and consider additional security measures.

Windows includes RDP servers and clients as part of its operating system. This functionality is also accessible on macOS and Linux using xrdp, which is a free, open-source implementation of Microsoft's RDP server. This makes RDP capabilities widely available across different platforms. For those using macOS, remote access is facilitated through the Screen Sharing feature. This feature is built upon Virtual Network Computing (VNC), a freeware solution similar to RDP in its functionality. Screen-sharing servers can be accessed by any VNC client, broadening the scope of remote access. VNC operates over port 5900, offering a similar experience to that of RDP.

**Figure 7-1   Windows Remote Desktop Connection Application**

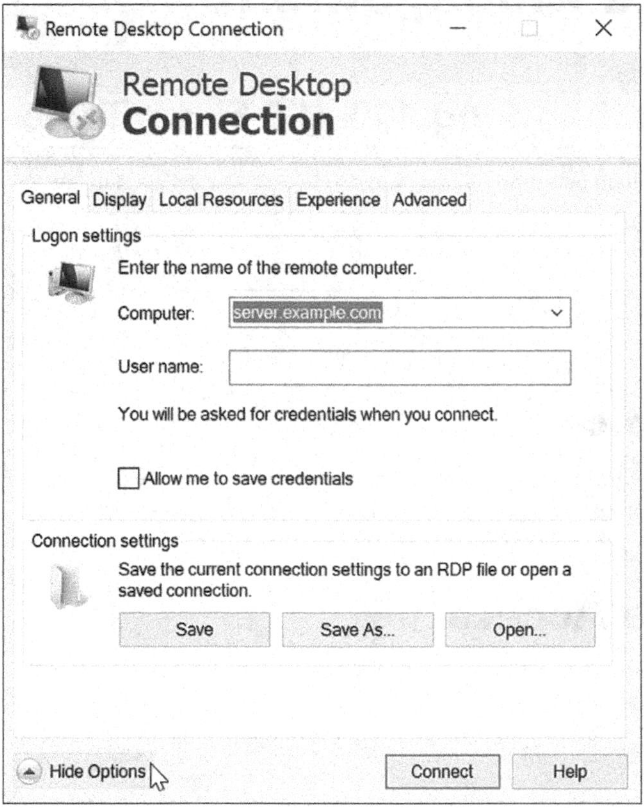

# SSH

SSH creates a secure channel over an unsecured network. It's most commonly used for remote login and executing commands on remote machines. Use the command **ssh** *username@hostname* to start your secure session. Replace *username* with your username on the remote server and *hostname* with the IP address or domain of the server.

The following requirements must be met before you will be able to gain remote access:

- The remote server must be running an SSH server (like OpenSSH).

- The SSH port (default is 22) must be open and accessible from your local machine.

- Your user account on the remote server must have permissions to access via SSH.

---

**NOTE**   You may also see the Windows SSH command shown as **ssh -l** *username hostname*. Although valid, this syntax is less commonly used.

---

# Telnet

Telnet allows users to communicate with a remote device or computer. A common use case might be to test a port on a remote machine, using a command like **telnet** *hostname port*. However, Telnet is not secure. It transmits all data, including login credentials, in plaintext. This lack of security makes Telnet a less desirable choice in environments where data protection is a priority.

# Virtual Private Networks (VPNs)

VPNs are a crucial technology in networking, offering a secure way to access a network over the Internet. They create a private network from a public Internet connection, masking your IP address so your online actions are virtually untraceable.

When you connect to a VPN, your data is encrypted before it goes out to the Internet. This encrypted data is then sent to a VPN server, where it's decrypted and sent to its destination. The response is encrypted by the VPN server before it's sent back to you. This process ensures that your data remains private and secure.

VPNs are especially useful for remotely accessing network devices securely. For example, network administrators working from home can use VPNs to securely connect to their corporate network and access devices and servers as if they were on site.

## Windows VPN Configuration

To set up a VPN connection on a Windows system, you would typically go through the following steps:

1. Click the **Start** button and then select **Settings > Network & Internet > VPN > Add a VPN connection**.

2. In **Add a VPN connection** (see Figure 7-2), choose **Windows (built-in)** or another VPN application that is installed. Then fill in the rest of the details provided by your VPN service or network administrator.

3. Click **Save**.

## Scripting a VPN Connection

Automating VPN connections can be handy. Example 7-1 shows a script in PowerShell to establish a VPN connection. This script adds a VPN connection with your specified parameters.

**Figure 7-2   Windows VPN Configuration Example**

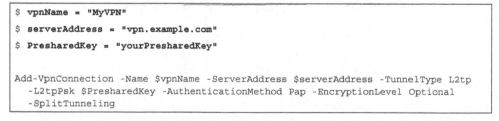

**Example 7-1   PowerShell Script to Automate a VPN Connection**

```
$ vpnName = "MyVPN"
$ serverAddress = "vpn.example.com"
$ PresharedKey = "yourPresharedKey"

Add-VpnConnection -Name $vpnName -ServerAddress $serverAddress -TunnelType L2tp
  -L2tpPsk $PresharedKey -AuthenticationMethod Pap -EncryptionLevel Optional
  -SplitTunneling
```

# Terminal Emulators

Terminal emulators are software programs that enable a user to access the command–line interface of a network device, such as a router or switch, from a remote location. They replicate the functionality of traditional hardware terminals but in a software format.

One popular terminal emulator is PuTTY (see Figure 7-3). PuTTY is commonly used to access Cisco devices. To connect to a device, you would open PuTTY, select the connection type (such as SSH or Telnet), enter the IP address of the device, and then click **Open** to start the session.

**Figure 7-3  The PuTTY Terminal Emulator**

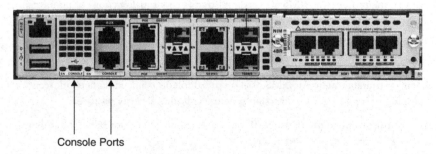

PuTTY Configuration

Category:
- Session
  - Logging
- Terminal
  - Keyboard
  - Bell
  - Features
- Window
  - Appearance
  - Behaviour
  - Translation
  - Selection
  - Colours
- Connection
  - Data
  - Proxy
  - SSH
  - Serial
  - Telnet
  - Rlogin
  - SUPDUP

Basic options for your PuTTY session

Specify the destination you want to connect to

Host Name (or IP address)     Port
10.1.1.1                      22

Connection type:
◉ SSH    ○ Serial    ○ Other:  Telnet ∨

Load, save or delete a stored session

Saved Sessions

Default Settings                    Load

                                    Save

                                    Delete

Close window on exit:
○ Always    ○ Never    ◉ Only on clean exit

About              Open         Cancel

# Consoles

The console is a physical port on a network device that provides direct access to the device's operating system. The Cisco 4461 ISR, shown in Figure 7-4, has two console ports: one for USB connections and one for older PCs with a serial COM port. There is also an auxiliary port that can be used to connect a modem for dialup console access.

**Figure 7-4  Console Ports on the Cisco 4461 ISR**

Console Ports

Console ports are typically used for initial configuration or troubleshooting purposes. Accessing a device through the console port is considered more secure and reliable, especially when network connectivity issues prevent remote access.

To access a Cisco switch through the console, you would connect a console cable from your computer to the console port on the switch. Then, using a terminal emulator like PuTTY, select the "Serial" connection type, specify the correct COM port, and establish the connection.

Console ports are typically used for one the following reasons:

- **Initial configuration:** Terminal emulators are often used to perform the initial setup of a device (for instance, configuring the basic settings of a Cisco router).

- **Routine monitoring:** Regular checks on network device status can be done remotely using terminal emulators.

- **Troubleshooting:** When problems arise, terminal emulators allow for quick diagnostics and troubleshooting.

- **Firmware updates:** Terminal emulators facilitate the process of updating a device's firmware.

For critical configurations and firmware or software updates, consider using console access to avoid interruptions due to network instability.

# Network Management Systems

Network management systems (NMSs) are essential for managing networks that are larger than a small office. They provide a centralized framework for monitoring, managing, and maintaining network devices and services. In essence, an NMS is the backbone that keeps the network's health in check, ensuring optimal performance and security.

## NMS Functions

Key functions of an NMS include the following:

- **Monitoring network performance:** An NMS continuously tracks various parameters like bandwidth usage, packet loss, latency, and error rates. Tools like SolarWinds, Nagios, and Cisco's ThousandEyes are popular for this purpose.

- **Fault management:** An NMS alerts administrators about malfunctions or performance degradation, often before users are even aware.

- **Configuration management:** An NMS allows for bulk changes and can roll back configurations to a previous state if needed.

- **Security management:** An NMS plays a crucial role in maintaining network security by managing firewalls, intrusion detection systems, and other security protocols.

- **Accounting management:** An NMS can track resource usage for billing or analysis purposes, ensuring efficient resource allocation.

## Network Management Tools

An NMS typically includes some or all of the following tools and functions.

## Simple Network Management Protocol (SNMP)

SNMP is widely used for monitoring network-attached devices. For example, to check the status of a router interface, you can use the command **snmpget –v2c –c public 192.168.1.1 1.3.6.1.2.1.2.2.1.8.2**, where **–v2c** specifies SNMP version, **–c** public is the community string, and **1.3.6.1.2.1.2.2.1.8.2** is the Object Identifier (OID) for interface status.

## Command-Line Interfaces (CLI)

Network administrators often use the CLI to configure and troubleshoot network devices. For example, in Cisco devices, the **show running-config** command displays the current configuration of the device.

## REST APIs

Modern NMSs use REST APIs for more flexible and programmable network management. Using a REST API to fetch network device details might involve a command like **curl -X GET https://nms.example.com/api/devices/12345**. This command might return a JSON file with details of all the **devices** at the location **12345**.

## Syslog

Syslog servers collect log messages from various network devices, aiding in troubleshooting and auditing. For example, configuring a Cisco router to send logs to a Syslog server might include the command **logging 192.168.1.100**.

## NetFlow

Used for network traffic analysis, NetFlow is used for network analysis and provides insights into traffic flow and volume. On a Cisco router, **ip flow-export destination 192.168.1.150 9996** configures NetFlow to export data to a collector at **192.168.1.150** at port number **9996**.

# Network Cloud Management Using Meraki

The Meraki cloud solution empowers users to manage all Meraki network devices via a unified, straightforward, and secure platform. The solution encompasses deployment, monitoring, and configuration of Meraki devices, accessible through the Meraki dashboard web interface or APIs.

The Meraki dashboard, shown in Figure 7-5, is a web-based tool enabling the configuration of Meraki devices and services. It's the core interface for managing Meraki organizations and networks.

**Figure 7-5   Meraki Dashboard**

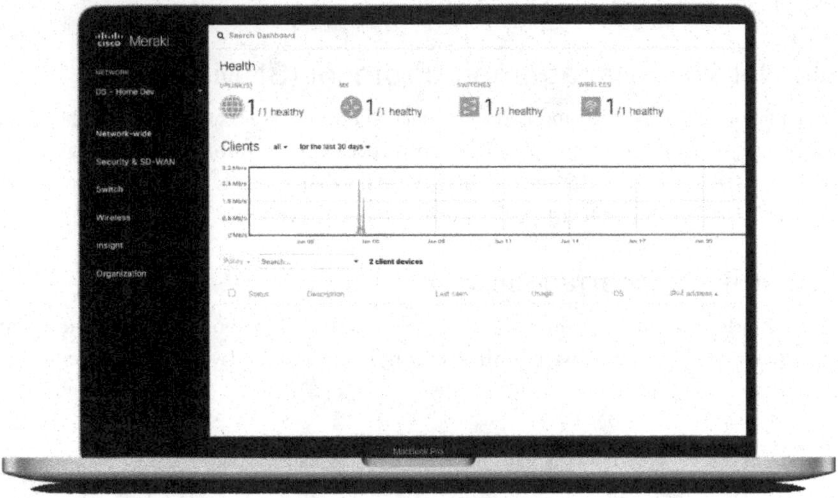

# Meraki Dashboard Features

Features of the Meraki dashboard include the following:

- **Data management and security**: Meraki distinguishes between management and user data. Management data is securely sent to the cloud, while user data flows directly through LAN/WAN.

- **High availability and data centers**: Meraki's highly available architecture includes real-time data replication across regional data centers and nightly backups, adhering to cybersecurity standards.

- **Device-to-cloud communication**: An event-driven remote procedure call (RPC) engine manages device-cloud communication, allowing for cloud-based configuration and automatic updates upon device reconnection.

- **Configuration management**: Device configurations are stored and updated securely in a backend container via dashboard or API changes.

- **Data storage and privacy compliance**: Meraki's cloud infrastructure respects regional and industry-specific privacy laws, integrating privacy features and PCI compliance in its security suite.

# APIs and Advanced Control

Meraki APIs provide granular control over the Meraki solution, offering capabilities beyond the dashboard's scope. These RESTful APIs use HTTPS for transport and JSON for serialization, allowing users to automate deployments, monitor networks, and develop custom solutions atop the Meraki platform.

# Study Resources

For today's exam topics, refer to the following resources for more study:

| Resource | Module or Chapter |
|---|---|
| SFA Self Enroll: Network Support and Security | 1 |
| SFA Instructor Led: Networking Essentials | 37 |
| CCST Networking 100–150 Official Cert Guide | 21 |

**NOTE**    SFA: https://skillsforall.com/

# Show Commands

## CCST Networking 100-150 Exam Topic

- 5.5. Run basic **show** commands on a Cisco network device.

  - *show run, show cdp neighbors, show ip interface brief, show ip route, show version, show inventory, show mac address-table, show interface, show interface x, show interface status; privilege levels; command help and auto-complete*

## Key Topics

Today, we review using the Cisco IOS help facility, command auto-completion, privilege levels, Cisco Discovery Protocol (CDP), and basic **show** commands used on Cisco devices to verify their configuration and operation.

## Cisco IOS Help Facility

Cisco IOS has extensive command-line input help facilities, including context-sensitive help. The following summarizes the two types of help available:

- **Word help**: Enter a character sequence of an incomplete command immediately followed by a question mark (**sh?**) to get a list of available commands that start with the character sequence.

- **Command syntax help**: Enter the **?** command to get command syntax help to see all the available arguments to complete a command (**show ?**). Cisco IOS then displays a list of available arguments.

As part of the help facility, Cisco IOS displays console error messages when incorrect command syntax is entered. Table 6-1 shows sample error messages, what they mean, and how to get help.

**Table 6-1  Console Error Messages**

| Example Error Message | Meaning | How to Get Help |
|---|---|---|
| switch# **cl**<br><br>% Ambiguous command:<br>"cl" | You did not enter enough characters for your device to recognize the command. | Reenter the command, followed by a question mark (?), without a space between the command and the question mark. The possible keywords that you can enter with the command will be displayed. |
| switch# **clock**<br><br>% Incomplete command. | You did not enter all the keywords or values required by this command. | Reenter the command, followed by a question mark (?), with a space between the command and the question mark. |
| switch# **clock ste**<br>             ^<br><br>% Invalid input<br>detected at '^' marker. | You entered the command incorrectly. The caret (^) marks the point of the error. | Enter a question mark (?) to display all the available commands or parameters. |

# Command Auto-Complete

To auto-complete a command, simply press the **Tab** key. If the number of letters you typed for a command or argument are unambiguous (meaning no other command or argument begins with that letter combination), the Cisco IOS will auto-complete the command. This feature is shown in Example 6-1.

**Example 6-1  Using the Help Facility and Auto-Complete**

```
R1# con
% Ambiguous command: "con"
R1# con?
configure  connect
R1# conf
R1# configure t
R1# configure terminal
Enter configuration commands, one per line.  End with CNTL/Z.
R1(config)#
```

In Example 6-1, **con** is ambiguous because there are two commands that begin with those letters. Adding an *f* makes it unambiguous and the network technician can press **Tab** to auto-complete. For **terminal**, there is no other argument for the **configure** command that begins with a *t*. Therefore, the network technician can simply enter **t** and presses **Tab**.

# Privilege Levels

Large IT departments in big organizations encompass a diverse range of job roles. It's crucial that not every role is granted equal access to the organization's infrastructure devices. To address this, Cisco IOS software offers two approaches to manage infrastructure access: privilege levels and role-based command-line interface (CLI). For the CCST Networking exam, you are responsible for knowing about privilege levels.

By default, the Cisco IOS software CLI has two levels of access to commands:

- **User EXEC mode (privilege level 1)**: This provides the lowest EXEC mode user privileges and allows only user-level commands available at the **Router>** prompt.

- **Privileged EXEC mode (privilege level 15)**: This is the highest-level privilege and includes all enable-level commands at the **Router#** prompt.

There are 16 privilege levels in total, as listed next. The higher the privilege level, the more router access a user has. Commands that are available at lower privilege levels are also executable at higher levels.

- **Level 0**: Predefined for user-level access privileges. Seldom used, but includes five commands: **disable, enable, exit, help,** and **logout.**

- **Level 1**: The default level for login with the router prompt **Router >**. A user cannot make any changes or view the running configuration file.

- **Levels 2–14**: May be customized for user-level privileges. Commands from lower levels may be moved up to another higher level, or commands from higher levels may be moved down to a lower level.

- **Level 15**: Reserved for the enable mode privileges (**enable** command). Users can change configurations and view configuration files.

Use the **privilege** global configuration mode command and the following syntax to assign commands to a custom privilege level.

```
Router(config)# privilege mode {level level|reset} command
```

Table 6-2 provides a description of the arguments for the **privilege** command.

**Table 6-2   Details of the *privilege* Command**

| Command | Description |
|---------|-------------|
| Mode | Specifies the configuration mode. Use the **privilege ?** command to see a complete list of router configuration modes available on your router. |
| Level | (Optional) Enables setting a privilege level with a specified command. |
| Level | (Optional) The privilege level that is associated with a command. You can specify up to 16 privilege levels, using the numbers 0 to 15. |
| Reset | (Optional) Resets the privilege level of a command. |
| Command | (Optional) Argument to use when you want to reset the privilege level. |

# Cisco Discovery Protocol (CDP)

CDP is a Cisco proprietary Layer 2 protocol used to gather information about Cisco devices on the same data link. In Figure 6-1, CDP sends advertisements to directly connected devices.

**Figure 6-1   CDP Sends Advertisements Between Directly Connected Devices**

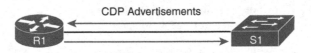

CDP runs on all Cisco-manufactured equipment. It gathers the protocol addresses of neighboring devices and discovers the platform of those devices. CDP runs over the data link layer only. This means that two systems that support different Layer 3 protocols can learn about each other.

CDP provides the following information about each CDP neighbor device:

- **Device identifiers**: The configured hostname of a switch, router, or other device

- **Address list**: Up to one network layer address for each protocol supported

- **Port identifier**: The name of the local and remote port in the form of an ASCII character string, such as FastEthernet 0/0

- **Capabilities list**: For example, whether a specific device is a Layer 2 switch or a Layer 3 switch

- **Platform**: The hardware platform of the device; for example, a Cisco 1841 series router

Refer to the topology in Figure 6-1 and the **show cdp neighbors** command output in Example 6-2.

**Example 6-2   *show cdp neighbors***

```
R3# show cdp neighbors
Capability Codes: R - Router, T - Trans Bridge, B - Source Route Bridge
                  S - Switch, H - Host, I - IGMP, r - Repeater, P - Phone,
                  D - Remote, C - CVTA, M - Two-port Mac Relay
Device ID        Local Intrfce    Holdtme    Capability  Platform   Port ID
S3               Gig 0/0/1        122              S I   WS-C2960+  Fas 0/5
Total cdp entries displayed : 1
R3#
```

**NOTE**   Cisco devices also support Link Layer Discovery Protocol (LLDP), which is a vendor-neutral open standard (IEEE 802.1AB). LLDP works with routers, switches, and wireless LAN access points. As with CDP, LLDP is a neighbor discovery protocol that is used for network devices to advertise information about themselves to other devices on the network.

# Common show Commands

The Cisco IOS CLI **show** commands display relevant information about the configuration and operation of the device. Network technicians use **show** commands extensively for viewing configuration files, checking the status of device interfaces and processes, and verifying the device operational status. The status of nearly every process or function of the router can be displayed using a **show** command.

Commonly used **show** commands and when to use them are listed in Table 6-3.

**Table 6-3  The *show* Commands**

| Command | Purpose |
|---|---|
| show running-config | To verify the current configuration and settings |
| show interfaces | To verify the interface status and see if there are any error messages |
| show ip interface | To verify the Layer 3 information of an interface |
| show arp | To verify the list of known hosts on the local Ethernet LANs |
| show ip route | To verify the Layer 3 routing information |
| show protocols | To verify which protocols are operational |
| show version | To verify the memory, interfaces, and licenses of the device |
| show interface status | To verify summary information for all the ports on a switch |
| show mac address-table | To verify the switch's static and dynamic MAC addresses |
| show inventory | To verify the product identification (PID) information for the switch's hardware |

Examples 6-3 through 6-12 display the output from each of these **show** commands.

**Example 6-3  *show running-config***

```
R1# show running-config

(Output omitted)

!
version 15.5
service timestamps debug datetime msec
service timestamps log datetime msec
service password-encryption
!
hostname R1
!
interface GigabitEthernet0/0/0
 description Link to R2
 ip address 209.165.200.225 255.255.255.252
 negotiation auto
!
```

```
interface GigabitEthernet0/0/1
 description Link to LAN
 ip address 192.168.10.1 255.255.255.0
 negotiation auto
!
router ospf 10
 network 192.168.10.0 0.0.0.255 area 0
 network 209.165.200.224 0.0.0.3 area 0
!
banner motd ^C Authorized access only! ^C
!
line con 0
 password 7 14141B180F0B
 login
line vty 0 4
 password 7 00071A150754
 login
 transport input telnet ssh
!
end
R1#
```

**Example 6-4**  *show interfaces*

```
R1# show interfaces
GigabitEthernet0/0/0 is up, line protocol is up
  Hardware is ISR4321-2x1GE, address is a0e0.af0d.e140 (bia a0e0.af0d.e140)
  Description: Link to R2
  Internet address is 209.165.200.225/30
  MTU 1500 bytes, BW 100000 Kbit/sec, DLY 100 usec,
     reliability 255/255, txload 1/255, rxload 1/255
  Encapsulation ARPA, loopback not set
  Keepalive not supported
  Full Duplex, 100Mbps, link type is auto, media type is RJ45
  output flow-control is off, input flow-control is off
  ARP type: ARPA, ARP Timeout 04:00:00
  Last input 00:00:01, output 00:00:21, output hang never
  Last clearing of "show interface" counters never
  Input queue: 0/375/0/0 (size/max/drops/flushes); Total output drops: 0
  Queueing strategy: fifo
  Output queue: 0/40 (size/max)
  5 minute input rate 0 bits/sec, 0 packets/sec
  5 minute output rate 0 bits/sec, 0 packets/sec
     5127 packets input, 590285 bytes, 0 no buffer
     Received 29 broadcasts (0 IP multicasts)
```

```
          0 runts, 0 giants, 0 throttles
          0 input errors, 0 CRC, 0 frame, 0 overrun, 0 ignored
          0 watchdog, 5043 multicast, 0 pause input
          1150 packets output, 153999 bytes, 0 underruns
          0 output errors, 0 collisions, 2 interface resets
          0 unknown protocol drops
          0 babbles, 0 late collision, 0 deferred
          1 lost carrier, 0 no carrier, 0 pause output
          0 output buffer failures, 0 output buffers swapped out
```

**Example 6-5  *show ip interface***

```
R1# show ip interface
GigabitEthernet0/0/0 is up, line protocol is up
   Internet address is 209.165.200.225/30
   Broadcast address is 255.255.255.255
   Address determined by setup command
   MTU is 1500 bytes
   Helper address is not set
   Directed broadcast forwarding is disabled
   Multicast reserved groups joined: 224.0.0.5 224.0.0.6
   Outgoing Common access list is not set
   Outgoing access list is not set
   Inbound Common access list is not set
   Inbound  access list is not set
   Proxy ARP is enabled
   Local Proxy ARP is disabled
   Security level is default
   Split horizon is enabled
   ICMP redirects are always sent
   ICMP unreachables are always sent
   ICMP mask replies are never sent
   IP fast switching is enabled
   IP Flow switching is disabled
   IP CEF switching is enabled
   IP CEF switching turbo vector
   IP Null turbo vector
   Associated unicast routing topologies:
         Topology "base", operation state is UP
   IP multicast fast switching is enabled
   IP multicast distributed fast switching is disabled
   IP route-cache flags are Fast, CEF
   Router Discovery is disabled
   IP output packet accounting is disabled
   IP access violation accounting is disabled
   TCP/IP header compression is disabled
   RTP/IP header compression is disabled
```

```
    Probe proxy name replies are disabled
    Policy routing is disabled
    Network address translation is disabled
    BGP Policy Mapping is disabled
    Input features: MCI Check
    IPv4 WCCP Redirect outbound is disabled
    IPv4 WCCP Redirect inbound is disabled
    IPv4 WCCP Redirect exclude is disabled

(Output omitted)
```

**Example 6-6** *show arp*

```
R1# show arp
Protocol  Address              Age (min)   Hardware Addr   Type   Interface
Internet  192.168.10.1              -      a0e0.af0d.e141  ARPA   GigabitEthernet0/0/1
Internet  192.168.10.10            95      c07b.bcc4.a9c0  ARPA   GigabitEthernet0/0/1
Internet  209.165.200.225           -      a0e0.af0d.e140  ARPA   GigabitEthernet0/0/0
Internet  209.165.200.226         138      a03d.6fe1.9d90  ARPA   GigabitEthernet0/0/0
R1#
```

**Example 6-7** *show ip route*

```
R1# show ip route
Codes: L - local, C - connected, S - static, R - RIP, M - mobile, B - BGP
       D - EIGRP, EX - EIGRP external, O - OSPF, IA - OSPF inter area
       N1 - OSPF NSSA external type 1, N2 - OSPF NSSA external type 2
       E1 - OSPF external type 1, E2 - OSPF external type 2
       i - IS-IS, su - IS-IS summary, L1 - IS-IS level-1, L2 - IS-IS level-2
       ia - IS-IS inter area, * - candidate default, U - per-user static route
       o - ODR, P - periodic downloaded static route, H - NHRP, l - LISP
       a - application route
       + - replicated route, % - next hop override, p - overrides from PfR
Gateway of last resort is 209.165.200.226 to network 0.0.0.0
O*E2  0.0.0.0/0 [110/1] via 209.165.200.226, 02:19:50, GigabitEthernet0/0/0
      10.0.0.0/24 is subnetted, 1 subnets
O        10.1.1.0 [110/3] via 209.165.200.226, 02:05:42, GigabitEthernet0/0/0
      192.168.10.0/24 is variably subnetted, 2 subnets, 2 masks
C        192.168.10.0/24 is directly connected, GigabitEthernet0/0/1
L        192.168.10.1/32 is directly connected, GigabitEthernet0/0/1
      209.165.200.0/24 is variably subnetted, 3 subnets, 2 masks
C        209.165.200.224/30 is directly connected, GigabitEthernet0/0/0
L        209.165.200.225/32 is directly connected, GigabitEthernet0/0/0
O        209.165.200.228/30 [110/2] via 209.165.200.226, 02:07:19,
   GigabitEthernet0/0/0
R1#
```

**Example 6-8** *show protocols*

```
R1# show protocols
Global values:
  Internet Protocol routing is enabled
GigabitEthernet0/0/0 is up, line protocol is up
  Internet address is 209.165.200.225/30
GigabitEthernet0/0/1 is up, line protocol is up
  Internet address is 192.168.10.1/24
Serial0/1/0 is down, line protocol is down
Serial0/1/1 is down, line protocol is down
GigabitEthernet0 is administratively down, line protocol is down
R1#
```

**Example 6-9** *show version*

```
R1# show version
Cisco IOS XE Software, Version 03.16.08.S - Extended Support Release
Cisco IOS Software, ISR Software (X86_64_LINUX_IOSD-UNIVERSALK9-M), Version
  15.5(3)S8, RELEASE SOFTWARE (fc2)
Technical Support: http://www.cisco.com/techsupport
Copyright (c) 1986-2018 by Cisco Systems, Inc.
Compiled Wed 08-Aug-18 10:48 by mcpre


(Output omitted)


ROM: IOS-XE ROMMON
R1 uptime is 2 hours, 25 minutes
Uptime for this control processor is 2 hours, 27 minutes
System returned to ROM by reload
System image file is "bootflash:/isr4300-universalk9.03.16.08.S.155-3.S8-ext.SPA.
  bin"
Last reload reason: LocalSoft


(Output omitted)


Technology Package License Information:
-------------------------------------------------------------------
Technology    Technology-package         Technology-package
              Current     Type           Next reboot
-------------------------------------------------------------------
appxk9        appxk9      RightToUse     appxk9
uck9          None        None           None
securityk9    securityk9  Permanent      securityk9
ipbase        ipbasek9    Permanent      ipbasek9
```

```
cisco ISR4321/K9 (1RU) processor with 1647778K/6147K bytes of memory.
Processor board ID FLM2044W0LT
2 Gigabit Ethernet interfaces
2 Serial interfaces
32768K bytes of non-volatile configuration memory.
4194304K bytes of physical memory.
3207167K bytes of flash memory at bootflash:.
978928K bytes of USB flash at usb0:.
Configuration register is 0x2102
R1#
```

**Example 6-10**  *show interface status*

```
S1# show interface status

Port        Name        Status       Vlan     Duplex  Speed Type
Gi1/0/1                 connected    1        a-full  a-1000 10/100/1000BaseTX
Gi1/0/2                 connected    1        a-full  a-1000 10/100/1000BaseTX
Gi1/0/3                 connected    1        a-full  a-1000 10/100/1000BaseTX
Gi1/0/4                 notconnect   1          auto    auto 10/100/1000BaseTX
Gi1/0/5                 notconnect   1          auto    auto 10/100/1000BaseTX
Gi1/0/6                 notconnect   1          auto    auto 10/100/1000BaseTX
Gi1/0/7                 notconnect   1          auto    auto 10/100/1000BaseTX
Gi1/0/8                 notconnect   1          auto    auto 10/100/1000BaseTX
Gi1/0/9                 notconnect   1          auto    auto 10/100/1000BaseTX
Gi1/0/10                notconnect   1          auto    auto 10/100/1000BaseTX
Gi1/0/11                notconnect   1          auto    auto 10/100/1000BaseTX
Gi1/0/12                notconnect   1          auto    auto 10/100/1000BaseTX
Gi1/0/13                notconnect   1          auto    auto 10/100/1000BaseTX
Gi1/0/14                notconnect   1          auto    auto 10/100/1000BaseTX
Gi1/0/15                notconnect   1          auto    auto 10/100/1000BaseTX
Gi1/0/16                notconnect   1          auto    auto 10/100/1000BaseTX
Gi1/0/17                notconnect   1          auto    auto 10/100/1000BaseTX
Gi1/0/18                notconnect   1          auto    auto 10/100/1000BaseTX
Gi1/0/19                notconnect   1          auto    auto 10/100/1000BaseTX
Gi1/0/20                notconnect   1          auto    auto 10/100/1000BaseTX
Gi1/0/21                notconnect   1          auto    auto 10/100/1000BaseTX
Gi1/0/22                notconnect   1          auto    auto 10/100/1000BaseTX
Gi1/0/23                notconnect   1          auto    auto 10/100/1000BaseTX
Gi1/0/24                notconnect   1          auto    auto 10/100/1000BaseTX
S1#
```

**Example 6-11**  *show mac address-table*

```
Switch# show mac address-table
          Mac Address Table
-------------------------------------------

Vlan    Mac Address      Type        Ports
----    -----------      --------    -----
All     0100.0ccc.cccc   STATIC      CPU
All     0100.0ccc.cccd   STATIC      CPU
All     0180.c200.0000   STATIC      CPU
All     0180.c200.0001   STATIC      CPU
All     0180.c200.0002   STATIC      CPU
All     0180.c200.0003   STATIC      CPU
All     0180.c200.0004   STATIC      CPU
All     0180.c200.0005   STATIC      CPU
All     0180.c200.0006   STATIC      CPU
All     0180.c200.0007   STATIC      CPU
All     0180.c200.0008   STATIC      CPU
All     0180.c200.0009   STATIC      CPU
All     0180.c200.000a   STATIC      CPU
All     0180.c200.000b   STATIC      CPU
All     0180.c200.000c   STATIC      CPU
All     0180.c200.000d   STATIC      CPU
All     0180.c200.000e   STATIC      CPU
All     0180.c200.000f   STATIC      CPU
All     0180.c200.0010   STATIC      CPU
All     0180.c200.0021   STATIC      CPU
All     ffff.ffff.ffff   STATIC      CPU
   1    188b.45eb.cc01   DYNAMIC     Gi1/0/1
Total Mac Addresses for this criterion: 22
S1#
```

**Example 6-12**  *show inventory*

```
S1# show inventory
NAME: "1", DESCR: "WS-C2960+24TC-L"
PID: WS-C2960+24TC-L   , VID: V01   , SN: FCQ1736X33Q

NAME: "GigabitEthernet0/1", DESCR: "100BaseBX-10D SFP"
PID:                   , VID:       , SN: NEC09050251

NAME: "GigabitEthernet0/2", DESCR: "100BaseBX-10U SFP"
PID:                   , VID:       , SN: NEC09050020
S1#
```

## The show ip interface brief Command

One of the most frequently used commands is the **show ip interface brief**. This command provides a more abbreviated output than the **show ip interface** command and provides a quick summary of the key information for all the network interfaces on a router.

For example, the **show ip interface brief** output shown in Example 6-13 displays all interfaces on the router, the IP address assigned to each interface, if any, and the operational status of the interface.

**Example 6-13   The *show ip interface brief* Command on a Router**

```
R1# show ip interface brief
Interface              IP-Address       OK? Method Status                Protocol
GigabitEthernet0/0/0   209.165.200.225  YES manual up                    up
GigabitEthernet0/0/1   192.168.10.1     YES manual up                    up
Serial0/1/0            unassigned       NO  unset  down                  down
Serial0/1/1            unassigned       NO  unset  down                  down
GigabitEthernet0       unassigned       YES unset  administratively down down
R1#
```

The **show ip interface brief** command can also be used to verify the status of the switch interfaces, as shown in Example 6-14.

**Example 6-14   The *show ip interface brief* Command on a Switch**

```
S1# show ip interface brief
Interface              IP-Address       OK? Method Status                Protocol
Vlan1                  192.168.254.250  YES manual up                    up
FastEthernet0/1        unassigned       YES unset  down                  down
FastEthernet0/2        unassigned       YES unset  up                    up
FastEthernet0/3        unassigned       YES unset  up                    up
(output omitted)
S1#
```

# Study Resources

For today's exam topics, refer to the following resources for more study:

| Resource | Module or Chapter |
|---|---|
| SFA Self Enroll: Networking Devices and Initial Configuration | 10 |
| SFA Instructor Led: Networking Essentials | 27 |
| CCST Networking 100–150 Official Cert Guide | 23 |

**NOTE**   SFA: https://skillsforall.com/

# Day 5

# Firewalls

## CCST Networking 100-150 Exam Topic

- 6.1. Describe how firewalls operate to filter traffic.
  - *Firewalls (blocked ports and protocols); rules deny or permit access*

## Key Topics

Firewalls are a crucial aspect of network security, acting as gatekeepers between networks or between a network and the Internet. They enforce security rules and policies, determining which traffic is allowed or denied. Today, we review the operation of firewalls, focusing on different types, their functionalities, and some examples in Cisco and Linux environments.

## Firewall Devices

Firewalls monitor and control incoming and outgoing network traffic based on predetermined security rules. They can block specific ports and protocols, thereby preventing unauthorized access. For example, a firewall might block TCP port 80 to prevent HTTP traffic or UDP port 53 to restrict DNS queries from external sources. Rules can also be based on IP addresses. For instance, a rule might allow all traffic from a specific IP range. Let's review four common types of firewall devices.

### Stateless Firewalls

Stateless firewalls filter traffic based on individual packet characteristics without considering the overall context of the network connection. Also called packet filtering firewalls, they inspect each packet in isolation, disregarding any connection history. These firewalls are typically part of a router firewall, which permits or denies traffic based on Layer 3 and Layer 4 information, as shown in Figure 5-1. They are suitable for environments where speed is more critical than intricate security checks.

**Figure 5-1  Stateless Firewalls and the OSI Model**

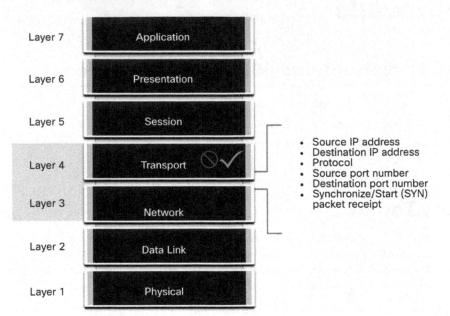

Advantages of stateless firewalls include the following:

- Stateless firewalls implement straightforward permit or deny rule sets, making them simple to use.

- They have minimal impact on network performance due to their basic operation.

- They are easy to implement and are widely supported by most routers.

- They provide a basic level of security at the network layer.

- They perform many functions of advanced firewalls but at a significantly lower cost.

Disadvantages of stateless firewalls include the following:

- They are susceptible to IP spoofing, allowing threat actors to bypass the filters if packets meet ACL criteria.

- They are ineffective in reliably filtering fragmented packets, potentially allowing some fragments to pass through unchecked.

- They rely on complex ACLs that can be challenging to implement and maintain effectively.

- They are unable to dynamically filter services that use dynamic port negotiations, requiring open access to a range of ports.

- Their stateless nature means they examine each packet in isolation, without considering the state of the connection, leading to potential security gaps.

## Stateful Firewalls

Stateful firewalls remember the state of active connections. This is essential for preventing unauthorized access while allowing legitimate responses. Stateful firewalls provide stateful packet filtering by using connection information maintained in a state table. For instance, if an internal user initiates a web session, the firewall records the session in its table and allows return traffic to the originating source. Stateful filtering is a firewall architecture that is classified at the network layer.

Advantages of stateful firewalls include the following:

- They serve as a primary defense mechanism by filtering unwanted or harmful traffic.

- They provide more stringent control over security compared to packet filters or proxy servers.

- They offer improved performance over packet filters or proxy servers.

- They defend against spoofing and denial of service (DoS) attacks by verifying the legitimacy of packets in the context of existing connections.

- They generate more detailed log information than packet filtering firewalls.

Disadvantages of stateful firewalls include the following:

- They are ineffective against application layer attacks because they do not inspect the actual contents of HTTP connections.

- They have limited support for filtering stateless protocols such as UDP and ICMP, which do not generate connection information for state tables.

- They have difficulty in tracking connections that use dynamic port negotiation, often requiring a range of ports to be opened for certain applications.

- They lack the capability to support user authentication.

## Application Gateway Firewalls

An application gateway firewall (proxy firewall), as shown in Figure 5-2, also functions at the application layer, inspecting the data within the packets. This allows for more granular control, like blocking specific content within web traffic or preventing certain types of database queries. Most of the firewall control and filtering is done in software. When a client needs to access a remote server, it connects to a proxy server. The proxy server connects to the remote server on behalf of the client. Therefore, the server only sees a connection from the proxy server.

## Next-Generation Firewalls

Next-generation firewalls (NGFWs) integrate traditional firewall technology with other security functions, like an intrusion prevention system (IPS) and application awareness. The Cisco Firepower 1000 Series, shown in Figure 5-3, offers advanced threat protection by using continuous analysis and retrospective security. With a connection to Cisco Talos delivering threat intelligence in real time, these NGFWs build in security resilience, allowing you to see and detect more intrusions.

**Figure 5-2   Application Gateway Firewalls and the OSI Model**

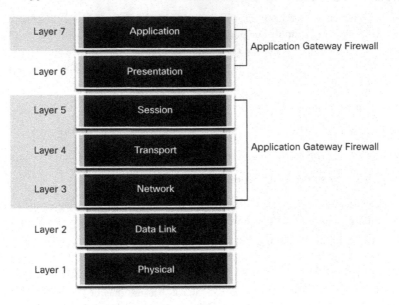

**Figure 5-3   Cisco Firepower 1000 Series**

# Cisco IOS Firewall Configuration Example

Firewall rules in the Cisco IOS can be configured to be as specific as needed. They can be based on source and destination IP addresses, port numbers, protocols, or even time of day. For example, the following three-step process configures a rule to allow SSH access (port 22) only from a network administrator's IP address during working hours:

**Step 1.**   Define the time range.

Assuming working hours are from 8 a.m. to 6 p.m., Monday to Friday, use the following to define the time range:

```
time-range WORK_HOURS
 periodic Monday Tuesday Wednesday Thursday Friday 8:00 to 18:00
```

**Step 2.**   Create an access control list (ACL).

Use the following to create an extended ACL that permits SSH (port 22) from the network administrator's IP address (192.168.1.100) during the defined time range:

```
access-list 101 permit tcp host 192.168.1.100 any eq 22 time-range
WORK_HOURS
access-list 101 deny tcp any any eq 22
access-list 101 permit ip any any
```

This ACL allows SSH from 192.168.1.100 during **WORK_HOURS**, denies SSH at all other times, and permits all other traffic.

**Step 3.**   Apply the ACL to the VTY lines.

Apply this ACL to the VTY lines (virtual terminal lines) to control remote access to the router:

```
line vty 0 15
 access-class 101 in
```

Applying the ACL to the VTY lines ensures that these rules are enforced for remote SSH access to the router.

# Host-Based Firewalls

Host-based personal firewalls are vital tools for protecting individual computers from unauthorized access and potential threats. These firewalls, which are essentially standalone software programs, effectively manage traffic entering and leaving a computer. Some examples of host-based firewalls are provided in the following sections.

## Windows Defender Firewall

Originally introduced in Windows XP and now known as Windows Defender Firewall, this firewall adopts a profile-based approach. It offers three distinct profiles, as shown in Figure 5-4, catering to different network environments:

- The Public profile for highly restrictive access on public networks

- The Private profile for computers shielded by other security devices such as home routers

- The Domain profile for trusted business networks with robust security infrastructures

Windows Defender Firewall is notable for its logging capabilities and the ability to be centrally managed with tools such as System Center 2012 Configuration Manager, allowing for tailored security policies across an organization.

**Figure 5-4   Windows Defender Firewall**

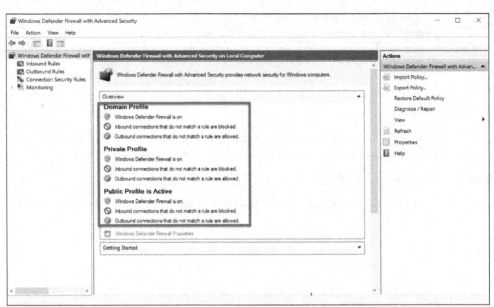

## iptables

In Linux, **iptables** is a common tool used by system administrators. It enables the configuration of network access rules directly within the Linux kernel's Netfilter modules. **iptables** provides granular control over incoming and outgoing network traffic. For example, the following command appends (**-A**) a rule to the **INPUT** chain to allow SSH traffic to the host:

```
iptables -A INPUT -p tcp --dport 22 -j ACCEPT
```

However, it is important to note that although the command itself modifies the current firewall rules in memory, these changes are not persistent across reboots. To make the rules persistent, you need to save them to a configuration file, which can vary based on the Linux distribution. On many systems, you can save the current **iptables** configuration using a command like **iptables-save > /etc/iptables/rules.v4** for IPv4 rules.

## nftables

**nftables** is a modern firewall solution for Linux systems, designed to replace legacy tools like **iptables**, **ip6tables**, **arptables**, and **ebtables**. It provides a more efficient and flexible way to manage network traffic filtering at various protocol layers. It uses a simplified syntax for defining rules, reducing the complexity of managing firewall rules. For example, the same **iptables** rule in **nftables** format is as follows:

```
nft add rule ip filter input tcp dport 22 accept
```

Note how this command is much easier to read and understand. For ease of transition, **nftables** includes a compatibility layer that allows it to interpret **iptables** rulesets.

## TCP Wrappers

TCP Wrappers is a rule-based access control and logging system. Its specialty lies in packet filtering based on IP addresses and network services. For example, the following configuration allows SSH connections from any host in the 192.168.1.* subnet and is written to the **/etc/hosts.allow** file:

```
sshd: 192.168.1.
```

The default policy is to deny all other access, but you can explicitly configure it in the **/etc/hosts. deny** file:

```
sshd: ALL
```

TCP Wrappers is particularly useful for administrators seeking to enhance security with minimal impact on system resources. However, it's important to note that TCP Wrappers should be part of a layered security approach, as it's not designed to replace more comprehensive firewall solutions.

# Study Resources

For today's exam topics, refer to the following resources for more study:

| Resource | Module or Chapter |
| --- | --- |
| SFA Self Enroll: Network Support and Security | 3 |
| SFA Instructor Led: Networking Essentials | 39 |
| CCST Networking 100-150 Official Cert Guide | 20 |

**NOTE**   SFA: https://skillsforall.com/

# Threats, Vulnerabilities, and Attacks

## CCST Networking 100-150 Exam Topic

- 6.2. Describe foundational security concepts.

  - *Confidentiality, integrity, and availability (CIA); authentication, authorization, and accounting (AAA); multifactor authentication (MFA); encryption, certificates, and password complexity; identity stores/databases (Active Directory); threats and vulnerabilities; spam, phishing, malware, and denial of service*

## Key Topics

We will spend the next two days reviewing foundational security concepts. Today, we review how cyber criminals target critical infrastructure and systems using various types of network attacks, including data exfiltration, penetration testing tool misuse, and different forms of malware. Tomorrow, our focus will be on mitigation techniques to reduce security threats.

## Security Fundamentals

Cyber criminals now have the expertise and tools necessary to take down critical infrastructure and systems. Specific terminology is used to describe their tools and attacks.

### Security Terms

Assets must be identified and protected. Vulnerabilities must be addressed before they become a threat and are exploited. Mitigation techniques are required before, during, and after an attack. Review the security terms in Table 4-1.

**Table 4-1  Security Terms**

| Security Terms | Description |
| --- | --- |
| Asset | An asset is anything of value to the organization. It includes people, equipment, resources, and data. |
| Vulnerability | A vulnerability is a weakness in a system, or its design, which could be exploited by a threat. |
| Threat | A threat is a potential danger to a company's assets, data, or network functionality. |
| Exploit | An exploit is a mechanism that takes advantage of a vulnerability. |

| Security Terms | Description |
|---|---|
| Mitigation | Mitigation is the countermeasure that reduces the likelihood or severity of a potential threat or risk. |
| Risk | Risk is the likelihood of a threat to exploit the vulnerability of an asset, with the aim of negatively affecting an organization. |

# Data Exfiltration

An attack vector is a path by which a threat actor can gain access to a server, host, or network. Attack vectors originate from outside or inside the network. For example, threat actors may target a network through the Internet, to disrupt network operations and create a denial of service (DoS) attack. An internal user, such as an employee, can accidentally or intentionally disrupt network operations through a variety of methods. Internal threats have the potential to cause greater damage than external threats because internal users have direct access to the building and its infrastructure devices.

Employees may also have knowledge of the corporate network, its resources, and its confidential data. Data loss or data exfiltration is when data is intentionally or unintentionally lost, stolen, or leaked to the outside world. Network security professionals must protect the organization's data. Various data loss prevention (DLP) controls must be implemented that combine strategic, operational, and tactical measures. Common data loss vectors are shown in Table 4-2.

**Table 4-2   Data Loss Vectors**

| Data Loss Vectors | Description |
|---|---|
| Email/social networking | Intercepted email or IM messages could be captured and reveal confidential information. |
| Unencrypted devices | If the data is not stored using an encryption algorithm, then the thief can retrieve valuable confidential data. |
| Cloud storage devices | Sensitive data can be lost if access to the cloud is compromised due to weak security settings. |
| Removable media | One risk is that an employee could perform an unauthorized transfer of data to a USB drive. Another risk is that a USB drive containing valuable corporate data could be lost. |
| Hard copy | Confidential data should be shredded when no longer required. |
| Improper access control | Passwords or weak passwords that have been compromised can provide a threat actor with easy access to corporate data. |

# Penetration Testing Tools

To validate the security of a network and its systems, many network penetration testing tools have been developed. It is unfortunate that many of these tools, shown in Table 4-3, can be used by threat actors for exploitation.

**Table 4-3  Types of Penetration Tools**

| Tool | Description |
| --- | --- |
| Password crackers | Password cracking tools are often referred to as password recovery tools and can be used to crack or recover a password. Password crackers repeatedly make guesses in order to crack the password. |
| Wireless hacking tools | Wireless hacking tools are used to intentionally hack into a wireless network to detect security vulnerabilities. |
| Network scanning and hacking tools | Network scanning tools are used to probe network devices, servers, and hosts for open TCP or UDP ports. |
| Packet crafting tools | These tools are used to probe and test a firewall's robustness using specially crafted forged packets. |
| Packet sniffers | These tools are used to capture and analyze packets within traditional Ethernet LANs or WLANs. |
| Rootkit detectors | This is a directory and file integrity checker used by white hats to detect installed root kits. |
| Forensic tools | These tools are used by white hat hackers to sniff out any trace of evidence existing in a computer. |
| Debuggers | These tools are used by black hats to reverse engineer binary files when writing exploits. They are also used by white hats when analyzing malware. |
| Hacking operating systems | These are specially designed operating systems preloaded with tools optimized for hacking. |
| Encryption tools | Encryption tools use algorithm schemes to encode the data to prevent unauthorized access to the encrypted data. |
| Vulnerability exploitation tools | These tools identify whether a remote host is vulnerable to a security attack. |
| Vulnerability scanners | These tools scan a network or system to identify open ports. They can also be used to scan for known vulnerabilities and scan virtual machines (VMs), bring your own devices (BYODs), and client databases. |

# Attack Types

Threat actors can use penetration tools, or a combination of the tools, to create attacks. Table 4-4 displays common types of attacks.

**Table 4-4  Common Types of Attacks**

| Attack Type | Description |
| --- | --- |
| Eavesdropping attack | This is when a threat actor captures and "listens" to network traffic. This attack is also referred to as sniffing or snooping. |
| Data modification attack | If threat actors have captured enterprise traffic, they can alter the data in the packet without the knowledge of the sender or receiver. |
| IP address spoofing attack | A threat actor constructs an IP packet that appears to originate from a valid address inside the corporate intranet. |

| Attack Type | Description |
|---|---|
| Password-based attacks | If threat actors discover a valid user account, the threat actors have the same rights as the real user. Threat actors could use that valid account to obtain lists of other users and network information, change server and network configurations, and modify, reroute, or delete data. |
| Denial of service attack | A DoS attack prevents normal use of a computer or network by valid users. A DoS attack can flood a computer or the entire network with traffic until a shutdown occurs because of the overload. A DoS attack can also block traffic, which results in a loss of access to network resources by authorized users. |
| Man-in-the-middle attack (MITM) | This attack occurs when threat actors have positioned themselves between a source and destination. They can now actively monitor, capture, and control the communication transparently. |
| Compromised-key attack | If a threat actor obtains a secret key, that key is referred to as a compromised key. A compromised key can be used to gain access to a secured communication without the sender or receiver being aware of the attack. |
| Sniffer attack | A sniffer is an application or device that can read, monitor, and capture network data exchanges and read network packets. If the packets are not encrypted, a sniffer provides a full view of the data inside the packet. |

## Types of Malware

Malware is short for malicious software. It is code or software specifically designed to damage, disrupt, steal, or inflict "bad" or illegitimate action on data, hosts, or networks. Viruses, worms, and Trojan horses are types of malware:

- A **worm** executes arbitrary code and installs copies of itself in the memory of the infected computer. The main purpose of a worm is to automatically replicate itself and spread across the network from system to system.

- A **virus** is malicious software that executes a specific, unwanted, and often harmful function on a computer.

- A **Trojan horse** is a non-self-replicating type of malware. It often contains malicious code that is designed to look like something else, such as a legitimate application or file. When an infected application or file is downloaded and opened, the Trojan horse can attack the end device from within.

Other types of malware are shown in Table 4-5.

**Table 4-5   Other Types of Malware**

| Malware | Description |
|---|---|
| Adware | - Adware is usually distributed by downloading online software.<br>- Adware can display unsolicited advertising using pop-up web browser windows or new toolbars, or it could unexpectedly redirect a web page to a different website.<br>- Pop-up windows may be difficult to control, as new windows can pop up faster than the user can close them. |

| Malware | Description |
|---------|-------------|
| Ransomware | ■ Ransomware typically denies a user access to their files by encrypting the files and then displaying a message demanding a ransom for the decryption key.<br>■ Users without up-to-date backups must pay the ransom to decrypt their files.<br>■ Payment is usually made using wire transfer or crypto currencies such as Bitcoin. |
| Rootkit | ■ Rootkits are used by threat actors to gain administrator account-level access to a computer.<br>■ They are very difficult to detect because they can alter the firewall, antivirus protection, system files, and even OS commands to conceal their presence.<br>■ They can provide a backdoor to threat actors, giving them access to the PC and allowing them to upload files and install new software to be used in a DDoS attack.<br>■ Special tools must be used to remove rootkits, or a complete OS reinstall may be required. |
| Spyware | ■ Spyware is similar to adware but is used to gather information about the user and send to threat actors without the user's consent.<br>■ Spyware can be a low threat (gathering browsing data), or it can be a high threat (capturing personal and financial information). |

# Network Attacks

Network attacks include reconnaissance attacks, access attacks, DoS attacks, social engineering attacks, and attacks to the vulnerabilities of the TCP/IP protocol suite.

## Reconnaissance Attacks

Reconnaissance is information gathering. Threat actors use reconnaissance (or recon) attacks to do unauthorized discovery and mapping of systems, services, or vulnerabilities. Recon attacks precede access attacks or DoS attacks. Some common reconnaissance attacks are described in Table 4-6.

**Table 4-6  Types of Reconnaissance Attacks**

| Technique | Description |
|-----------|-------------|
| Perform an information query of a target. | The threat actor is looking for initial information about a target. Various tools can be used, including the Google search feature, the organization's website, whois, and more. |
| Initiate a ping sweep of the target network. | The information query usually reveals the target's network address. The threat actor can now initiate a ping sweep to determine which IP addresses are active. |
| Initiate a port scan of active IP addresses. | This is used to determine which ports or services are available. Examples of port scanners include Nmap, SuperScan, Angry IP Scanner, and NetScanTools. |
| Run vulnerability scanners. | This is to query the identified ports to determine the type and version of the application and operating system that is running on the host. Examples of tools include Nipper, Secunia PSI, Core Impact, Nessus v6, SAINT, and OpenVAS. |
| Run exploitation tools. | The threat actor now attempts to discover vulnerable services that can be exploited. A variety of vulnerability exploitation tools exist, including Metasploit, Core Impact, Sqlmap, and Social Engineer Toolkit. |

## Access Attacks

The purpose of these types of attacks is to gain entry to web accounts, confidential databases, and other sensitive information. Threat actors use access attacks on network devices and computers to retrieve data, gain access, or to escalate access privileges to administrator status. Access attacks are described in Table 4-7.

**Table 4-7   Types of Access Attacks**

| Access Attack | Description |
|---|---|
| Password attacks | In a password attack, the threat actor attempts to discover critical system passwords using various methods. Password attacks are very common and can be launched using a variety of password cracking tools. |
| Spoofing attacks | In spoofing attacks, the threat actor device attempts to pose as another device by falsifying data. Common spoofing attacks include IP spoofing, MAC spoofing, and DHCP spoofing. These spoofing attacks will be discussed in more detail later in this module. |
| Trust exploitation attacks | In a trust exploitation attack, a threat actor uses unauthorized privileges to gain access to a system, possibly compromising the target. |
| Port redirection attacks | In a port redirection attack, a threat actor uses a compromised system as a base for attacks against other targets. |
| Man-in-the-middle attacks | In a man-in-the-middle attack, the threat actor is positioned in between two legitimate entities in order to read or modify the data that passes between the two parties. |
| Buffer overflow attacks | In a buffer overflow attack, the threat actor exploits the buffer memory and overwhelms it with unexpected values. This usually renders the system inoperable, creating a DoS attack. |

## Social Engineering Attacks

Social engineering is a type of access attack in which the threat actor attempts to manipulate individuals into performing actions or divulging confidential information. Social engineering techniques are described in Table 4-8.

**Table 4-8   Types of Social Engineering Attacks**

| Social Engineering Attack | Description |
|---|---|
| Pretexting | A threat actor pretends to need personal or financial data to confirm the identity of the recipient. |
| Phishing | A threat actor sends fraudulent email that is disguised as being from a legitimate, trusted source to trick the recipient into installing malware on their device, or to share personal or financial information. |
| Spear phishing | A threat actor creates a targeted phishing attack tailored for a specific individual or organization. |

| Social Engineering Attack | Description |
|---|---|
| Spam | Also known as junk mail, this is unsolicited email that often contains harmful links, malware, or deceptive content. |
| Something for something | Sometimes called "quid pro quo," this is when a threat actor requests personal information from a party in exchange for something such as a gift. |
| Baiting | A threat actor leaves a malware-infected flash drive in a public location. A victim finds the drive and unsuspectingly inserts it into their laptop, unintentionally installing malware. |
| Impersonation | This type of attack is where a threat actor pretends to be someone they are not to gain the trust of a victim. |
| Tailgating | This is where a threat actor quickly follows an authorized person into a secure location to gain access to a secure area. |
| Shoulder surfing | This is where a threat actor inconspicuously looks over someone's shoulder to steal their passwords or other information. |
| Dumpster diving | This is where a threat actor rummages through trash bins to discover confidential documents. |

## DoS and DDoS Attacks

A denial of service (DoS) attack creates some sort of interruption of network services to users, devices, or applications. DoS attacks are created in two ways:

- **Overwhelming quantity of traffic:** The threat actor sends an enormous quantity of data at a rate that the network, host, or application cannot handle. This causes transmission and response times to slow down. It can also crash a device or service.

- **Maliciously formatted packets:** The threat actor sends a maliciously formatted packet to a host or application and the receiver is unable to handle it. This causes the receiving device to run very slowly or crash.

DoS attacks are relatively simple to conduct, even by an unskilled threat actor. A distributed DoS (DDoS) is similar to a DoS attack, but it originates from multiple, coordinated sources. For example, a threat actor builds a network of infected hosts, known as zombies. A network of zombies is called a botnet. The threat actor uses a command and control (CnC) program to instruct the botnet of zombies to carry out a DDoS attack.

## IP Attacks

The Internet Protocol (IP) does not validate whether the source IP address contained in a packet actually came from that source. For this reason, threat actors can send packets using a spoofed source IP address. Threat actors can also tamper with the other fields in the IP header to carry out their attacks. Security analysts must understand the different fields in both the IPv4 and IPv6 headers. Some of the more common IP-related attacks are shown in Table 4-9.

**Table 4-9   Types of IP Attacks**

| IP Attack Techniques | Description |
|---|---|
| ICMP attacks | Threat actors use Internet Control Message Protocol (ICMP) echo packets (pings) to discover subnets and hosts on a protected network, to generate DoS flood attacks, and to alter host routing tables. |
| Amplification and reflection attacks | Threat actors attempt to prevent legitimate users from accessing information or services using DoS and DDoS attacks. One type of amplification and reflection attack is where the threat actor forwards ICMP echo request messages to many hosts. These messages contain the source IP address of the victim. Therefore, these hosts all reply to the spoofed IP address of the victim to overwhelm it. |
| Address spoofing attacks | Threat actors spoof the source IP address in an IP packet to perform blind spoofing or non-blind spoofing. In non-blind spoofing, the threat actor can see the traffic that is being sent between the host and the target. The threat actor uses non-blind spoofing to inspect the reply packet from the target victim. Non-blind spoofing determines the state of a firewall and sequence-number prediction. It can also hijack an authorized session. In blind spoofing, the threat actor cannot see the traffic that is being sent between the host and the target. Blind spoofing is used in DoS attacks. |
| Man-in-the-middle attack | Threat actors position themselves between a source and destination to transparently monitor, capture, and control the communication. They could eavesdrop by inspecting captured packets, or they could alter packets and forward them to their original destination. |
| Session hijacking | Threat actors gain access to the physical network and then use an MITM attack to hijack a session. |

# Transport Layer Attacks

Threat actors conduct port scans of target devices to discover which services are available. A threat actor can exploit TCP and UDP in the following ways:

- **TCP SYN flood attack**: This attack exploits the TCP three-way handshake. The threat actor continually sends TCP SYN session request packets with a randomly spoofed source IP address to a target. The target device replies with a TCP SYN-ACK packet to the spoofed IP address and waits for a TCP ACK packet. Those responses never arrive. Eventually the target host is overwhelmed with half-open TCP connections, and TCP services are denied to legitimate users.

- **TCP reset attack**: A threat actor could do a TCP reset attack and send a spoofed packet containing a TCP RST to one or both endpoints. This creates a DoS for the connection.

- **TCP session hijacking**: A threat actor takes over an already-authenticated host as it communicates with the target. The threat actor must spoof the IP address of one host, predict the next sequence number, and send an ACK to the other host. If successful, the threat actor could send, but not receive, data from the target device.

- **UDP flood attack:** The threat actor uses a tool to send a flood of UDP packets, often from a spoofed host, to a server on the subnet. The program will sweep through all the known ports trying to find closed ports. This will cause the server to reply with an ICMP port unreachable message. Because there are many closed ports on the server, this creates a lot of traffic on the segment, which uses up most of the bandwidth. The result is very similar to a DoS attack.

# Study Resources

For today's exam topics, refer to the following resources for more study:

| Resource | Module or Chapter |
| --- | --- |
| SFA Self Enroll: Network Support and Security | 2, 3 |
| SFA Instructor Led: Networking Essentials | 38, 39 |
| CCST Networking 100-150 Official Cert Guide | 18, 19 |

**NOTE**   SFA: https://skillsforall.com/

# Day 3

# Security Protocols and Practices

## CCST Networking 100-150 Exam Topic

- 6.2. Describe foundational security concepts.

    - *Confidentiality, integrity, and availability (CIA); authentication, authorization, and accounting (AAA); multifactor authentication (MFA); encryption, certificates, and password complexity; identity stores/databases (Active Directory); threats and vulnerabilities; spam, phishing, malware, and denial of service*

# Key Topics

Today, we will review the key aspects of security protocols and practices, focusing on foundational security concepts such as confidentiality, integrity, and availability, as well as other crucial elements like authentication, authorization, accounting (AAA) and various security mechanisms. We also review the role of identity stores such as Active Directory in managing user access and the importance of a robust security program for organizational safety.

# Security Fundamentals

Cyber criminals now have the expertise and tools necessary to take down critical infrastructure and systems. Specific terminology is used to describe their tools and attacks.

## The Cybersecurity Cube

The cybersecurity cube, also known as the McCumber cube, is a conceptual model designed to guide policies and procedures for information security within an organization. It provides a comprehensive framework for considering information security from three key dimensions: security principles, data states, and safeguards.

## Security Principles

The first dimension of the cybersecurity cube, shown in Figure 3-1, focuses on the foundational security principles of the confidentiality, integrity, and availability (CIA) of data:

- **Confidentiality** ensures that information is accessible only to those authorized to have access.

- **Integrity** ensures that data cannot be tampered with or altered by unauthorized people.

- **Availability** ensures that authorized users have access to information and associated assets when needed.

**Figure 3-1   Security Principles Dimension of the Cybersecurity Cube**

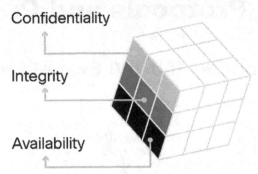

Confidentiality

Integrity

Availability

## Data States

The second dimension of the cybersecurity cube, shown in Figure 3-2, represents the three possible data states:

- **Processing:** This is data in process and pertains to information in the process of being used or manipulated.

- **Storage:** This is data at rest. Information is in a static state, stored in some form of physical or digital medium.

- **Transmission:** This is data in motion and involves information being transmitted or communicated across some distance.

**Figure 3-2   Data States Dimension of the Cybersecurity Cube**

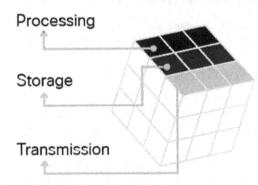

Processing

Storage

Transmission

## Safeguards

The third dimension of the cybersecurity cube, shown in Figure 3-3, defines three safeguards our cybersecurity defenses need in order to protect data and infrastructure:

- **Technology:** This includes firewalls, encryption, intrusion detection systems, and other hardware or software solutions.

- **Policy and practices:** This includes policies such as acceptable use policies, access control policies, and security protocols.

- **People**: This involves training, awareness programs, and the management of human resources to ensure that individuals understand and follow security policies.

**Figure 3-3    Safeguards Dimension of the Cybersecurity Cube**

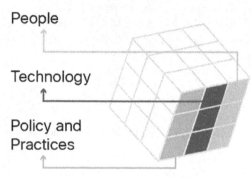

## The CIA Triad

The CIA Triad, shown in Figure 3-4, is a widely accepted model for framing information security policies. Confidentiality, integrity, and availability each represent a fundamental objective of security best practices.

**Figure 3-4    The CIA Triad Circle**

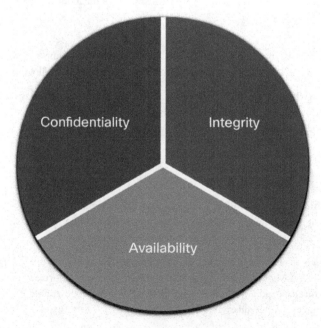

# Confidentiality

Confidentiality refers to the protection of information so that it is not disclosed to unauthorized individuals, entities, or processes. Techniques used to ensure confidentiality include the following:

- **Encryption**: Utilizes algorithms to convert data into a format unreadable to unauthorized users. Common encryption tools include AES (Advanced Encryption Standard) and RSA (Rivest-Shamir-Adleman). For example, the following SQL statement creates and encrypts a table with the key **my_key** and uses an AES algorithm.

  ```
  CREATE TABLE encrypted_table (...) ENCRYPTED WITH (COLUMN_ENCRYPTION_KEY = my_key,
  ALGORITHM = 'AEAD_AES_256_CBC_HMAC_SHA_256');
  ```

  The ellipsis (...) would be replaced with the definitions of columns that you want in the table, such as their names and data types.

- **Access control**: Involves setting permissions and privileges to restrict data access to authorized users only, such as implementing role-based access control (RBAC) in a network environment. RBAC is a method of restricting access to certain commands and features based on the user's role.

- **Secure communication protocols**: SSL (Secure Sockets Layer) and TLS (Transport Layer Security) are fundamental for ensuring the confidentiality and integrity of data transmitted over the Internet. These protocols encrypt data sent between a client (like a web browser) and a server (such as a website), safeguarding it from eavesdropping, tampering, or message forgery.

# Integrity

Integrity ensures information is accurate and reliable and has not been tampered with or altered by unauthorized individuals. Techniques used to ensure integrity include the following:

- **Hashing algorithms**: Like SHA-256, these are used to create a unique hash value for data. Any modification in the data changes this hash, thereby detecting alterations. Hashes are commonly used to verify file integrity. For example, the following Linux command would create a hash for **myfile.txt**:

  ```
  sha256sum myfile.txt
  ```

- **Digital certificates**: These provide assurance about the origin and authenticity of digital data. For example, signing software with a digital certificate ensures that the software comes from a trusted source and has not been tampered with since it was signed.

- **Audit trails**: These are used to keep track of who accessed or modified information. For example, consider a MySQL database to store sensitive customer information. To monitor who accesses this data and any changes made, you would enable logging for connection and modification queries and regularly review the logs.

## Availability

Availability ensures that information and resources are accessible to authorized users when needed. Techniques used to ensure availability include the following:

- **Redundancy:** This involves creating additional or duplicate systems, data, and connections. For example, you might use RAID (redundant array of independent disks) for data storage redundancy or install backup power supplies.

- **Failover mechanism:** This involves automatic switching to a backup system or network in case of failure. For example, you might configure SQL Server database mirroring for automatic failover or configure routers and switches with mechanisms like Hot Standby Routing Protocol (HSRP) or types of Spanning Tree Protocol (STP).

- **Regular maintenance:** This includes updating and patching systems to prevent failures. It is a best practice to schedule regular updates and backups for critical systems.

# Access Control

An essential goal of network security is controlling access to the network.

## Types of Access Control

Access control can be broadly categorized into three types: physical access control, logical access control, and administrative access control.

## Physical Access Control

Physical access control is designed to prevent unauthorized physical entry into a facility or area. It ensures that only authorized personnel can access physical resources such as buildings, rooms, and data centers. This can include locks, security guards, biometric systems (such as fingerprint or retina scanners), key cards, and barriers like turnstiles and gates. It also encompasses surveillance systems such as CCTV cameras.

## Logical Access Control

Logical access control, also known as digital access control, manages access to computer networks, system files, and data. It is about ensuring that only authorized users can access and manipulate digital resources. This involves the use of usernames, passwords, access control lists (ACLs), encryption, digital certificates, and multifactor authentication. Firewalls and intrusion detection systems also play a role in logical access control.

## Administrative Access Control

Administrative access control refers to the policies and procedures that dictate how physical and logical access controls are implemented and managed. It's about the governance of access control. This includes the development of policies, guidelines, and procedures for access control, such as defining user roles and responsibilities, establishing protocols for granting and revoking access, and conducting regular security audits. Administrative access control is essential for ensuring that the physical and logical access controls are effective and comply with regulatory standards.

# Authentication, Authorization, and Accounting (AAA)

AAA is a framework used in computing to control access to computer resources, enforce policies, audit usage, and provide the information necessary to bill for services.

## Authentication

Authentication is the process of verifying the identity of a user or device. Common methods used for authentication include the following:

- **Passwords:** The most common form of authentication. It's a secret known only to the user and the system.

- **Smart cards:** A physical token used in conjunction with a PIN. The card carries user credentials.

- **Biometrics:** Involves identifying a user based on unique physical characteristics, such as fingerprints, facial recognition, or iris scans.

- **Multifactor authentication (MFA):** Combines two or more different authentication methods, often something you know (a password) and something you have (a mobile device or token) or something you are (fingerprint).

## Authorization

After a user is authenticated, authorization is the process of determining if they have the right to access a resource or perform a certain action. Common methods used for authorization include the following:

- **RBACs:** Users are assigned roles, and each role is granted specific access rights.

- **File permissions in Linux:** In a Linux system, each file and directory have permissions that control whether users can read (**r**), write (**w**), or execute (**x**) them.

- **ACLs:** Used in network devices to manage network traffic access rights.

## Accounting

Accounting is the process of tracking user activities and system resource usage. It's important for auditing, billing, and resource management. Common methods used for accounting include the following:

- **Log files:** Systems and applications maintain log files that record user activities.

- **Network device logs:** Routers and switches can log accounting data such as session duration and volume of data transferred.

- **Billing systems:** In ISPs or cloud services, accounting data is used for billing purposes.

# Identity Stores

Identity stores, or identity management systems, are used to manage user identities and control their access to resources. Active Directory (AD) from Microsoft is one of the most widely used identity stores, especially in Windows-based environments.

AD is a directory service included in most Windows Server operating systems. AD provides a centralized location for network administration and security. It stores information about objects on the network and makes this information easy for administrators and users to find and use.

## AD Functions

Core functions of AD include the following:

- **Directory services**: These services store data as objects. An object is a single element, such as a user, group, application, or device, such as a printer.

- **Centralized resource and security administration**: Allows network administrators to assign policies, deploy and update software, and apply critical updates to an entire organization.

- **Authentication and authorization**: These functions handle access to resources within a network. Users' login credentials are checked against the information stored in AD.

## AD Key Components

Key components of AD include the following:

- **Domains**: A domain is a group of objects, such as users, groups, and devices, which share the same AD database.

- **Trees and forests**: A tree is a collection of one or more domains and domain trees in a contiguous namespace, linked in a transitive trust hierarchy. At the top is the forest, a collection of trees sharing a common global catalog, directory schema, logical structure, and directory configuration.

- **Organizational units (OUs)**: OUs are containers used to organize objects within domains. OUs can contain other OUs, accounts, groups, and resources, and they can be used to apply and enforce policies.

# Security Program

An organization should educate its user community through a security program. An effective security program should have the following basic elements:

- **User awareness**: All users should be made aware of the need for data confidentiality to protect corporate information, as well as their own credentials and personal information. They should also be made aware of potential threats, schemes to mislead, and proper procedures to report security incidents. Users should also be instructed to follow strict guidelines regarding data loss.

- **User training**: All users should be required to participate in periodic formal training so that they become familiar with all corporate security policies.

- **Physical access control**: Infrastructure locations, such as network closets and data centers, should remain securely locked. Administrators should control physical access and quickly remove access when an employee is dismissed.

# Study Resources

For today's exam topics, refer to the following resources for more study:

| Resource | Module or Chapter |
|---|---|
| SFA Self Enroll: Network Support and Security | 2, 3 |
| SFA Instructor Led: Networking Essentials | 38, 39 |
| CCST Networking 100–150 Official Cert Guide | 18, 19 |

**NOTE**   SFA: https://skillsforall.com/

# Secure Wireless Access

## CCST Networking 100-150 Exam Topic

- 6.3. Configure basic wireless security on a home router (WPAx).

  - WPA, WPA2, WPA3; choosing between Personal and Enterprise; wireless security concepts

## Key Topics

A wireless local area network (WLAN) is open to anyone within range of a wireless access point (AP) and the appropriate credentials to associate to it. Today, we review the methods for securing wireless access.

## Wireless Attacks and Security

Attacks on wireless networks can originate from a variety of sources, including outsiders and disgruntled employees, or they can even occur accidentally. These networks face several specific threats, including the following:

- Data interception

- Unauthorized users trying to access network resources

- Denial of service (DoS) attacks

- Rogue access points (APs)

To defend against these attacks, you should implement a variety of security measures including SSID cloaking, MAC address filtering, and strong authentication.

### DoS Attacks

DoS attacks can arise from various causes, including the following:

- Improperly configured devices, where either an administrator might accidentally change settings and disable the network or an intruder with administrative access could intentionally do so

- Malicious users who aim to disrupt the wireless communication entirely, preventing any legitimate device from accessing the network

- Accidental interference from devices such as microwave ovens, cordless phones, and baby monitors on the 2.4-GHz band

To minimize the risk of DoS attacks, harden all devices, maintain secure passwords, create backups, and implement configuration changes during off-hours. To address accidental interference, the quickest solution is to switch to the 5-GHz band.

## Rogue Access Points

A rogue AP is an unauthorized wireless router or AP connected to a corporate network, potentially enabling access to secure resources. These can be installed either maliciously or inadvertently. Rogue APs pose serious security risks, including data interception and network attacks. Personal network hotspots can also act as rogue APs, bypassing security protocols. To mitigate these risks, organizations should configure wireless LAN controllers (WLCs) with specific rogue AP policies, such as the policy configuration shown in Figure 2-1, and use monitoring software to detect unauthorized APs.

**Figure 2-1   Configuring Rogue Policies on a Cisco WLC**

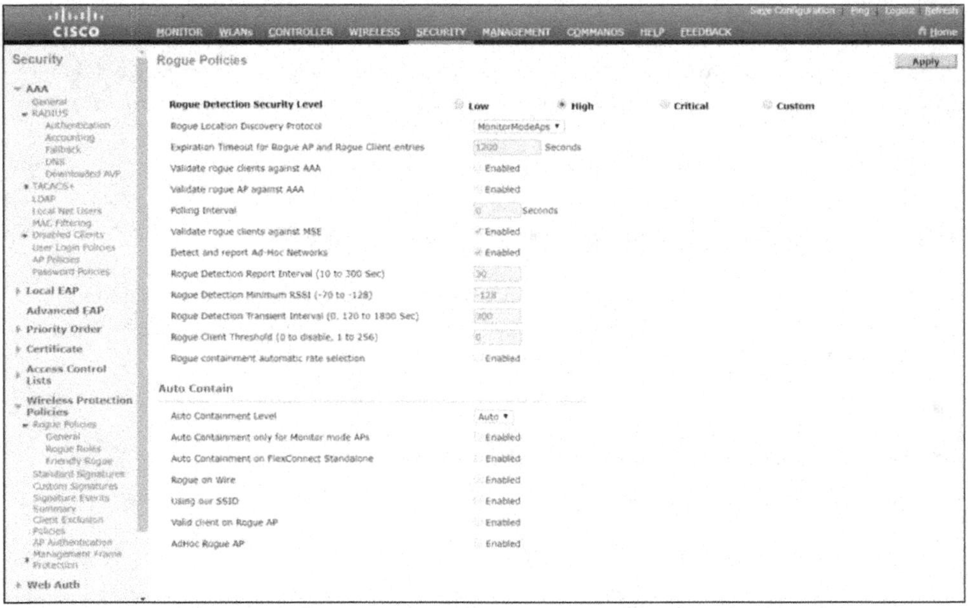

## Man-in-the-Middle Attack

In a man-in-the-middle (MITM) attack, the hacker is positioned in between two legitimate entities in order to read or modify the data that passes between the two parties. A popular wireless MITM attack is called the "evil twin AP" attack, where an attacker introduces a rogue AP and configures it with the same SSID as a legitimate AP, as shown in Figure 2-2.

**Figure 2-2    Example of a MITM Attack**

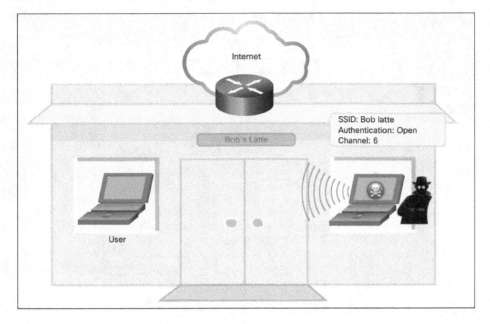

## SSID Cloaking

APs and some wireless routers allow the SSID beacon frame to be disabled, as shown in Figure 2-3. Wireless clients must manually configure the SSID to connect to the network.

**Figure 2-3    Example of Disabled SSID Broadcast**

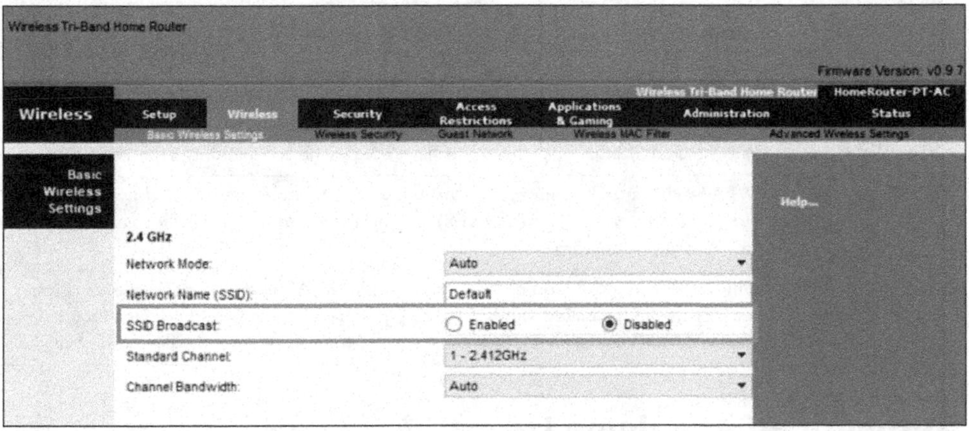

## MAC Addresses Filtering

An administrator can manually permit or deny clients wireless access based on their physical MAC hardware address. In Figure 2-4, the router is configured to permit two MAC addresses. Devices with different MAC addresses will not be able to join the 2.4-GHz WLAN.

**Figure 2-4   Example of Filtering MAC Addresses**

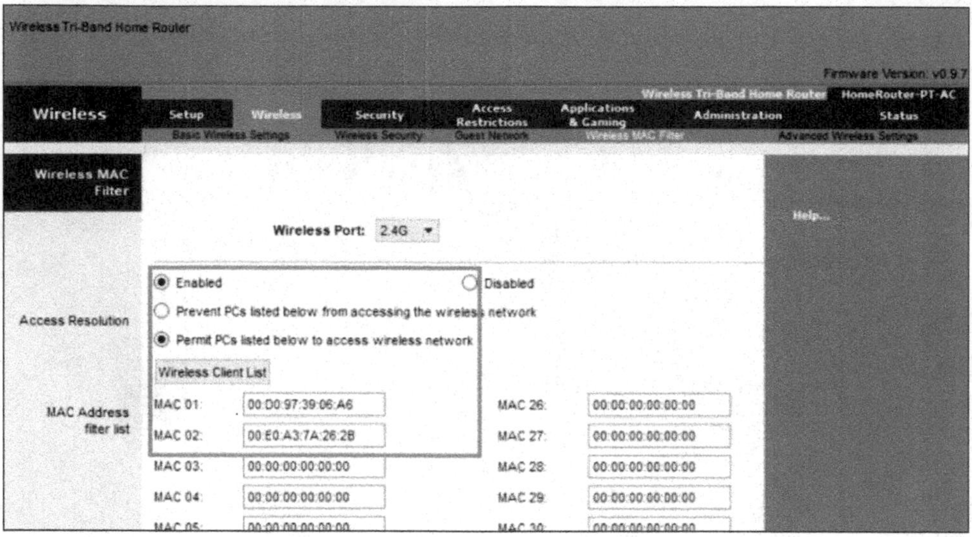

## Shared Key Authentication Methods

The best way to secure a wireless network is to use one of the four authentication and encryption methods shown in Table 2-1.

**Table 2-1   802.11 Shared Key Authentication Techniques**

| Authentication Method | Description |
| --- | --- |
| Wired Equivalent Privacy (WEP) | The original 802.11 specification using Rivest Cipher 4 (RC4) encryption method with a static key. WEP is no longer recommended and should never be used. |
| Wi-Fi Protected Access (WPA) | A Wi-Fi Alliance standard that uses WEP but secures the data with the much stronger Temporal Key Integrity Protocol (TKIP) encryption algorithm. TKIP changes the key for each packet, making it much more difficult to hack. WPA is not secure and should only be used in situations where you have a legacy device that only supports WPA. |
| WPA2 | WPA2 is the current industry standard for securing wireless networks. It uses the Advanced Encryption Standard (AES) for encryption. AES is currently considered the strongest encryption protocol. |
| WPA3 | This is the next generation of Wi-Fi security. All WPA3-enabled devices use the latest security methods, disallow outdated legacy protocols, and require the use of Protected Management Frames (PMF). However, devices with WPA3 are not yet readily available. |

## Authenticating a Home User

Until WPA3 becomes more widespread and available, home routers typically have two choices for authentication: WPA and WPA2. WPA2 is the stronger of the two. Figure 2-5 shows the option to select the WPA2 personal authentication method. Enterprise WPA2 is used in an organizational setting where users connect with their credentials.

**Figure 2-5   Example of Configure WPA2 Personal Authentication**

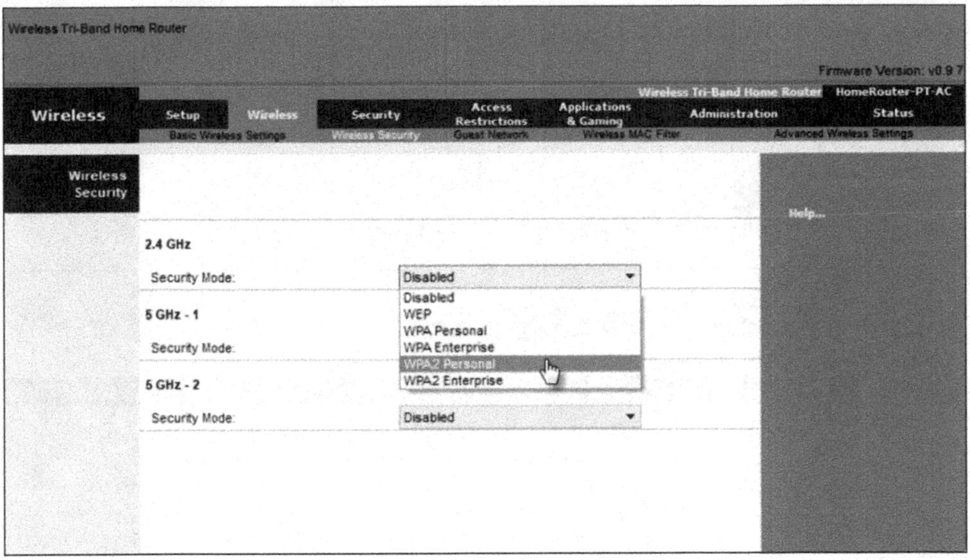

# Encryption Methods

Encryption is used to protect data. The WPA and WPA2 standards can use Temporal Key Integrity Protocol (TKIP) and Advanced Encryption Standard (AES). AES is preferred for its much stronger encryption. In Figure 2-6, the administrator is configuring the wireless router to use WPA2 Personal with AES encryption on the 2.4-GHz band.

**Figure 2-6   Example of Configuring AES Encryption for WPA2**

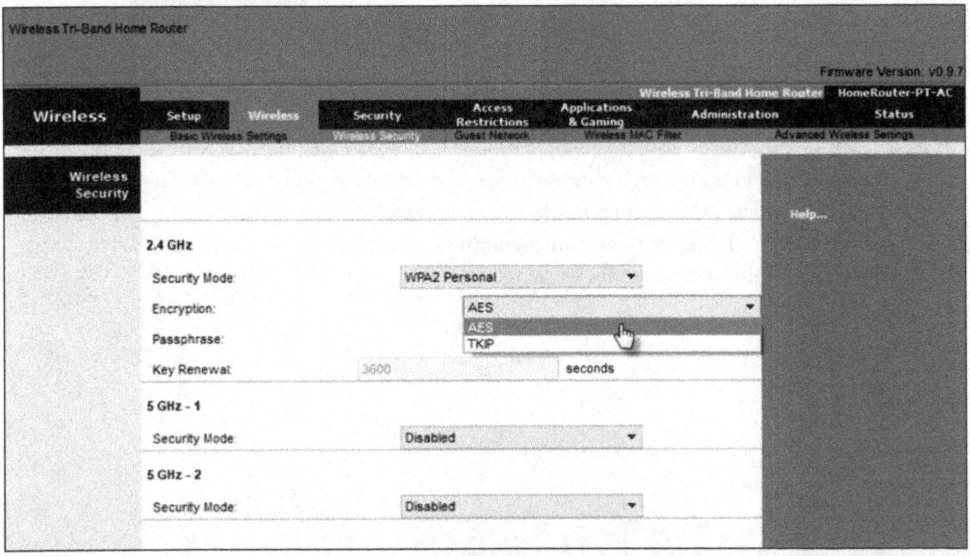

# Home Router Configuration

Remote workers, small branch offices, and home networks often use a small office and home router. Let's review how to configure a basic home router for network connectivity. For this, we will use the wireless home router available in Packet Tracer (see Figure 2-7). If you don't already have Packet Tracer, you can get it at https://skillsforall.com/resources/lab-downloads. You will need to register and log in.

**Figure 2-7   The Wireless Home Router in Packet Tracer**

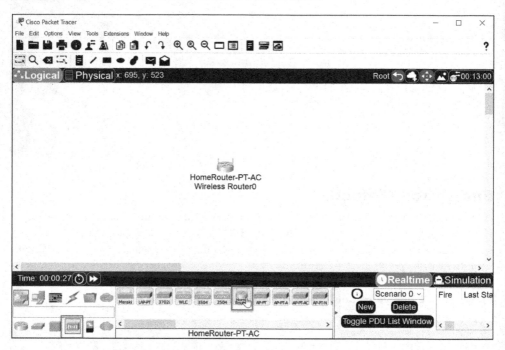

## Log in to the Wireless Router

To gain access to the wireless router's configuration GUI, open a web browser. In the address field, enter the default IP address for your wireless router. Figure 2-8 shows the IPv4 address 192.168.0.1, which is a common default for many manufacturers. A security window prompts for authorization to access the router GUI. The word **admin** is commonly used as the default username and password, but this could be different for other models.

**Figure 2-8    Log in with Default Credentials**

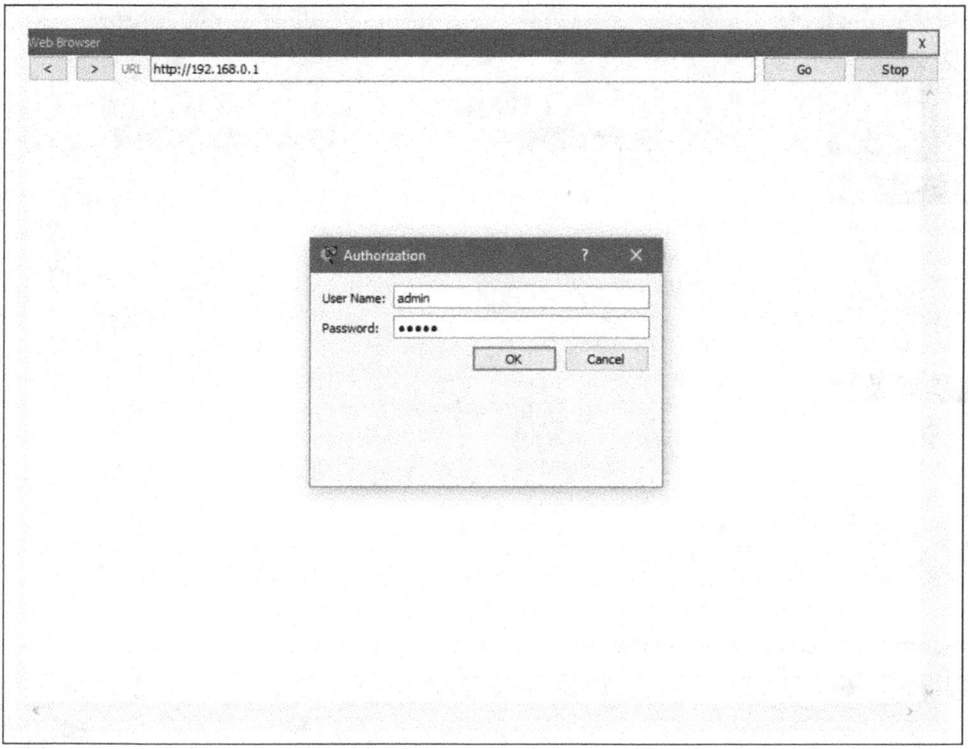

## Basic Network Setup

Basic network setup includes the following steps.

### Step 1: Log in to the router from a web browser.

After you log in, a GUI opens, as shown in Figure 2-9. At this point, it is a best practice to make changes to the default settings.

### Step 2: Change the default administrative password.

To change the default login password, find the administration portion of the router's GUI. On some devices, such as the one in Figure 2-10, you can only change the password.

**Figure 2-9   Basic Network Setup – Step 1**

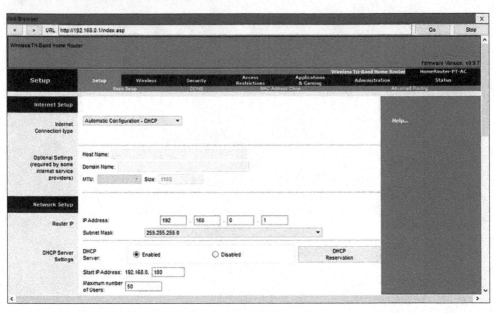

**Figure 2-10   Basic Network Setup – Step 2**

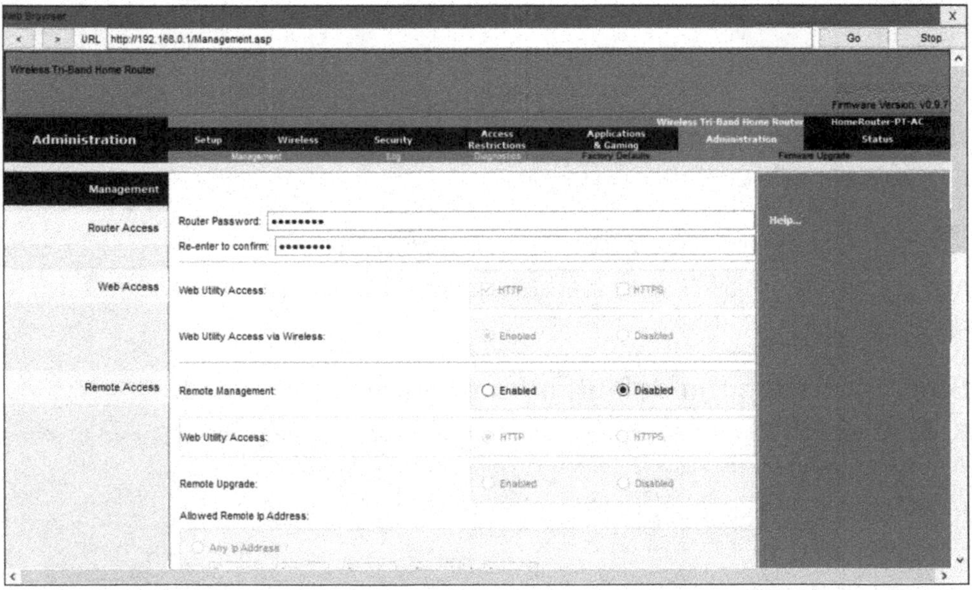

## Step 3: Log in with the new administrative password.

After you save the new password, the wireless router will request authorization again, as shown in Figure 2–11.

**Figure 2-11   Basic Network Setup – Step 3**

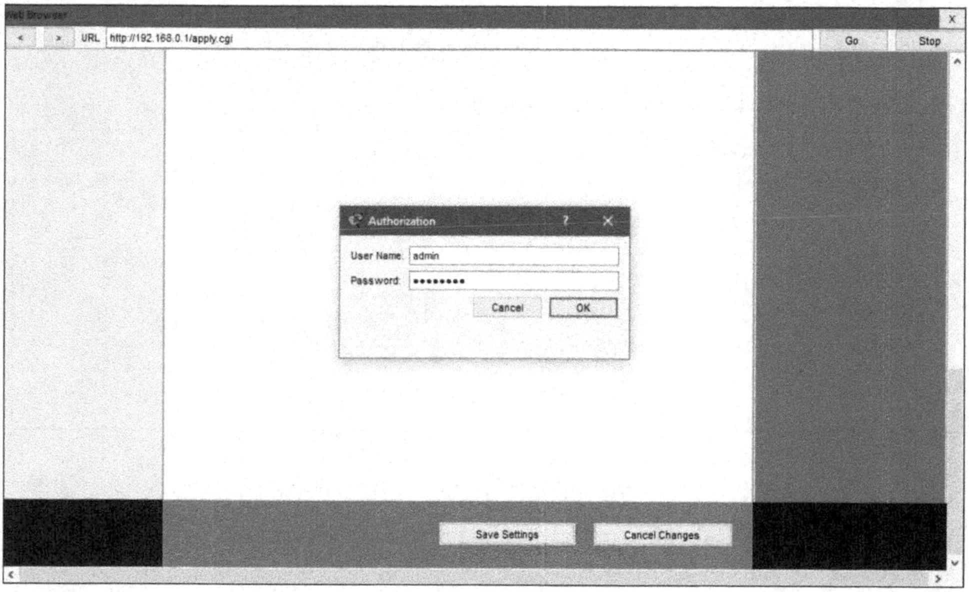

## Step 4: Change the default DHCP IPv4 addresses.

Change the default router IPv4 address. The IPv4 address 10.10.10.1 is used in Figure 2-12.

**Figure 2-12   Basic Network Setup – Step 4**

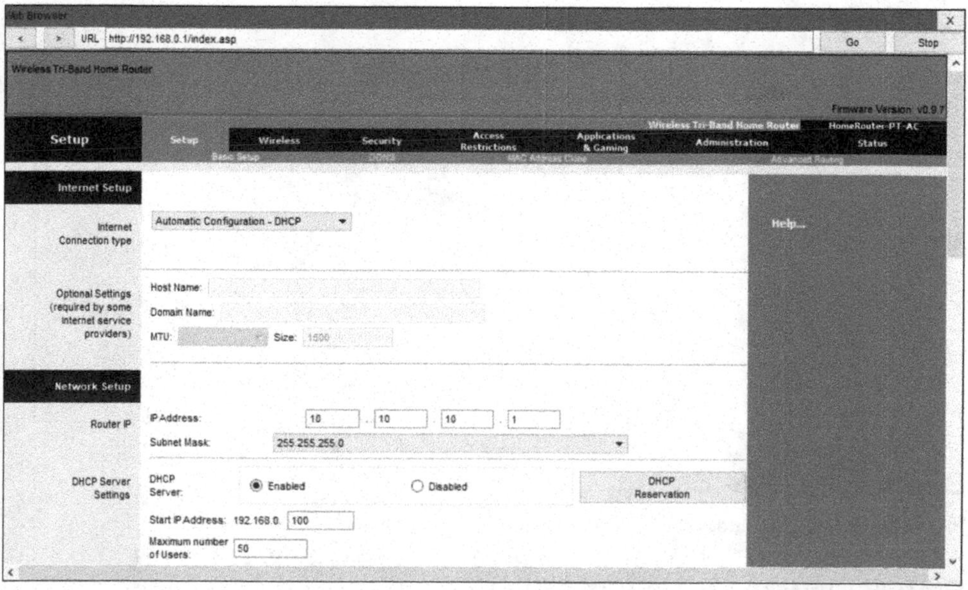

## Step 5: Renew the IP address.

When you click **Save**, you will temporarily lose access to the wireless router. Open a command window and renew your IP address with the **ipconfig /renew** command, as shown in Example 2-1.

**Example 2-1  Basic Network Setup – Step 5**

```
Packet Tracer PC Command Line 1.0
C:\> ipconfig /renew

    IP Address.....................: 10.10.10.100
    Subnet Mask....................: 255.255.255.0
    Default Gateway................: 10.10.10.1
    DNS Server.....................: 0.0.0.0

C:\>
```

## Step 6: Log in to the router with the new IP address.

Enter the router's new IP address to regain access to the router configuration GUI, as shown in Figure 2-13.

**Figure 2-13  Basic Network Setup – Step 6**

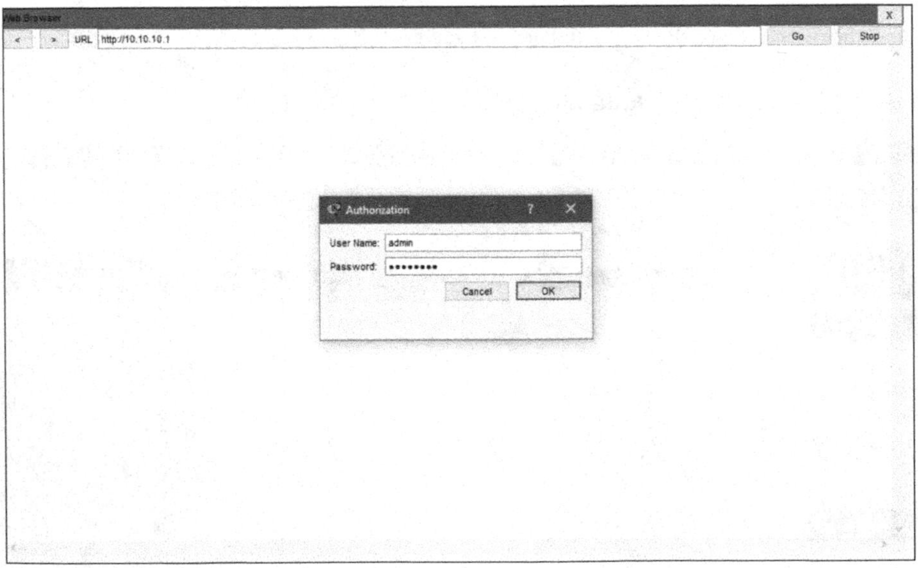

## Basic Wireless Setup

Basic wireless setup includes the following steps.

## Step 1: View the WLAN defaults.

Locate the basic wireless settings for your router to change these defaults, as shown in Figure 2-14.

**Figure 2-14    Basic Wireless Setup – Step 1**

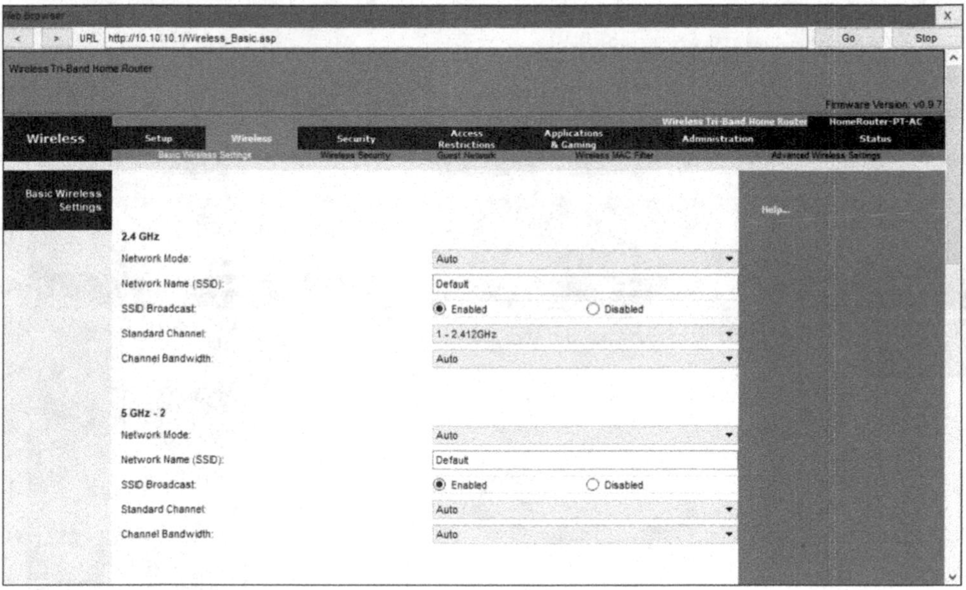

## Step 2: Change the network mode.

Some wireless routers allow you to select which 802.11 standard to implement. Figure 2-15 shows that "Legacy" has been selected. Today's wireless routers configured for legacy or mixed mode most likely support 802.11a, 802.11n, and 802.11ac NICs.

**Figure 2-15    Basic Wireless Setup – Step 2**

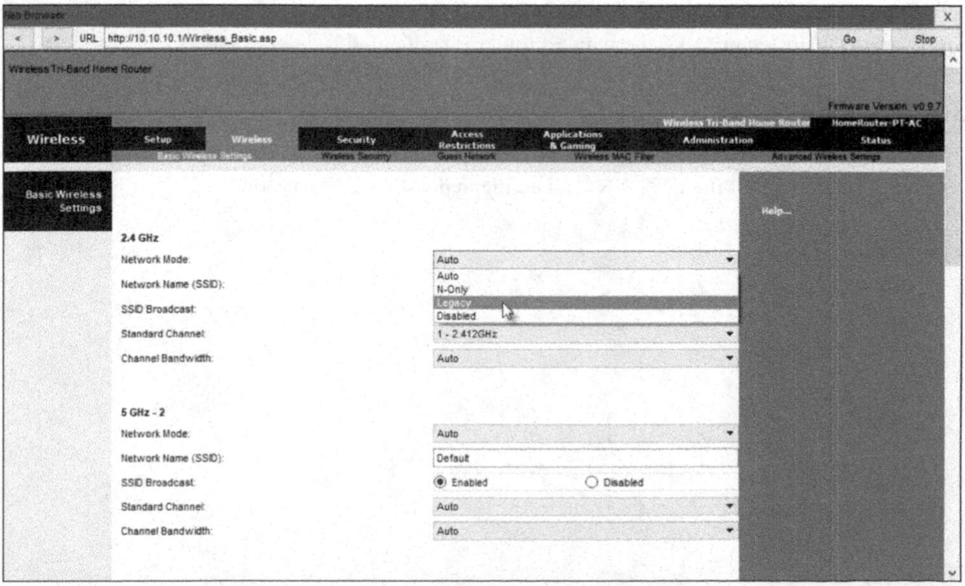

## Step 3: Configure the SSID.

Assign a new Service Set Identified (SSID) to the WLANs. **OfficeNet** is used in Figure 2-16 for all three WLANs (the third WLAN is not shown).

**Figure 2-16   Basic Wireless Setup – Step 3**

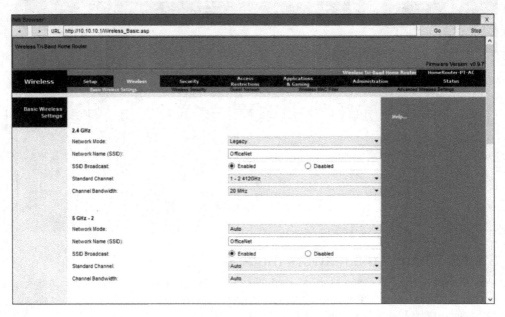

## Step 4: Configure the channel.

To avoid 2.4 GHz overlapping with other devices, configure non-overlapping channels on the wireless routers and access points that are near to each other. Specifically, channels 1, 6, and 11 are non-overlapping. In Figure 2-17, the wireless router is configured to use channel 6.

## Step 5: Configure the security mode.

Out of the box, a wireless router may have no WLAN security configured. In Figure 2-18, WPA2 Personal is selected for all three WLANs and configured with AES encryption.

**Figure 2-17    Basic Wireless Setup – Step 4**

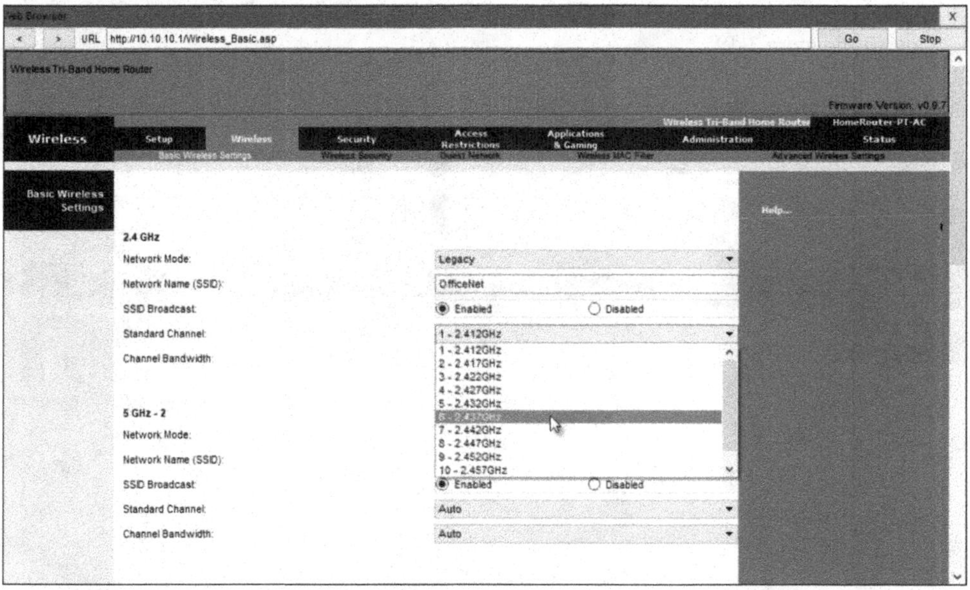

**Figure 2-18    Basic Wireless Setup – Step 5**

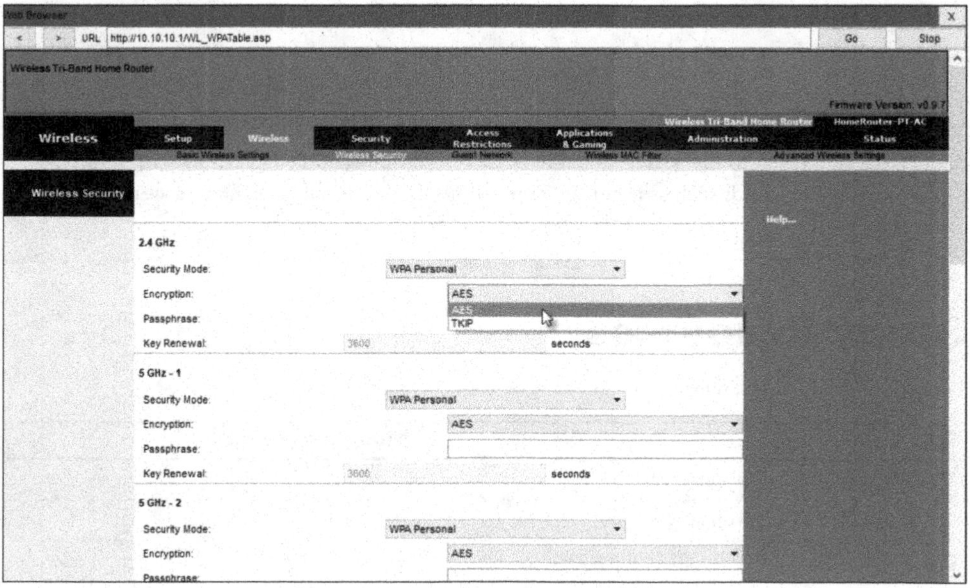

## Step 6: Configure the passphrase.

WPA2 Personal uses a passphrase to authenticate wireless clients. The passphrase **cisco123** is configured in Figure 2-19.

**Figure 2-19   Basic Wireless Setup – Step 6**

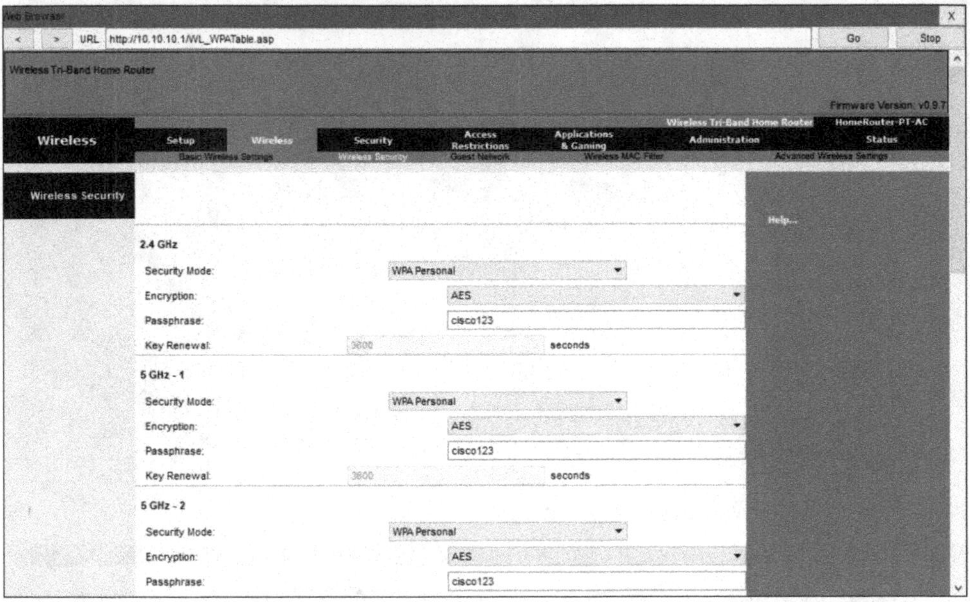

## Step 7: Verify connectivity for devices connected to the router.

All devices connected to the router should have DHCP enabled. Some devices may need to be renewed with commands such as **ipconfig /renew**. Verify the devices can access a website like www.cisco.com.

# Study Resources

For today's exam topics, refer to the following resources for more study:

| Resource | Module or Chapter |
| --- | --- |
| SFA Self Enroll: Network Support and Security | 3 |
| SFA Instructor Led: Networking Essentials | 39 |
| CCST Networking 100-150 Official Cert Guide | 11 |

**NOTE**   SFA: https://skillsforall.com/

# Review and Practice

Today is primarily a day for relaxation, a bit of practice, and some light review. Quickly review the topics for the exam, focusing on areas where you need a refresher. However, avoid dedicating the entire day to intense study. It's important to maintain a low stress level, eat nutritious meals, engage in some gentle physical activity, and ensure you get plenty of rest, in preparation for your exam tomorrow.

While it's uncertain what specific questions will appear on the exam, there's a chance you might encounter a brief simulation. To help you prepare for this scenario, I've created a simple Packet Tracer exercise for you to practice with. Don't worry if you're unable to configure everything perfectly. Some difficulties might arise from your unfamiliarity with Packet Tracer. The exam will not be using Packet Tracer. This activity is designed to offer you some hands-on simulation experience, potentially useful for the CCST Networking exam.

If you have trouble with the activity because you are unfamiliar with Packet Tracer, then you may want to spend the one or two hours it takes to complete the **Getting Started with Packet Tracer** mini-course at **www.skillsforall.com**.

As specified in **Readers Services** on page viii, **Register your copy of this book** at www.ciscopress.com/title/9780138222918 for convenient access to downloads, updates, and corrections as they become available. Here you will find the Packet Tracer activity for this Day.

# Configure a Home Network

The instructions for the activity are embedded in the Packet Tracer file. They are repeated here for your convenience.

## Instructions

The **Home Router** is locked. Use the **Web Browser** desktop app on PC0 to access the router. To access the router, discover its IP address by looking at the default gateway assigned to PC0 by DHCP.

Complete the following requirements:

- After you access the router with username **admin** and password **admin**, change the administrator's password to **adminonly**. If the router is not accessible yet, you can click the **Fast Forward Time (Alt+D)** button to speed up convergence.

- Change the DHCP configuration to the 10.10.10.0/24 network with 10.10.10.1 assigned to the router.

- Change the **Static DNS 1** IP address to 198.51.100.10.

- Refresh the DHCP settings on PC0, if necessary, and reconnect to the **Home Router** at its new IP address.

- Configure the 2.4GHz WLAN to use **Legacy**. *This is not graded by Packet Tracer.*

- Configure **OfficeNet** as the SSID for all three WLANs.

- Change the channel to 6 for the 2.4GHz WLAN. *This is not graded by Packet Tracer.*

- Configure AES encryption and set **cisco123** as the passphrase.

- Use the **PC Wireless** desktop app to configure the laptop to use the new SSID and passphrase.

- Verify that both the laptop and the PC can access the Cisco server. The network may take a few minutes to converge. You can click the **Fast Forward Time (Alt+D)** button to speed up convergence.

# Exam Day

Today is your opportunity to prove that you have what it takes to manage a small enterprise branch network. Just 50 minutes stand between you and your CCST Networking certification. Use the following information to focus on the process details for the day of your CCST Networking exam.

# What You Need for the Exam

To take a Certiport certification exam, you have two options: taking the exam in person at a local Certiport Authorized Testing Center and taking the exam remotely from home.

## In-Person Exam at a Local CATC

- Certification exams must be taken at a Certiport Authorized Testing Center (CATC) under the supervision of an authorized proctor.

- Locate a nearby CATC using the Locator feature or check if your school has one.

- Purchase an exam voucher and receive a 16-digit code via email.

- Bring the printed or written voucher code to the CATC, or assign it to yourself for easy access during the exam.

- Confirm the CATC's policies and fees before your exam.

- Bring your Certiport username, password, and voucher code. Phones and other electronics are not allowed during the exam.

- The CATC will provide the required software.

## Remote Exam from Home

- Certiport offers a virtual solution, Exams from Home, in partnership with a CATC.

- Purchase an exam voucher and a separate proctoring service fee from Get Certified America.

- Receive a 16-digit voucher code and separate instructions via email.

- Ensure you have a compatible system: Windows 10/11 or MacOS X Sierra 10.12 or higher, high-speed Internet, webcam, full keyboard and mouse, screen resolution of at least 1280×800, and a preferred browser like Chrome.

- Chromebook users need to install the Compass for Individuals app.

- No software installation is required for Windows or Mac users, but a small program file is run through the browser.

- The webcam is used for identity verification, and the exam is monitored by a proctor. Electronic device usage is prohibited during the exam.

- Have your Certiport username, password, voucher code, and an Exams from Home access code ready on the exam day. Instructions and the access code are provided by Get Certified America after scheduling the exam.

In both cases, it's crucial to create a Certiport profile and have the necessary credentials and codes on the exam day.

# What You Should Receive After Completion

When you complete the exam, you will see an immediate electronic response on whether you passed or failed. The proctor will give you a certified score report with the following important information:

- Your score report, including the minimum passing score and your score on the exam. The report also includes a breakout displaying your percentage for each general exam topic.

- Identification information required to track your certification. *Do not lose your certified examination score report.*

# Summary

Your state of mind is a key factor in your success on the CCST exam. If you know the details of the exam topics and the details of the exam process, you can begin the exam with confidence and focus. If taking it in person, arrive early to the exam. Bring earplugs just in case a testing neighbor has a bad cough or any loud nervous habits. If taking it remotely, begin to prepare your test-taking area an hour before the exam is scheduled to begin. Do not let an extremely difficult or specific question impede your progress. You cannot return to questions on the exam that you have already answered, so answer each question confidently and move on.

# Post-Exam Information

Signing up for and actually taking the CCST exam is no small accomplishment. Many network engineers have avoided certification exams for years. The following sections discuss your options after exam day.

## Receiving Your Certificate and Badge

If you passed the exam, you can log in at https://app.certiport.com/portal/ and then click **My Transcripts**. Click the orange PDF link and use the options within your PDF viewer to print or save a copy of the certificate.

You can also access your badge for use with current and future employers. Although procedures change often, currently you can find out more by visiting https://certiport.pearsonvue.com/Certifications/Cisco/Certified-Support-Technician/Badging.

Unlike other Cisco certifications, entry-level CCST certifications are valid for a lifetime and do not have an expiration date.

## Determining Career Options

After you pass the CCST exam, be sure to add your CCST certification to your résumé. Matthew Moran provides the following advice for adding certifications to a résumé in his book *Building Your I.T. Career: A Complete Toolkit for a Dynamic Career in Any Economy*, Second Edition (Pearson IT Certification, 2013):

> "I don't believe you should place your certifications after your name. It is presumptuous to pretend that your latest certification is the equivalent to someone who has spent 4–7 years pursuing a Ph.D. or some other advanced degree. Instead, place your certifications or degrees in a section titled *Education and Certifications*. A master's degree might be the exception to this rule."

Moran also discusses good strategies for breaking into the IT industry after you have earned your CCST Networking certification:

> "The most important factor is that you are moving toward a career goal. You might not get the title or job you want right out of school. If you can master those skills at your current position, while simultaneously building your network of contacts that lead to your dream position, you should be satisfied. You must build your career piece by piece. It won't happen all at once."

Moran outlines in his book that certifications such as CCST Networking are part of an overall professional skill set that you must continually enhance to further your IT career.

Your CCST Networking certificate proves that you are disciplined enough to commit to a rigorous course of study and follow through with your professional goals. You won't likely be hired simply because you have a CCST Networking certificate, but you will be placed ahead of other candidates. To supplement the CCST Networking certification, be sure to highlight any networking skills that pertain to CCST Networking in the job and skills descriptions on your résumé.

# Examining Certification Options

Passing the CCST Networking exam is no easy task, but it is the starting point for more advanced Cisco certifications, such as CCNA- and CCNP-level exams. To learn more about other Cisco certification exams beyond CCST Networking, visit https://www.cisco.com/c/en/us/training-events/training-certifications/exams.html.

# If You Did Not Pass the Exam

If you did not pass your first attempt at the CCST Networking exam, you must wait at least two calendar days after the day of the exam to retest. Stay motivated and sign up to take the exam again within 30 days of your first attempt. The score report outlines your weaknesses. Find a study group and use The Cisco Learning Network (http://learningnetwork.cisco.com) online community to help you with those topics.

If you are familiar with the general concepts, focus on taking practice exams and memorizing the small details that make the exam so difficult. Review the curriculum at https://www.skillsforall.com. Hopefully, you bought the *Cisco Certified Support Technician CCST Networking 100-150 Official Cert Guide* (Cisco Press, 2023). Review the chapters and topics that cover your weak areas. Consider your first attempt as a formal practice exam and excellent preparation to pass the second attempt.

# Summary

Whether you display your certificate and update your résumé or prepare to conquer the exam on your second attempt, remember to marvel at the innovation and creativity behind each concept you learn. The ability of our society to continually improve communication will keep you learning, discovering, and employed for a lifetime.

# CCST Networking Countdown Calendar

The lines after the countdown number allow you to add the actual calendar days for reference.

| 31 _____ | 30 _____ | 29 _____ | 28 _____ | 27 _____ | 26 _____ | 25 _____ |
|---|---|---|---|---|---|---|
| Networking Models | TCP/IP Layer Functions | Data Encapsulation | Measuring Network Performance | Network Topologies | Cloud Computing | Transport Protocols |
| **24** _____ | **23** _____ | **22** _____ | **21** _____ | **20** _____ | **19** _____ | **18** _____ |
| FTP, NTP, and ICMP | HTTP, DHCP, and DNS | Private Addressing and NAT | IPv4 Addressing | IPv6 Addressing | Cables and Connectors | Wireless Technologies |
| **17** _____ | **16** _____ | **15** _____ | **14** _____ | **13** _____ | **12** _____ | **11** _____ |
| Endpoint Devices | Configure PC and Mobile Device Access | Device Status Lights | Connecting Cables | Device Ports | Routing Concepts | Switching Concepts |

| 10 _____ | 9 _____ | 8 _____ | 7 _____ | 6 _____ | 5 _____ | 4 _____ |
|---|---|---|---|---|---|---|
| Trouble-shooting and Help Desks | Wireshark | Diagnostic Commands | Device Management | Show Commands | Firewalls | Threats, Vulnerabilities, and Attacks |

| 3 _____ | 2 _____ | 1 _____ | EXAM DAY | | | |
|---|---|---|---|---|---|---|
| Security Protocols and Practices | Secure Wireless Access | Review and Practice | Time _____ Location _____ | | | |

# Exam Checklist

**CCST Networking Checklist Days 31–25**

| Checkbox | Date | Objective |
|---|---|---|
| | | Schedule to take the CCNA 200-301 exam at http://www.vue.com. |
| | | Take at least one practice CCST Networking exam. |
| | | Create a diagram from memory of the layered models and a brief description of each layer's function. |
| | | Describe in detail the process of requesting and sending a web page. |
| | | Describe the encapsulation process, including the headers and PDUs at each layer. |
| | | Explain to a friend why bandwidth is not a true measurement of throughput or goodput. |
| | | Practice drawing and labeling various types of topologies. |
| | | Describe to a friend the concept of cloud computing. Include a discussion of virtualization. |
| | | Describe the difference between TCP and UDP, including which types of applications use each or both. |
| | | Read and review Days 31–25 in this book. |

**CCST Networking Checklist Days 24–18**

| Checkbox | Date | Objective |
|---|---|---|
| | | Take at least two practice CCST exams. |
| | | Practice using FTP and SFTP commands. |
| | | Describe the operation of NTP and its stratums. |
| | | Describe the operation of ICMPv4, including the **ping** and **trace** commands. |
| | | Describe the operation of ICMPv6, including its message types. |
| | | Describe the operation of DHCP, including the message types for both IPv4 and IPv6. |
| | | Dissect a URL, labeling each of its parts. |
| | | Explain to a friend how web addresses are translated into IP addresses. |
| | | Explain to a friend why you can each have the same IP address but be on different networks. |
| | | Describe the structure and operation of IPv4. List and describe the uses for the various types of IPv4 addresses. |

| Checkbox | Date | Objective |
|---|---|---|
| | | Describe the structure and operation of IPv6. List and describe the uses for the various types of IPv6 addresses. |
| | | Explain to a friend the different types of media, including sources of interference for each. |
| | | Explain the difference between wireless networks and cellular networks. |
| | | Read and review Days 24–18 in this book. |

## CCST Networking Checklist Days 17–10

| Checkbox | Date | Objective |
|---|---|---|
| | | Take an additional CCNA practice exam. |
| | | Describe the various types of endpoints, including mobile and IoT devices. |
| | | Practice configuring and verifying the configuration of computers and mobile devices. |
| | | Look up different Cisco equipment status lights. |
| | | Use Packet Tracer or another simulator to practice connecting cables to various devices and port types. |
| | | Practice identifying and describing port types by looking up the backplane description of various Cisco routers and switches. |
| | | Describe the difference between directly connected and remote networks from the router's perspective. |
| | | Describe the various methods that a router can use to learn about and share knowledge of remote networks. |
| | | Explain to a friend how a switch populates its Mac address table. |
| | | Explain to a friend why you might use a VLAN and describe the different types. |
| | | Describe the various troubleshooting methodologies and when you might use each. |
| | | Describe basic security threats and the methods used to mitigate them. |
| | | Explain how help desks prioritize and escalate tickets. |
| | | Read and review Days 17–10 in this book. |

**CCST Networking Checklist Days 9–1**

| Checkbox | Date | Objective |
|---|---|---|
| | | Practice using Wireshark to capture and filter traffic on your network. Explore the details of common TCP and HTTP packets. |
| | | Practice using all the diagnostic commands, including on Windows and macOS or Linux. Be sure you are familiar with the output of each. |
| | | Describe the various methods a technician can use to remotely access another device. |
| | | Describe the purpose of a VPN and explain how to configure one in Windows. |
| | | Describe popular Network Management Systems and tools. |
| | | Use a configured Packet Tracer activity to practice using the various **show** commands listed in the 5.5 exam topic. |
| | | Explain to a friend the various types of firewalls and the benefits and challenges of each. |
| | | Describe basic security threats and the methods used to mitigate them. |
| | | Describe security threats that are unique to wireless networks. |
| | | Practice configuring and securing the wireless networks on a home router. |
| | | Read and review Days 9–1 in this book. |
| | | Visit the testing center and talk with the proctor at least two days before the exam. If taking the exam remotely, complete the setup process to get your environment approved for testing. |
| | | Eat a decent meal, watch a good movie, and get a good night's rest before the exam. |

# Index

Register your product at **ciscopress.com/register**
to unlock additional benefits:

- Save 35%* on your next purchase with an exclusive discount code
- Find companion files, errata, and product updates if available
- Sign up to receive special offers on new editions and related titles

Get more when you shop at **ciscopress.com**:

- Everyday discounts on books, eBooks, video courses, and more
- Free U.S. shipping on all orders
- Multi-format eBooks to read on your preferred device
- Print and eBook Best Value Packs

**Cisco Press**